Liberia: The Rise and Fall of the First Republic

G.E. Saigbe Boley

MACMILLAN PUBLISHERS

First published 1983
Reprinted 1984

Published by
Macmillan Publishers
London and Basingstoke
Companies and representatives in Lagos, Zaria, Manzini,
Nairobi, Singapore, Hong Kong, Delhi, Dublin, Auckland,
Melbourne, Tokyo, New York, Washington, Dallas

ISBN 0 333 36624 7   Paper
ISBN 0 333 36623 9   Cased

Typeset in Hong Kong by Asco Trade Typesetting Limited
Printed in Hong Kong

Acknowledgements

The author and publishers wish to thank the following who have kindly given
permission for the use of copyright material:
Frank Cass & Co. Ltd. for extracts from *The Native Problem in Africa*,
Vol. II, by Raymond Leslie Buell
Cornell University Press for extracts from *Liberia: The Evolution of Privilege*
by J. Gus Liebenow
Doubleday & Co. Inc. for extracts from *Liberia Rediscovered* by James C.
Young (Copyright 1934 by Doubleday & Co. Inc.)
Harper & Row, Publishers Inc. for extracts from *Liberia: Black Africa in
Microcosm* by Charles Morrow Wilson
C. Hurst & Co. (Publishers) Ltd. for extracts from *The Love of Liberty: The
Rule of William V.S. Tubman in Liberia 1946–1971* by Tuan Wreh.

Every effort has been made to trace all the copyright holders but, if any have
been inadvertently overlooked, the publishers will be pleased to make the
necessary arrangements at the first opportunity.

To the Liberian people, victims of the ills (for which every Liberian must stand equally responsible) of the First Republic;

From some of us – very few of us indeed – with the 'will' and 'conscience' to challenge the evils and stand for principle;

To the rest of us – so many of us – spineless, remiss and unprincipled, willing to do anything, under any circumstance, at any cost only to remain in grace with the powers-that-be;

Let us, by adopting a change in attitude for the better, allow the Second Republic to be considerate of us – all of us!

About the Author

George Eutychianus Saigbe Boley was born on December 7, 1949 at Doublee, Putu Chiefdom, Grand Gedeh County. He attended elementary school at St Philomena's in Zwedru, Grand Gedeh County and graduated from Ricks Institute in Virginia, Liberia in 1969.

Dr Boley matriculated to the State University of New York College at Brockport, New York, where he earned a B.Sc degree in Political Science in 1974. He received his M.S.Ed. degree in Educational Administration at the same institution in 1975.

In the fall of 1975, Dr Boley entered the University of Akron, Ohio, and earned an Ed.D degree in Educational Administration in 1977.

Dr Boley returned home in 1978 and joined the Ministry of Education as Director of Planning. In February 1979 he was appointed Assistant Minister of Education for Administration, a position he held until March 1980 when he was arrested and charged with treason and sedition.

Following the coup of April 12, 1980, Dr Boley was among those released from further detention by the People's Redemption Council of the Armed Forces of Liberia (AFL). Dr Boley was appointed Minister of State on April 12, 1980 by the People's Redemption Council. In February 1981, Dr Boley was appointed Minister of Posts and Telecommunications. In November 1981, he was again appointed Minister of Education.

Contents

Preface

This book is an attempt to reconstruct the value system, attitudes and thought processes which led to the founding and ultimate demise of the First Liberian Republic. I will have achieved my objective in writing it if succeeding generations of Liberians will use it as a warning against those values and attitudes likely to destroy the Second Republic.

I have tried to detach myself from personal problems which could have blurred my objectivity by not submitting to them. Accordingly, I have recorded my observations and experiences as clearly and objectively as possible, realizing that a slightly different analytical approach to historical events may possibly have altered my impression of the First Republic.

I would not pretend to maintain, nor do I maintain, that this book contains all the historical facts pertaining to the First Liberian Republic. As I write of the First Liberian Republic, I do so solely to put into perspective – to make clearer to succeeding generations of Liberians – the reality of that past within the scope of defined objectives.

It is possible that some of the things in this book may have been said somewhere else, but perhaps a different manner of expression may be found in my version. Most importantly, I trust the reader will find this book different in that some new thoughts and information have been provided. All the documents contained in the Appendixes, except for the 1928 Fernando Poo Labor Agreement, are in the original form and have never been circulated. The reader should find these documents useful as they relate to crucial national problems experienced by the First Republic. Some of these problems, perhaps under slightly different circumstances and perhaps to a greater extent, might undoubtedly continue to plague the Second Republic.

Many of the issues discussed in this book could have been pursued further by quoting extensively from original sources and by padding them out with illustrations and boring statistics. However, for the sake of simplicity and precision, I have elected to record the facts and information as I know them, keeping quotations, illustrations and statistics to a necessary minimum.

During my seventeen-month tenure of service (October 1978 – March 1980) in the Tolbert/True Whig Party regime, I came as close to the corridors of power as the 'system' would allow someone with my kind of background. The information provided in this book (especially information relating to recent developments) is, therefore, the result of my exposure to, and experiences at, all levels of the social, economic and political structure of the First Republic.

I consider it a privilege to recount the issues dealt with in this book and I am optimistic that all Liberians will, in the light of the recent past and national experience, resolve to chart a course in the direction of change for the better. Let me hasten to add that the past is instanced merely as a warning against repeating the mistakes of old as we venture into the unknown future of constitutional rule in the Second Republic.

In thanking the many individuals whose efforts have made this book possible, I must first express gratitude to the seventeen-member People's Redemption Council of the Armed Forces of Liberia, led by C-in-C Dr Samuel Kanyon Doe (then Master Sergeant) for skillfully effecting my release, along with others, from prison on April 12, 1980. I must express thanks to Professor J. Gus Liebenow of Indiana University for his guiding comments in reviewing the initial draft of this manuscript. To Margaret A. Rich of the State University of New York College at Brockport, New York, I owe a special debt for invaluable assistance in obtaining source materials for me during the review of literature for this book. I must also acknowledge the assistance of Mrs Ruth Armstrong of the University of Liberia Libraries. For critically reviewing the manuscript and offering suggestions to improve it, I am thankful to Dr Peter L. Naigow, Minister of Information, and Dr Amos Sawyer, Dean, College of Liberal Arts, University of Liberia and Chairman of the National Constitution Commission.

I am most grateful for the assistance of Mr E. Wa-Valentine, Director of Archives at the Executive Mansion. To Mrs Cerue Darby, my secretary, for invaluable assistance in typing, proofreading and putting together the various drafts of this book, I am most grateful. I owe a special debt of gratitude to Mr Jacob S. Dogbeh for truly 'educating' me over the last few years in the realities of Liberian politics. Mr Dogbeh's analytical ability, coupled with his recollection and interpretation of events in the Liberian body politic, has been an added source of inspiration in the writing of this book.

Finally, to my wife Kathryn, for securing the original manuscript during my detention, and my children – Saigbe Jr, Mahnseah and Todd – for their encouragement and understanding during the writing of this book, I say a big 'Thank you'.

For all errors of omission and commission, including the shortcomings of this book, I stand solely responsible.

Zwedru, Liberia
7 December, 1982

x

CHAPTER ONE

West Africa before Liberia

The coastal area of West Africa, some two thousand miles in length, embraces peoples whose languages and customs indicate a common ancestry far in the distant past. When the European nations commenced their overseas exploration and expansion, Portugal led the way to Africa and the East, while Spain at about the same time was engaged in establishing an empire in America. In England, prior to the reign of Elizabeth I, Englishmen never conceived of the economic power and universal recognition that overseas exploration and expansion would bring to them.

Europeans knew very little about Africa and Africans. The works of Richard Hakluyt (1552–1616), an English clergyman and historian, aroused the interest of Europeans in general, and the English in particular, in Africa. Some of Hakluyt's writing included a twelve-volume compilation entitled *The Principal Navigations, Voyages, Traffiques and Discoveries of the English Nation* (1598). Hakluyt's interesting descriptions of exciting expeditions and excursions to many parts of the world stirred the curiosity of English society and awakened it to the potential of Africa. (It is important to note that Richard Hakluyt later helped to organize the settling of the Virginia Colony in the United States of America.) In the early seventeenth century another account of voyages of adventure was compiled by Samuel Purchas, a successor of Richard Hakluyt. The accounts of these two men 'first acquainted Englishmen at home with the newly discovered lands of Africa'.[1]

However, as the taste for overseas empires developed among Englishmen in the early sixteenth century, 'English voyagers did not touch upon the shores of West Africa until after 1550',[2] nearly a century after Prince

1

Henry the Navigator had mounted the sustained Portuguese drive southward for a sea passage to the Orient. Some earlier European description of West Africa was the work of fortune-seeking Englishmen whose desire to exploit the inhabitants of this region seemingly surpassed their willingness to regenerate them.

Nothing so astonished the English when they first came into contact with Africans, according to numerous descriptions, as did their skin color which was described as 'black'. The skin color of the Africans made a great impact on the Englishmen who first established contact with them for 'really black men were virtually unknown (to the Englishman) except as vaguely referred to in the hazy literature about the sub-Sahara which had filtered down from antiquity'.[3] Another factor which affected the Englishman's perception of the skin color of the African was the fact that England's first principal contact with Africa was confined to Western Africa and the Congo, where men were not merely of a dark complexion 'but almost literally black'.[4] The Englishman's initial experience of Africans was therefore limited and quite different from that of the Spanish and Portuguese who had for centuries been in contact with Africans of varying complexions and had in fact been invaded, conquered and ruled by people of a 'darker complexion and more highly civilized than themselves'.

The pre-sixteenth century perception of 'black' is described in the *Oxford English Dictionary* as: 'Deeply stained with dirt; soiled, dirty, foul ... Having dark or deadly purposes, malignant; pertaining to or involving death, deadly; baneful, disastrous, sinister ... Foul, iniquitous, atrocious, horrible, wicked ... Indicating disgrace, censure, liability to punishment, etc'.[5] Blackness was associated with 'baseness and evil', a 'sign of danger and repulsion'. The perception of whiteness was the exact opposite. White was associated with purity, beauty, virginity, virtue, and good. Black, on the other hand, meant filthiness, sin, baseness, ugliness and evil.

Early English explorers were quick to describe in strange fashion Africans with whom they came in contact. 'Travelers rarely failed to comment upon it (color); indeed, when describing Negroes they frequently began with complexion and then moved on to dress (or rather the lack of it) and manners.'[6] At Cape Verde, one explorer wrote, 'the People are all black, and are called Negroes without apparel, saving their privities'.[7]

Recapitulating two of his visits to West Africa in 1562 and 1663, Robert Baker, another English voyager, described the African in a poem as follows:

> And entering (a river), we see
> a number of black soules

Whose likeliness seem'd men to be
But all as black as coles
Their Captain comes to me
as naked as my naile,
Not having witte or honestie
To cover once his taile.[8]

Englishmen obviously perceived Africans as wholly different from themselves. They were 'black', their religion unorthodox and their manners anything but English. However, full scale participation in the slave trade by Englishmen did not occur until the eighteenth century.

In the early stages of the European exploration of the New World, Negroes came along as porters, servants and slaves.[9] As early as 1501[10] Spain repealed her earlier proscription and permitted Negroes to go into Spanish colonies in the New World. Some thirty Negroes accompanied Balboa when he discovered the Pacific Ocean. Vasco Nunez De Balboa (1475–1519) was a Spanish explorer who is credited with being the first European to see the eastern shore of the Pacific Ocean. Negroes were with the French in their exploration of the New World. During the Canadian expeditions, Negroes went with the Jesuit missionaries.[11] Thus, although Englishmen were predisposed to regard Negroes as members of an inferior race because of their 'blackness' and mannerisms, they were, however, not first to transport them to the New World.

Many factors contributed to the English migration to the New World, including religious persecution by the government of King James I which caused the Pilgrim Fathers to sail from Plymouth to seek freedom of worship in the New World. While the colonies and plantations established by the English in the West Indies prospered, those Englishmen who crossed the Atlantic Ocean and colonized British North America (originally Jamestown, Virginia, Massachusetts Bay and other eastern seaboard colonies) encountered unexpected restraints. The land was virgin wilderness, and the colonists were subject to attack by hostile Indians.

The early English colonists made extreme efforts to capitalize on the labor of the Indians. All such effort was to no avail, and African labor was a final resort. As a step towards coping with the unexpected conditions in their new colonies (ie clearing the wilderness for farming) the first group of Negroes arrived at Jamestown, Virginia in 1619[12], though their exact status during the next twenty years was not clear. 'Between 1640 and 1660 there is evidence of enslavement, and after 1660 slavery crystalized on the statute books of Maryland, Virginia and other colonies'[13] in North America.

Several African kings vehemently detested the exportation of their subjects. King Agaja of Dahomey, for example, 'in 1727 attempted to expell the European slavetraders from his portion of the Guinea Coast by burning their factories to the ground'.[14] The King further petitioned London by 'sending a certain Bulfinch Lamb, an English prisoner of war at Abomey, the Dahomean capital, to England as an envoy'.[15] Lamb informed his colleagues that the African would be willing to labor on British-owned plantations established in Africa rather than be exported to strange lands. The British were not interested in the proposal and Africans continued to be shipped into the New World.

Africans herded in shackles aboard slave vessels missed no opportunity to escape or commit suicide. The captain of one vessel carrying slaves to North America recorded the following:

> On the 14th of March we found a great deal of discontent among the Slaves, particularly the men, which continued till the 16th about five o'clock in the evening, when to our great amazement about one hundred men slaves jumped overboard, and it was with great difficulty we saved so many as we did; out of the whole we lost 33 of as good men slaves as we had on board, who would not endeavor to save themselves, but resolved to die and sunk directly down ...[16]

The new social and economic conditions in English America impressed indelibly on the Negro the peculiar quality of bondage to which he was subjected, as other servants escaped the general degradation that had originally been the common lot of all. 'Not only did the organization of the plantation with its separate quarters, hierarchy of overseers and absentee owners widen the gulf between black and white, but the involvement of the whole Southern economy in plantation production created an effective interest against any change of status.'[17]

By the turn of the seventeen century, Africans began to outnumber whites in such colonies as Virginia, Maryland and on major plantations in the Carolinas (North and South) and adjacent southern states and territories. In 1708 the Negro and white population in South Carolina was almost equal, with 4,100 Negroes and 4,080 whites. By 1715 the Negroes led the whites with 10,500 to 6,250. In 1724 there were three times as many Negroes as whites; in 1765, the Negro population was 90,000 while the whites totalled only 40,000.[18] Consequently, stricter laws were imposed upon Negroes to control their movement and activities and drastic penalties were restored for trivial offenses.

American Revolution and Negro freedom

Although the American Revolution did not advance the abolition of slavery in the eighteenth century, it can be said to have triggered a sense of motivation among Negroes as well as a few whites. 'On New Year's

Day of 1804 the Republic of Haiti became the second independent Nation in the Hemisphere (Western) ruled by triumphant revolutionaries who were, of all things, black.'[19] The end of the French Empire came after a battle between blacks and whites on the French-controlled island of Haiti which took thousands of lives, as millions of whites everywhere wondered what had gone wrong.

The news of the Haitian Revolution especially disturbed the white citizens of the State of Virginia, where the number of emancipated Negroes was increasing rapidly. After 1790[20] it became increasingly evident that white Southerners were less worried and exasperated by Negro slaves than by freed Negroes. From 1790 to 1810 the proportion of freed Negroes as a percentage of the total Negro population in the United States rose from almost 8 percent to more than 13 percent.[21] However, as a result of restraints upon Negro emancipation, the latter figure remained stationary until 1840 when it declined.

Table 1   *Proportion of Free Negroes, Coastal States, 1790*[22]

States	1790	1810
Delaware	30.5%	75.9%
Maryland	7.2%	23.3%
Virginia	4.2%	7.2%
North Carolina	4.8%	5.7%
South Carolina	1.7%	2.3%
Georgia	1.3%	1.7%

Everywhere in the United States, particularly in the South, whites were no longer at ease. The imported African laborers who had been, and would continue to be, a source of tremendous wealth, had now become an unequivocal threat to their masters.

CHAPTER TWO

Negro Removal from America

The repatriation of black people to Africa was not the result of a mere accident, nor was it done solely on a philanthropic basis as some would have us believe. The designs of the white man, in attempting to remove totally from the continent of North America all black people, especially those blacks who had been emancipated, reflected the prevailing attitude of whites generally toward blacks in eighteen-century America.

These designs, though conveniently labelled philanthropic by their proponents, must be carefully examined in relation to the circumstances which led to the repatriation of free black slaves to Liberia. The fear that America would lose its racial and cultural identity if the Negroes were allowed to mix with the whites was initially one of the principal reasons for the planned removal of black people from America under the auspices of the American Colonization Society.

Several prominent Americans who supported the colonization of foreign lands by Negroes had strong motives for giving so generously of their time as well as their financial and moral support to the cause of the American Colonization Society. Firstly, it was hoped that the resettlement of Negroes in foreign lands would alleviate the 'pitiable lot of the free Negroes [and] rid the community of the care and danger of a poor and disgruntled element', thus leading ultimately to the abolition of the institution of slavery. Secondly, the total removal of Negroes from North America and their subsequent resettlement elsewhere was seen by some supporters cf the colonization scheme as a 'means of removing the competition of cheap domestic labor and thereby encouraging white immigration from Europe'.[1] Thirdly, colonization was viewed by some as a possible solution to the problem of the rapidly increasing Negro population in America. By 1820, four years after the founding of the American Colonization Society, the total Negro population in America was recorded as being in excess of more than 1,500,000.

A possible fourth motive which induced some Americans to favor the Negro colonization movement was the belief that 'such settlements in Africa would furnish the nucleus from which Negro Missionaries would spread the doctrines of Christianity among the African natives'.[2] A fear of rebellions and insurrections by slaves, especially emancipated Negroes, was another motive for colonizing foreign lands with Negroes. This motive is evidenced by the fact that immediately following the Nat Turner incident[3] in Southampton County, Virginia in 1831, three States, Virginia, Mississippi and Maryland, and several organizations and private agencies (such as the Young Men's Colonization Society of Pennsylvania, founded in 1834, and the Colonization Society of the City of New York, founded in 1831) organized local Colonization Societies for the express purpose of repatriating Negroes to Liberia.

In this letter dated October 22, 1831, to Reverend Ralph R. Gurley, a pioneering agent of the American Colonization Society resident in Liberia, a White Virginian named Colin H. Minge wrote:

> There is not an enemy of the cause of colonization in Virginia at this time ... The whites are running away from the blacks, the masters from the slaves in lower Virginia, the place of insurrection. I received an invitation from a gentleman yesterday to go to his house to advise his negroes, eight in number, mostly young ones, to embark for Liberia, as he was willing to emancipate them.[4]

Some supporters of the colonization scheme sought the opportunity to use the Society for 'political purposes'. It was publicly alleged that Henry Clay, the famous Senator from Kentucky, used the Colonization Society as a political machine. Still other supporters of the Society considered it a sort of 'labor union' from which cheap labor could be obtained to amass wealth for themselves.

Fear of racial intermixture

In eighteen-century America there was a universal belief that racial inter-mixture would become uncontrollable as former Negro slaves were set free by their white masters or acquired their freedom by some form of payment mutually acceptable to themselves and their owners. Though it was commonly accepted that racial inter-mixture was an inevitable consequence of the emancipation of Negroes, no one attempted seriously to advance reasons why this should be so.

Winthrop D. Jordan, a contemporary American historian, explains why eighteen-century Americans believed that 'emancipation of Negroes from slavery would inevitably lead to increased racial inter-mixture'.[5] According to Jordan:

Perhaps the real reason for this expectation (those other kinds of human 'reasons') lay in the hopes that white men had invested in America. A darkened nation would present incontrovertible evidence that sheer animal sex was governing the American destiny and that the great experiment in the wilderness (Colonial North America) had failed to maintain the social and personal restraints which were the hallmarks and the very stuff of civilization. A blackened posterity would mean that the basest of energies had guided the direction of the American experiment and that civilized man had turned beast in the forest. Retention of whiteness would be evidence of purity and of diligent nurture of the original body of the folk. Could a blackened people look back to Europe and say they had faithfully performed their errand?[6]

The primary concerns of most Americans at the time were firstly, a fear that inter-racial mixture (socially) and miscegenation (marriage or interbreeding between members of different races) would produce a race of mulattoes not worthy of America and inconsistent with their European origin and ancestry; and secondly, a fear that free or emancipated Negroes would be the cause of constant agitation for Negro freedom and possible Negro insurrection.

The issue of racial inter-mixture in America gave rise to varying opinions, though generally in the same vein, from many quarters. One view was advanced by young Jonathan Edwards, the famous Puritan pastor of New England and a leading intellectual figure in colonial America. In 1792, before the assembled members of the Connecticut Abolition Society, Edwards asserted that the future generation of whites in the West Indies and the Southern States of North America 'will infallibly be a mongrel breed, or else, they must quit the country to the Negroes whom they have hitherto holden in bondage'.[7] Edwards further stated:

Thus it seems that they will be necessitated by Providence to make in one way or another compensation to the Negroes for the injury they have done them. In the first case, by taking them into affinity with themselves, giving them their own sons and daughters in marriage and making them and their posterity the heirs of all their property and all their honours, and by raising their colour to a partial whiteness, whereby a part at least of that mark which brings on them so much contempt will be wiped off. In the other case, by leaving to them all their real estates ... If therefore our Southern brethren, and the inhabitants of the West Indies, would balance their accounts with their Negro slaves at the cheapest possible rate, they will doubtless judge it prudent to leave the country, with all their houses, lands and improvements, to their quiet possession and dominion; as otherwise Providence will compel them to much dearer settlement, and one attended with a circumstance inconceivably more mortifying than the loss of all their real estates. I mean the mixture of their blood with that of the Negroes into one common posterity.[8]

It was believed by Americans at the time that the most serious challenge to the survival of America as a nation was the establishment and maintenance of a white identity. Such were the prevailing sentiments when Patrick Henry (1736–1799), a native of Virginia and a distinguished American statesman and orator, asked: 'Our country will be peopled. The question is, shall it be with Europeans or with Africans?'[9]

In keeping with the opinion of the time, marriage between Negroes and whites was prohibited by law in America. Some Americans, however, considered 'radicals' at that time, held their own views about laws forbidding marriage between Negroes and whites. Charles Crawford, an intellectual who was considered a 'radical', made public his view 'that Negroes ought to be allowed to marry white women without prosecution'.[10] Professor Samuel Stanhope Smith, a lecturer at the College of New Jersey, also suggested 'that emancipated Negroes might be settled on the Western lands and white persons encouraged to go there and intermarry'.[11] According to Professor Smith's thinking, this would be 'to bring the two races nearer together, and, in a course of time, to obliterate those wide distinctions which are now created by diversity of complexion' and augmented 'by prejudice'.[12]

Those Americans who defended slavery as a legitimate institution and advocated its continuation spared no efforts to attack proponents of the removal of emancipated Negroes from the American continent. Attention often veered from the merits of emancipation to the issue of racial inter-mixture. In 1790 when concern was voiced in the US Congress with respect to the 'color' of future generations of Americans, William Loughton Smith of South Carolina stated that 'a mixture of the races would degenerate the whites, without improving the blacks'.[13]

While Smith and his adherents expressed grave concern about the question of racial intermingling, they seemed either unable or unwilling to attend to the greater problem of the future of emancipated Negroes. America was faced with the dilemma of not wanting the Negroes to mix with the whites but at the same time lacking the political will to effect the removal of all such unwanted Negroes from the continent of North America.

As discussions about a possible solution to this dilemma continued among civic leaders and intellectuals, proposals emerged urging the establishment of a 'Negro Colony'. Americans of anti-slavery conviction supported the idea in their own bid to accelerate the process of Negro emancipation. In a Philadelphia newspaper in 1768, a contributor 'denounced Negro slavery and went on to propose a Negro Colony on some lands which His Majesty might be petitioned to cede to the Southward'.[14]

Some free Negroes favored the emancipation and colonization of Negroes in territories uninhabited by white men. Others did not favor the colonization scheme. Thomas Jefferson (1743–1826), a native of Virginia and third President of the United States (1801–1809), who amassed enormous wealth from the labor of his slaves, proclaimed that when freed the Negro was 'to be removed beyond reach of mixture,' so that he would not stain 'the blood of his master'.[15] The first public mention of Africa as a possible place to establish a 'Negro Colony' was made by an anonymous New Hampshire writer who suggested that all freed slaves be put in 'a state of dependence and discipline' because they were unused to freedom. 'Perhaps some should be sent to Africa...'.[16]

The educated as well as the uneducated and culturally unrefined whites promulgated the removal of Negroes from America. The concept of removing Negroes 'beyond reach of mixture' became generally and unquestioningly accepted by those who feared the 'mixture of the races' as well as by the advocates of the emancipation movement. A consensus had been reached that the black and white races were incompatible and definitely ought to live apart.

Toward colonization

Though Americans first had the idea of resettling freed Negroes in some distant land, the basis for the decision can be traced once again to England. The success of an experiment made in Sierra Leone, which lies to the north-west of Liberia on the west coast of Africa, by an association of British philanthropists between 1786 and 1794[17] aroused enthusiasm among American philanthropists and heightened their hopes that a similar 'Colony' could be established for the purpose of repatriating freed American slaves. In 1787 Thomas Jefferson stirred public debate on the problems affecting Negroes residing in Virginia. Other prominent Virginians joined Mr Jefferson in his efforts to find a solution to the problem of the rapidly-increasing number of black people living in the State of Virginia. In 1788 another Virginian, James Madison, communicated with Dr William Thornton, a British physician and supporter of the British abolitionist movement, on the subject of removing the Negroes residing in the State of Virginia. Dr Thornton migrated to America from the Virgin Islands and subsequently adopted American citizenship. It was Dr Thornton who briskly proposed Africa as an appropriate place to which to repatriate the Negroes in the State of Virginia in particular and America in general. Dr Thornton's rationale for the proposal was that it would be an impetus to the abolitionist and emancipation movements.

In the State of Virginia, the home of Thomas Jefferson, James Madison, James Monroe and other prominent Americans, the issue of what to do with the Negroes was a matter of concern to all Virginians as the Negro population there continued to increase rapidly. In the early nineteenth century 40 percent of all Negroes in America lived in the State of Virginia. Dr Thornton's proposal, as communicated to James Madison in 1788, was an attempt to solve this 'problem'. The plan was acceptable because it offered the basic security sought by the concerned citizens of the State of Virginia and white Americans in general. For Thomas Jefferson, James Madison and others of like mind, 'a settlement on the African Coast was preferable to the American interior because Negroes in the West would be destroyed by the "savages" (native American Indians) if too distant and would soon be at war with the whites if too near'.[18] It would seem that the decision to establish a Negro colony in Africa was calculated not only to remove the Negro 'beyond the reach of mixture' but also to keep him beyond the possibility of an insurrection against his master.

The American plan for a Negro colony in Africa attracted the support of many persons of varying backgrounds and interests. Paul Cuffee, a Negro Quaker, a businessman of good fortune and a resident of the State of Massachusetts, visited the British-established Negro colony at Sierra Leone at his own expense in 1811. Paul Cuffee's mother was an Indian and his father a Negro slave. Paul Cuffee was known to be the only man who actually transported Negroes to Africa at his own expense until the war of 1812.

President James Madison of the United States (1809–1817) declared war on Britain in 1812 because of indignation at the harassment of American commercial vessels by British and French warships. The activities of the American colonization movement were retarded by this war. Several thousand unwanted and nonstatused American Negroes fought gallantly against the British for the economic independence and survival of America.

By 1815 the crusade for the colonization of Negroes was clearly revived. Robert Findley, a pastor from Basking Ridge, New Jersey, resumed his 'proselytizings for Church participation in free-slave colonization in Africa'.[19] Some Negro churches and clergymen expressed their desire to join the cause. There were others who saw colonization merely as a means of ridding the country of Negroes.

In 1816 James Monroe was elected the fifth President of the United States of America. Like Thomas Jefferson and James Madison, President Monroe was a native of the State of Virginia and readily embraced the proposed scheme for the colonization of Negroes in Africa. Encouraged by President Monroe's support, Reverend Findley began to solicit financial support from the Federal Government of the United States, although Dr William Thornton, the original proponent of the colonization scheme, had not envisaged the use of public funds for such a purpose. In Thornton's view, the colonization of emancipated Negroes to Africa could best be accomplished through 'sincere missionary efforts by morally committed Churches and all true Christian believers'.[20] The funding required for an undertaking of the magnitude proposed by Dr Thornton was however, beyond the reach of 'missionary efforts,' 'committed Churches' and 'all true Christian believers'.

Organizing the Society to Colonize Free People of Color

America's efforts to colonize free Negroes 'beyond reach of mixture' gained momentum following the war of 1812 with Britain. Reverend Robert Findley recruited several prominent leaders to support the cause. Those recruited included such personalities as Elias Caldwell, Clerk of the Supreme Court of the United States of America and Findley's foster-brother-in-law, Francis Scott Key and Bushrod Washington, nephew of America's first President, George Washington. Bushrod Washington was, at the time of the founding of the American Colonization Society, an Associate Justice of the United States Supreme Court.

On December 21, 1816, the first organizational meeting was held for the purpose of forming a society for the colonization of emancipated American Negroes in a foreign land – preferably Africa. Henry Clay of Kentucky, a renowned slaver, an established lawyer and a great orator, was presiding officer. Also present at the historic first meeting were Daniel Webster of Massachusetts, another great American statesman and orator, and a Senator from the State of Maryland, a sister state of Virginia. Other Virginians present at the founders' meeting of the American Colonization Society included 'John Randolph, John Stull, Fernando Fairfax, Richard and Edmund Lee (elder brothers of

General-to-be Robert E. Lee) and several front-pew personalities including Presbyterian Elder Stephen Balch, the irrepressible Bishop Mead of the Virginia Episcopalians, and Reverend W.H. Wilmer, founder of the Virginia Theological Seminary'.[21] Henry Clay delivered the opening address and admitted that 'he was a slave owner without chagrin, that he cherished the humble, hardworking darkies who made the Clay plantation and cattle farms an internationally revered success'.[22] Like most Americans of his time, Henry Clay was tolerant of obedient, hardworking Negroes who knew their place, but as for the liberated, unowned black creatures, 'hell or back to Africa for them'.[23]

One week later, on December 28, 1816, a group of about fifty white Americans met and formally established the American Society for Colonizing Free People of Color. Bushrod Washington was elected the Society's first president and Elias Caldwell was elected first secretary. The number of Virginians instrumental in organizing and establishing the American Colonization Society might lead one to conclude that it was founded almost exclusively by Virginians.

When the Society was officially founded, Thomas Jefferson, who had retired from public service, endorsed its objectives and petitioned fellow-Virginian and United States President-elect James Monroe to support the cause of the American Colonization Society. At the same time the Society's new president Bushrod Washington, using his influence as Associate Justice of the United States Supreme Court, urged the Congress of the United States, through the House Committee on the Slave Trade, to support the cause of the Society by 'acquiring' a colony in Africa. Mr Washington also urged that the Congress secure 'a territory great enough to accommodate the entire Negro race'.[24]

Mr Washington's statement seems to suggest that the ultimate objective of the American Colonization Society was the total removal of all persons of Negro descent from America.

The Society and land acquisition

The American Colonization Society, conceived as a philanthropic venture, soon became a political instrument. Using the Anti-Slave Trade Act of 1807 as the authority to provide public funds to promote and achieve the objectives of the Society, President Monroe, with some difficulty, provided the sum of $100,000 to aid the cause of the American Colonization Society.

In 1821 the American Colonization Society dispatched two of its agents – Ephraim Bacon and Reverend Joseph R. Andrus – to the West African Coast to negotiate a 'land treaty' with the African natives.

The efforts of Andrus and Bacon to negotiate with King Jack Ben[25] and other chiefs of the Bassa tribe proved unsuccessful. Records of the land negotiations by Andrus and Bacon are sketchy and there is no certainty as to what actually occurred. The tribesmen and chiefs could not have readily accepted the sale of tribal lands, especially to white Americans, firstly because it went against tradition to sell tribal property, particularly land, and secondly because there was the fear that such a sale or any arrangement favoring the settling of Americans on tribal land would pose a threat to the survival of the tribal people. The experiences of the tribal peoples in withstanding slavers and the slave trade had been most horrifying. Many of the smaller and weaker tribes, including those residing at such coastal points then known as the Mosquito, Gold, Pepper (now Liberia) and Ivory Coasts, were the most ravaged. Other tribal communities along the West African coast 'were decimated, while entire tribes and once-abundant farming centers had been reduced to scatterings of distressed, harried and fearful survivors'.[26] The fear of being led into slavery haunted the tribesmen. Many of the slavers who frequented West Africa at the time were known to be Americans.

In December of 1821, following the failure of Andrus and Bacon to secure lands for the use of the American Colonization Society on the West Coast of Africa, the United States Government instructed Captain Robert F. Stockton of the United States Navy and Eli Ayres, a United States Navy surgeon, to proceed to the West African coast to obtain a 'land treaty' with the African natives in the interests of the American Colonization Society. Eli Ayres was appointed by President Monroe as his personal envoy to assist Captain Stockton, commander of the United States Navy schooner *Alligator*. Under the Anti-Slave Trade Act of 1807, the United States Navy was ordered to patrol the coasts of Africa and the high seas to ensure that vessels carrying Africans into slavery did not enter American waters or territories. The discharge of such 'illegal cargo' (ie slaves) on United States territory was not permitted under the Act. At the same time the United States Government, acting on instructions from President James Monroe, took the assignment of procuring through the Navy a 'land treaty' with the chiefs and natives of Cape Mesurado (site of present-day Monrovia).

Many 'would-be-slaves' were captured from slave vessels by the United States Navy and returned to Liberia. These became known as the 'recaptured slaves'.

Several writers, including Jehudi J. Ashmun, Director of the new colony in Liberia from 1822 through 1826, wrote about the 'land treaty' negotiation between Captain Stockton and Dr Ayres on the one hand and King George and the natives of Cape Mesurado on the other. In reporting the activities of the American colony in Liberia during the

14

period December 1821 to 1823, Ashmun related the Cape Mesurado negotiation as follows:

> After the preliminary negotiation, the tribesmen reconsidered and refused to allow the settlers to land (the first shipment of settlers was anchored at Shebro Island, Sierra Leone, while the 'land treaty' for the Cape was being negotiated). Dr Ayres was taken prisoner and obtained his release by consenting, as a condition for his freedom, to reaccept the remnant of the goods which had been advanced the month preceding in part payment for the lands; but contrived to evade the injunction for the immediate removal of the people from the country, by alleging the want of *vessels* for the purpose.[27]

To purchase the Cape, Ashmun wrote, 'a secret ex-parte agreement' was conducted with King George who resided on the Cape and claimed jurisdiction over the northern district of the peninsula of Montserrado.[28] Ashmun's account, for what it is worth, suggests that some force was used by the United States Navy to obtain the 'land treaty' for the Cape.

P.J. Staudenraus, in his book, *The African Colonization Movement, 1821–1865*, clearly describes the Stockton-Ayres encounter with King Peter and the natives of Cape Mesurado. According to Staudenraus, King Peter left the negotiation site for his village when the two parties could not reach a compromise. Stockton and Ayres pursued the King inland, where they encountered enormous resistance by the tribesmen, and King Peter declined to 'sell' any land. Stockton pointed a pistol at the King's head and procured a signed 'treaty' giving the American Colonization Society rights to Cape Mesurado, 'a stretch of land thirty-six miles long and three miles wide'.[29]

The reports of other writers about the Stockton-Ayres land negotiations with the chiefs and natives of Cape Mesurado confirmed the account given by Staudenraus. Davis[30] acknowledged that the success of the Stockton-Ayres land acquisition was the result of the dominance of the United States. The *Alligator*, Captain Stockton's warship, was dispatched to the West African coast by President Monroe to acquire land there in the name of the American Colonization Society, a task which the Society's agents, Andrus and Bacon, had failed to accomplish. By means of the US armed war vessel, 'the tribesmen were "persuaded" to sell a strip of land on the coast'.[31]

Liebenow wrote that the negotiations at the Cape were protracted and heated. 'At gunpoint, Captain Stockton attempted to convince King Peter and other Bassa and Dey Chieftains that the settlers came as benefactors, not enemies.'[32] Wilson also wrote that Captain Stockton and Dr Ayres 'went ashore and energetically persuaded the natives to sell . . . a strip of land one hundred and thirty miles long and forty miles deep . . .'[33] Wilson further indicated that 'there is no record of what the chiefs were paid for the coastal strip.'[34] There is also no consensus as to how much land was supposedly bought from the natives by Captain Robert F. Stockton and Dr Eli Ayres for the American Colonization Society. Foote concluded that, upon Ashmun's arrival in the colony in 1822, 'he found no documents defining the limits of the purchased territory.'[35] Many questions about the Cape Mesurado purchase remain unanswered and the details of this 'land treaty' can never be accurately reconstructed because there is no conclusive evidence as to what actually happened between Captain Stockton and Dr Ayres and the chiefs and tribesmen of Cape Mesurado.

CHAPTER THREE

A Commonwealth
of Colonies

Virginia-Caldwell Settlement

The settlement of the first colonists on Cape Mesurado, the site of present-day Monrovia, was followed by several other settlements in various parts of the new American colony on the West African coast soon to become the Commonwealth of Liberia. In 1824, two years after the arrival of the first American freed slave settlers at Cape Mesurado, the name Liberia was conferred on the settlement by Robert G. Harper, a white racialist of Baltimore, Maryland, USA. Liberia's capital Monrovia is named in honor of America's fifth President, James Monroe (1817–1825).

As the new colony of Liberia took form, various states and individual philanthropists in America began to lose interest in the parent American Colonization Society. Consequently, several local 'colonization movements' were organized. In 1831 the State of Virginia organized a state-sponsored colonization society to address itself to the problems of Negroes in that State. United States Chief Justice John Marshall was elected its first president. The Virginian Assembly, following the Nat Turner insurrection, set aside the sum of $90,000 for the local society to defray the cost of removing free Negroes from the State of Virginia. At a meeting held in 1837, the Colonization Society of the State of Virginia adopted the following resolution:

> Resolved, That the Managers of the Society be, and they are hereby, instructed to take proper measures for obtaining a suitable tract of territory on the coast of Africa for the establishment of a new plan-

tation, to be called New Virginia; and to be settled by free people of color, including manumitted slaves, from our own State, as soon as the necessary funds can be obtained for the purpose, from the patriotic contributions of our fellow-citizens, and the generous aid of the Legislature of our Commonwealth.[1]

The proposer of the resolution concluded:

I call it a new 'plantation,' Sir, because it was the term originally applied to our own colony, and I wish our new one to be, as it were, a slip from the old stock. I mean, however, that our plantation shall be, to all intents and purposes, a state – 'a free, sovereign and independent state,' in all the fullest and freest sense of the term; yet not a solitary, or single one, but bearing such relation to Liberia, and to the American Colonization Society of course, as our State does to the United States, or to the Union, and to the General Government; for we must have in due time, a union there also – another constellation, Sir, if you please, of social stars, mingling their rays together in another hemisphere.[2]

The Colonization Society of the State of Virginia acquired a site on the St Paul River and established a settlement opposite Caldwell. The settlement formed a part of the Commonwealth of Liberia. 'In 1850, 107 emigrants were sent from the State of Virginia, at a cost of $4,350; in 1851, 141 persons were colonized at a cost of $7,050; and, in 1851, 192 colonists arrived in Liberia from Virginia at a cost of $11,520.'[3]

Maryland Settlement

As in other states, the citizens of the State of Maryland were supportive of the efforts of the American Colonization Society when the parent society was founded. Between 1827 and 1831 the State of Maryland, through the State Legislature, set aside an annual sum of money for the American Colonization Society 'to be expended in the transportation to and maintenance in Africa of free Negroes inhabiting Maryland at the time of their emigration'. By 1832, however, Marylanders had lost interest in the American Colonization Society and resolved to form an independent State society. The society was named the Maryland State Colonization Society.

Chartered by the Legislature of the State of Maryland in 1832, the Maryland State Colonization Society was empowered to:

purchase, have and enjoy, to them and their successors, in fee, or otherwise, any lands, tenements and hereditaments by gift, grant, bargain and sale, devise, or other act of any person or persons, body politic or corporate whatsoever ... and to occupy, use and enjoy, or sell, transfer or otherwise dispose of, all such lands, tenements and hereditaments, goods or chattels, in such manner as they shall determine the best adapted and most conducive to the object of colonizing, with their own consent, in Africa the free people of color in Maryland, and such slaves as may be manumitted for the purpose, and which is declared to be the sole and exclusive object of the said Society.[4]

The Maryland State Colonization Society established a settlement in south-eastern Liberia and named in 'Maryland in Liberia'. The State of Maryland in Liberia remained independent of the other colonies in Liberia until February 28, 1857, when it agreed to join the Republic of Liberia.

Sinoe Settlement

The problem of free Negroes was considered in the State of Mississippi, as in other states, as a state (ie local) and not a national problem. Adopting the 'Maryland Plan', Mississippi decided to establish an independent colony, preferably in Africa, to which all free Negroes from the State of Mississippi would emigrate.

By 1824, white residents of Mississippi had embarked upon a campaign to encourage free Negroes residing in the State of Mississippi 'to emigrate to Haiti or to British Guyana or Trinidad'. In 1831 the Mississippi State Colonization Society was organized with the express purpose of aiding 'the Parent Institution (the American Colonization Society) in Washington, D.C., in the Colonization of free people of color of the United States, on the Coast of Africa'.[5] Between 1831 and 1866, the total number of Negroes who emigrated from the State of Mississippi to 'Mississippi in Africa' (ie Liberia) did not exceed six hundred. More than half of these settlers 'arrived after Mississippi in Africa ceased to exist as an independent settlement'.[6] Unlike other Negroes in Virginia, Maryland and other northern States, Negroes in the State of Mississippi showed unusual interest in colonization in Africa. In 1831, members of the Negro community in the State of Mississippi who favored colonization in Africa dispatched two of their number, Gloster Simpson and Archy Moore, to Liberia to investigate and report on conditions there. Encouraged by favorable reports from Simpson and Moore, the first expedition sent out by the Mississippi Society sailed from the port of New Orleans on the brig *Rover* on March 4, 1835, and arrived at Monrovia in April 1835. The party consisted of:

71 emigrants of whom 69 were from Mississippi. Two were free born. Of the remainder, eighteen had purchased their freedom, the others were slaves emancipated by Judge James Green and Mrs Mary Bul-

lock. Of the emigrants 22 were females, and 21 were children of ten years or under. Seventeen of the emigrants were literates. As the Mississippi Society has not as yet acquired a site for a colony, the emigrants were settled in Liberia, most of them at Millsburg, the rest at Monrovia. Five returned in the same year to the United States. A great number went to Mississippi in Africa, after that Settlement was founded.'[7]

Determined to establish an independent settlement in Africa, the Mississippi Society, with the help of the agent of the American Colonization Society, acquired title for a portion of land at the mouth of the Sinoe River from the native chiefs. The new settlement was called Mississippi in Africa, and the principal town was named Greenville, 'in honor of Judge James Green, who by his will had freed his slaves and left $25,000 for their transportation and support'.[8]

By early 1870, long after the independent settlement of Mississippi in Africa had ceased to exist and was in fact part and parcel of the Republic of Liberia, Negroes residing in the State of Mississippi expressed the desire to emigrate to Liberia. From some four hundred manumitted Mississippi Negroes, Blanche K. Bruce, the first and only Negro Senator from the State of Mississippi to serve a full six-year term, received petitions 'asking the government (ie the Mississippi State Government) for $100,000 so they could move to Liberia'.[9] Though Senator Bruce did not favor the request of his constituents, he defended the action of Negroes as they sought to flee the State of Mississippi to 'escape the harshness of white supremacy'.

Bassa Settlement

The settlement at Bassa was made possible by the merger of two independent colonization societies organized to pursue two distinct objectives. These societies were the Young Men's Colonization Society of Pennsylvania (YMCSP) and the Colonization Society of the City of New York (CSCNY). The Young Men's Colonization Society was organized in April 1834, principally to ensure that the 'large numbers of slaves emancipated under the will of a Virginian, Dr Aylett Hawes', a deceased member of the society, were transported to Liberia.

The Colonization Society of the City of New York, on the other hand, was organized to deal with the problems of ex-slaves in Savannah, Georgia, awaiting transportation to Africa. To accomplish their respective objectives, the two Societies combined their financial and human resources and, with the aid of the American Colonization Society, acquired a portion of land between the colonies of Mesurado and Mississippi in Africa (Sinoe), called Bassa Cove. The Societies further instructed that, to distinguish their settlements from other settlements already established in Liberia,' particular settlements at the Bassa Cove should be designated by the names of "New York" and "Pennsylvania" respectively'.[10]

On December 9, 1834, the first group of settlers, sponsored by the Young Men's Colonization Society of Pennsylvania and the Colonization Society of the City of New York, arrived at Monrovia on the *Ninus* 'and proceeded to the Bassa Cove on the following day'.[11] Prior to their departure for Liberia, the new settlers were advised, in keeping with the objectives of the Young Men's Colonization Society of Pennsylvania and the Colonization Society of the City of New York, to maintain 'the virtue of Sobriety' and withhold from 'all the common temptations and means for carrying on war, or for engaging in any aggressive steps with the native population of Africa ...'[12]

On June 10, 1835, barely six months after the establishment of the colony at Bassa Cove, the colonists alleged intrusions into their territory by the surrounding natives and almost completely abandoned the settlement. Many colonists proceeded to Monrovia and other nearby settlements. On October 9, 1835, Mr Ezekiel Skinner wrote a letter to the authorities of the Young Men's Colonization Society of Pennsylvania regarding developments at Bassa Cove. The following is an excerpt from Mr Skinner's communication, written apparently from Monrovia:

> I am sorry that I have time to write only a few lines to you, and to say that in removing the survivors of the late wars, also the last emigrants, and cargo to this place until after the rains, we have consulted both their comfort and safety and your interest. I propose now as soon as possible going to the Cove and making arrangements for the re-possessing of the establishment. I anticipate no difficulty in re-establishing the Colony. A small fortification and a few big guns will be sufficient to prevent future attacks. The natives, knowing that the Colony has the means of defense, will not, in my opinion, make any unlawful intrusions. Rest assured that so far as lies in my power, no opportunity for the promotion of your specific objects shall pass by unimproved.[13]

When the managers of the Societies (YMCSP and CSCNY) sponsoring the colony at Bassa Cove received reports of the occurrences there, they appointed Thomas Buchanan governor of the colony. Buchanan left America for Bassa Cove in December 1835, on the *Independence* 'which carried out only four emigrants and supplies for the Bassa Cove sufferers',[14] arriving in Monrovia on January 1, 1836. With the support of the United States Navy, the alleged harassment of the colonists by the natives was repelled and the colony at Bassa Cove was re-established under the leadership of Thomas Buchanan.

Table 2 *Status and Recorded Numbers of Negro Emigrants to Liberia 1822 – 1867 Under the Auspices of the American Colonization Society and Others**

Born free	4,541
Purchased their freedom	344
Emancipated to go to Liberia	5,957
'Free men'	753
From Barbados	304
Unknown	68
Total	12,009**
Settled by Maryland Society	1,227
Recaptured African slaves settled in Liberia by US Government	5,722
Grand Total	18,958

*Adapted from *American Journal of International Law*, Supplement, Vol. 4 (1910) (New York: Johnson Reprint Corporation), pp. 532–33.
**Note correction: Total number of emigrants settled by American Colonization Society is 12,009 instead of 11,909. Grand total of settlers is 18,958. See J. Gus Liebenow, *Liberia: The Evolution of Privilege* (Ithaca, New York: Cornell University Press, 1969), p.8.

On February 22, 1836, the Pennsylvania Society presented a report to its Board of Managers with the following contents:

Our Agent, while instructed to carry out the original design of the Society, by prosecuting our humane and benevolent purposes in a spirit of affectionate regard for the best interest of the natives, and using every effort for the preservation of the most friendly relations with them, has been furnished by the Navy Department with the means of defending the people under his charge against any fresh aggressions. From the well-known characteristics of those tribes, it is believed that the very fact of the colonists being possessed of the means of defense, will, in the language of our Constitution, operate as a 'dissuasion from warfares'.[15]

With the United States Navy providing 'protection' for the settlers, the emigrants voluntarily left America because, according to the United States Supreme Court Associate Justice Bushrod Washington, 'the so-called free slaves were in no legal sense citizens of the United States, and should therefore seize the opportunity to earn citizenship in Africa or another comparable distant place'.[16] Despite the material and moral support provided to the colonization movement by the American Government, 'less than twenty thousand Negroes left America'[17] for Liberia.

These settlers came from different parts of the United States with different experiences and backgrounds. They emigrated to Liberia to 'earn citizenship' and be free to determine their own destiny.

Discrimination in colonial Liberia

The *Strong*, last of the four ships which transported free American Negroes to Liberia under the auspices of the American Colonization Society, also returned to the African colony the first shipment of 're-·captured slaves' (fifteen in number) taken by United States naval vessels off the coast of the State of Georgia. Jehudi Ashmun, acting in the dual capacity of agent for both the American Colonization Society and the United States Government, received the 'recaptured' Africans. Ashmun immediately proceeded to arrange the living conditions and life-style to be adopted by the recaptured Africans and reported as follows to the American Colonization Society's Board of Managers:

1 They (the recaptured Africans) are to form a community by themselves, entirely unconnected, except in worship, and as here-after stated, with other colonists.

2 Their Superintendent is to control their hour of rising and sleep-ing, leading the family devotions,... instruct them ... in the principles of Christianity, from three to four hours, daily.

3 D. George is appointed to take charge of them at a particular hour every day, lead them into the fields, and teach them Agriculture, for several hours; subject to future designation.

4 Draper (Major T. Draper) is to be responsible for the good order, cleanliness, and good conduct of the boys ... rules, premiums, penalties are established ... [18]

Thus, offically, colonial Liberia had distinctly become a class-divided society. The colonists were provided with homes for themselves and their families; the recaptured Africans were under close supervision – to the extent that a member of the colony slept in adjacent quarters. If a colonist settled in Monrovia, he was assigned a lot in town plus five acres on the outskirts for farming.'[19] The same land allocation techniques employed in Virginia, Plymouth, Massachusetts Bay and other colonies in former British North America were used to distribute land in colonial

Liberia. 'If he (a colonist) settled in the country (this was a later date when the colonists began to move out of Monrovia), he was given 50 acres of land with the stipulation that he build a permanent house on it and put at least two acres of it into cultivation within a stipulated period of time.'[20] Such privileges were never accorded the recaptured Africans.

While all had advisory duties, only selected members from the colonists' midst occupied positions of leadership. 'Mr Johnston was named Commissary of Stores, Mr Sampson was Commissary of Ordinance, Lott Carey became Health Officer and General Inspector; others were named to various posts in the colonial government.'[21] Recaptured Africans, on the contrary, were told when to get up, when to sleep, when to learn, when to work. Most of the recaptured Africans returned to Liberia by US naval authorities were used and treated by the Negro settlers as menials. In 1827 some 127 recaptured Africans returned to Liberia by a US Navy vessel were forcibly indentured and 'apprenticed to Liberian subjects, the adults for seven years and the children till the age of twenty-one ...'[22]

Between 1826 and 1837, two new settlements, namely New Georgia[23] and Marshall, were established by the colonial government exclusively for these recaptured Africans. Several writers described these settlements and their inhabitants. In 1833, Reverend C.M. Waring mentioned one of the settlements in a letter, though not by name. 'These native Africans are located four miles from Monrovia, where they have built themselves a meeting-house sufficient for their worship.... I attend at that place once a month to administer the sacrament.'[24]

As they saw no difference culturally and socially between themselves and the indigenous natives from whom most of them had been separated for only a few years or less than one generation, the recaptured Africans began to relate to and intermarry with the natives.[25] Many members of the colonists' settlement group expressed concern about the relationship and intermixture between the recaptured Africans and natives. Some colonists took pains to report to Reverend Ralph R. Gurley, then Secretary-General of the American Colonization Society, the activities of the recaptured Africans. A Mr Mechlin wrote the following:

> Our recaptured Africans of the Ebo and Passo tribes, were in the habit of procuring wives from the adjacent tribes; this they effected by paying a small sum to the parent of the girl; the women thus obtained were brought into the colony, clothed after our own fashion, and we compelled them to be married according to the forms of some one of the churches (Christian), or to acknowledge themselves to be husband and wife before the Clerk of the Court of Sessions.[26]

The cultural differences are understandable. The colonists who were emancipated to embrace freedom and, according to one white American official, to 'introduce Christianity and promote civilization in Africa',[27] came with an adopted culture incompatible with that of the natives.

Reverend J.P. Pinney in a letter to the Brethren of the Western Foreign Missionaries Board, regretted the sentiments among the colonists:

The natives are, as to wealth and intellectual cultivation, related to the colonists as the Negro of America is to the white man; and this fact, added to their mode of *'dress'* ... leads to the same distinction, as exists in America between *colors*. A colonist of any dye (and many there are of darker hue than the Vey, or Dey, or Kree, or Basso), would if at all respectable, think himself degraded by marrying a native. The natives are in fact menials, (I mean those in town), and I am to be obliged to say, that so little effort is made by the colonists to elevate them, as is usually made by the higher classes in the United States, to better the condition of the lower.[28]

The emergence of social, economic and political classes took root in colonial Liberia. By 1837, the various settlements at Cape Mesurado, Greenville, Bassa Cove, Caldwell, Millsburg, Virginia and others, torn by internal strife, united and formed a Commonwealth. Adopted by the Board of Directors of the American Colonization Society on January 5, 1839, Article I of the Constitution of the Commonwealth of Liberia reads:

The Colonies or settlements of Monrovia, New Georgia, Caldwell, Millsburg, Marshall, Bexley, Bassa Cove, and Edina, and such other Colonies hereafter established by this Society, or by Colonization Societies adopting the Constitution of the American Colonization Society, on the Western Coast of Africa, are hereby united into one Government, under the name and style of the Commonwealth of Liberia.[29]

The settlements of New Georgia and Marshall, though embraced as part of the Commonwealth of Liberia, did not receive equal consideration for development with other settlements because these two were exclusively inhabited by the recaptured Africans. New Georgia is situated four miles from Monrovia while Marshall is only twenty miles outside Monrovia.

The emergence of Liberia as Black Africa's first independent republic was the result of social and political events in American history. Liberia's existence is so closely linked to America's that one American journalist referred to Liberia as 'America's Black Stepchild.' Despite

America's support for Liberia, some problems soon developed which were beyond the control of the United States. One of the major problems which confronted the leadership of the Commonwealth of Liberia was the handling of matters relating to the commercial activities carried on between the native Liberians and British traders and explorers. The fear of encroachment on its territory by Britain, France and Germany caused the Commonwealth to request American intervention. With assurances of support, the colonists began to interfere with British subjects engaged in commerce with Liberian natives outside the recognized limits of the Commonwealth of Liberia.

Disturbed by the action of the Commonwealth of Liberia against British subjects, Mr Fox, Britain's Minister to the United States, made an official inquiry of Mr Upshur, then US Secretary of State, in a letter date 9 August 1843:

> I had recently the honour to state to you ... that Her Majesty's Government have, for some time past, been desirous of ascertaining authentically, the nature and extent of the connexion subsisting between the American Colony of Liberia, on the Coast of Africa, and the Government of the United States. Certain differences which have arisen ... between British subjects trading with Africa on one hand, and the authorities of Liberia on the other, render it very necessary ... that Her Majesty's Government should be accurately informed what degree of official patronage and protection if any, the United States Government extend the colony of Liberia ... as a national establishment; ... and consequently ... if at all, United States Government hold themselves responsible toward foreign countries for the acts of the authorities of Liberia.[30]

In response to Mr Fox's inquiry, Mr Upshur, after relating why and how Liberia was founded, concluded:

> It is due to Her Majesty's Government that I should inform you that this Government regards it (Liberia) as occupying a peculiar position, and as possessing peculiar claims to the friendly consideration of all Christian powers; that this Government will be, at all times, prepared to interpose its good office to prevent any encroachment by the colonies upon any just right of any nation; and that it would be very unwilling to see it despoiled of its territory rightfully acquired, or improperly restrained in the exercise of its necessary rights and powers as an independent settlement.[31]

America's expression of unwillingness to see Liberia despoiled of its territory lessened British commercial animation; relieved temporarily the leadership of the Commonwealth; and ignited once again the path-finding torch to independence – the declaration of a sovereign, independent and universally recognized Nation of Liberia.

The American Colonization Society, being a private organization based in America, was not internationally recognized and could not, therefore, negotiate international treaties. Neither could it any longer afford properly to direct and instruct the overseas colony, since matters relevant to the existence of the Commonwealth of Liberia had been elevated to the international platform. A decision by the Society to relinquish the colony was not long in coming.

Four years later, on July 26, 1847, Liberia declared independence, embraced a republican form of Government and adopted a Constitution modeled on that of the United States. It is interesting, however, that the United States did not officially recognize Liberia as an independent nation for fifteen years following independence. Britain, ironically, was the first to recognize Liberia as a sovereign and independent nation.

Table 3 *Countries Recognizing Liberia as a Sovereign and Independent Nation*

Country	Date of recognition
Great Britain	1848
France & Germany	May 29, 1855
Denmark	May 29, 1855
Maryland in Liberia	January 4, 1856
Belgium	March 29, 1858
USA	October 10, 1862
Italy	October 26, 1865
Netherlands	December 20, 1865
Portugal	March 4, 1865
Norway & Sweden	September 1, 1865
Australia	September 1, 1865
North Germany Confederation	October 3, 1867
Spain	December 12, 1894

A Constitution from without

Every form of government, democratic or otherwise, must meet a final test and obligation; that of being acceptable and suitable to the needs of the governed. For Liberia, 'the new government was founded improvidently, without sufficient study or knowledge of the conditions to be met'.[32] The First Liberian Republic was modeled on the republican form of government in the United States, and the Constitution was written by a Professor Simon Greenleaf of Harvard University. The Constitution of the First Republic was beyond the comprehension of the people whom it was meant to govern as well as those entrusted with its implementation because:

1 The Constitution of the First Liberian Republic did not evolve out of the natural conditions and surroundings and/or orientations of the Liberian experience;
2 The leadership of the country at the time had no experience of the education of the schools from which the organic statutory laws of the adopted constitution evolved; and,
3 For the natives, the term constitution or its content was incompatible with their traditional political philosophies.

Though the Constitution of the First Republic was a good instrument, its implementation by the leadership was the source of many of the problems which led to the overthrow of the First Republic on April 12, 1980 by seventeen enlisted men of the Armed Forces of Liberia.

The survival of any national government depends on its ability to maintain stability and peace amongst the various elements within its jurisdiction. In the First Liberian Republic, despite the constitutional guarantee of freedom, justice and equality, a native or aboriginal Liberian was considered inferior to an Americo-Liberian by reason of his alleged 'heathenism'; similarly, a native of Liberia was not considered a full citizen unless he was, by the standards of the settlers, completely detribalized or 'civilized', a concept beyond the grasp of a tribesman in the same manner that it is difficult for a Westerner to appreciate fully the significance of some African tribal customs.

Absence of national consciousness

In spite of the achievement of independence, there was a clear division between the natives and the officials of the Government of the new Republic. The Declaration of Independence, an interestingly worded document, confirms the cultural, political, religious, and social differences between the peoples of the new Republic. These differences explain in part the absence of the national consciousness in the new Republic. The second statement in the Declaration of Independence reads:

... While announcing to the nations of the world the new position which the people of the Republic have felt themselves called upon to assume, courtesy to their opinion seems to demand a brief accompanying statement of the causes which induced them, first to expatriate themselves from the LAND OF THEIR NATIVITY and to form a settlement on this BARBAROUS coast ...[33]

Here, as we see, America, not Africa, was the land of their nativity and Africa, not America which denied the colonists every imaginable claim to human dignity, was regarded as barbarous. The pleas continue:

... Removed beyond those influences which oppressed us in OUR NATIVE LAND, it was hoped we would be enabled to enjoy those rights and privileges and exercise and improve those faculties which the God of nature has given us in common with the rest of mankind.[34]

The attitude of the colonists, who subsequently became the organizers and leaders of the New Republic, toward the natives or aboriginal Liberians was of vital importance in determining the degree of participation by indigenous Liberians in the political process. The indigenous Liberians or natives have through a thousand years developed a unique culture and a civilization different from that of America, the country claimed by the 'former slaves' and 'founding fathers' of the Liberian Republic as the land of their nativity. Without any regard for their customs, laws and traditions, the natives were referred to as 'heathens, infidels and savages'.[35]

The perceived differences between the minority element comprizing the colonists or Americo-Liberians and the aborigines, who comprized some 95 percent of the national population, continued uncorrected. The meagre resources of the Republic were diverted to warfare against indigenous Liberians by the Americo-Liberian controlled Government, and toward the settlement of countless numbers of internal disputes and rivalries.

In his First Inaugural Address, President Arthur Barclay (1904–1912), considering the prerequisites for national unity, said:

Two questions have for many years agitated and vexed the minds of thinking citizens:
1 How can we best develop and utilize the resources of our land?
2 In what way can the Government best satisfy, control and attach the native populations to the interest of the State?

Of these questions, the first interests more the Americo-Liberian population, intent on material prosperity; but the latter is most important. We cannot develop the interior effectively until a satisfactory understanding with the resident populations is arrived at.

The efforts which we have, in the past, made to coerce these populations by arms, have deservedly failed. Government must rest on the consent of the governed. We made a great initial mistake in the beginning of our national career. We sought to obtain, and did succeed in grasping an enormous mass of territory, but we neglected to conciliate and attach the resident populations to our interest. Our present narrow and jealous trade policy, initiated in the sixties, has had the worst possible effect upon our political relations with the outlying native populations. Take for instance the Manna and Gallinas territories, formerly a part of Liberia. Why did we lose these? Because we neglected to look after and conciliate the populations. We thought their wishes and desires unworthy of serious consideration, and after enduring the situation for many years they detached themselves from the interest of Liberia, and carried their territories with them. The same thing happened with respect to the territory below the Cavalla, and although we regarded the secession of those districts a great national loss, we have never drawn the proper lesson from the incident and we are still inclined to proceed on the old mistaken lines. Our old attitude of indifference toward the native populations must be dropped. A fixed and unwavering policy with respect to the Native, proceeding on the lines of interest their local affairs, protection, civilization and safeguarding their institutions when not brutal or harmful, should at once be set on foot ...

When we came here in 1822, the country was indeed divided among a large number of tribes, but there were signs, not only in this territory but along the whole West Coast, of a desire to merge the tribal governments into wider political organizations which would secure the peace of the country, put a stop to incessant raids, devastations, and consequent loss of life and property and give the working class a chance to secure progress and development.[36]

In his own Inaugural Address twelve years later (1916), President Daniel Edward Howard (1912–1920) expressed concern about the state of disunity among the native and Americo-Liberian populations of Liberia. Speaking of the military officers loaned to Liberia by the United States Government to organize and train Liberian military personnel for the purpose of maintaining 'peace and order on the coast and in the interior', President Howard said:

All of the officers so far secured have been under fire, the following wars have been fought: Tappi, August 1912 to January 1913, under Captain Brown; Rivercess and Rockcess, October, 1912 to April 1913, under Major Ballard; Bandi, July to November, 1913 under Captain Hawkins; Gissi, November, 1914 to February 1915, under Lieutenants Martin and Miller; Pahn (Cape Palmas) April to June 1915, under Captain Hawkins; Planh and Secomb, May, 1915, under Major York, and I may mention the present war at Sinoe.[37]

In the 1916 issue of the *Official Gazette*, President Howard expressed his disappointment about the numerous wars in which his administration had engaged and remarked: 'What manner of Government is this, which recounts civil strife as if it were an honorable adventure and a credit to themselves?' All of these wars between the government forces and the aborigines were fought during the first four-year term of President Howard's administration.

CHAPTER FOUR

Roots of Crisis: Mismanagement and Official Abuse

The problems of the First Liberian Republic had many roots. From the arrival of the colonists through to Independence and the post World War II period, Liberia experienced social and political problems. External problems, in the form of encroachment, or threat of encroachment, on Liberian territory by foreign powers, were beyond the control of the Republic. Though Britain and France posed the most serious threat to the poverty-stricken Republic, Portugal, Spain and Germany exerted considerable pressure in their own attempts to despoil Liberia of its territory. Internally, a lack of the arts of administration and management, coupled with official abuse of power, further reduced whatever chances existed for progress in the Republic.

Until the post World War II era, Liberia's economy was in a state of near-disaster. As early as 1864 it was observed that the Government was not receiving all the money to which it was rightfully entitled. A Special Committee on Public Accounts was empowered by the Legislature to investigate the affairs of the Secretary of the Treasury. The Special Committee complained that its investigation had been hampered by the 'habitual absence of the Secretary of the Treasury from his office'. The Committee, in its final report, noted that 'there has been much irreregularity and looseness in keeping the public accounts.'[1] Enormous sums of money paid out of the public accounts went unreported to the Secretary of the Treasury. During the previous years a national deficit of $118,957 was supported by funds allocated by the United States Government for the transportation and support of recaptured African slaves resettled in Liberia.

It appeared also that part of the public fund had been used for private speculation for the benefit of President Stephen Allen Benson[2], second President of the Republic of Liberia. Large amounts of merchandise invoiced to the government were redirected to President Benson's account at very low prices; and the goods were afterwards sold by the Government Storekeeper at high prices, the profit being credited to the President ... [3] Other questionable activities on the part of public officials were also uncovered by the Special Committee on Public Accounts.

In 1871 Liberia succeeded in securing her first foreign loan. The Legislature empowered President Edwin James Roye (1870–1871) to negotiate a $500,000 loan of which $100,000 was to be used to buy up Government paper of any kind outstanding; another $100,000 was to be deposited with the public exchequer as security for the issue of treasury notes; and the balance was to be deposited in a bank as an emergency fund.[4] President Roye appointed two Liberians, along with the British Consul in Liberia, to go to London to negotiate the loan. 'The bankers agreed to lend the nominal sum of $500,00 at a discount of 30 percent, and seven percent interest, repayable in fifteen years.' That is to say, in return for issuing bonds amounting to $500,000 and paying seven percent interest, the Liberian Government was to receive only $350,000.[5] The British Consul who headed the delegation to negotiate the loan was an agent for the banking firm from which the loan was secured. President Roye did not advise the Legislature of the terms and conditions on which the loan was obtained. It was later discovered that a large portion of the proceeds from the loan was converted to the personal use of President Roye and his friends and that 'the Liberian Government actually received only $100,000 out of the $500,000 which was borrowed'.[6] Although the loan funds had not been accounted for by President Roye, he attempted unconstitutionally to extend his two-year term of office to four without the approval of the Legislature.

On October 19, 1871, President Edward James Roye was impeached and removed from office. He was the first and only President to be impeached during the tenure of the First Republic.

Joseph Jenkins Roberts who was the first President of the First Republic (1848–1856) became President for the second time when President Roye was removed from office. In his inaugural speech on January 1, 1872, Mr Roberts admitted that 'there has been culpable laxity and want of system at the Treasury Department'. President Roberts indicated further that 'we have been reduced to our present monetary condition by gross official corruption and a lavish misapplication of the public funds'.[7]

The 'gross official corruption and lavish misapplication of the public funds' referred to by President Roberts in 1872 can be traced to the administration of President Stephen Allen Benson (1856–1864), the second President of the First Republic. It was during President Benson's administration that the National Legislature formed a committee known as the Special Committee on Public Accounts. This Committee, empowered to investigate the management of the public funds by the Secretary of the Treasury, implicated President Benson in its report to the Legislature as having used public funds for his own personal benefit.

In analyzing further the double-edged problem of 'mismanagement' and 'gross official corruption', President Roberts remarked:

> Since 1864 this question of the public finance has been a source of perplexing anxiety. In consequence of a seriously defective financial policy .... the legal tender of the country became greatly depressed. The Legislature, from time to time, applied remedies which they hoped would relieve the Treasury, and restore the finances to a healthy state. Their measures, however, were to increase the revenue, without descending to the root of the evil .... unfavourably affecting all the operation of government and producing vexatious inconveniences and distress upon the community at large.[8]

Referring to the disastrous experience of the Republic with regard to the first $500,000 loan involving President Roye, President Roberts thought it useless to apportion blame. However, he made the following observation:

> It (the loan) has not only increased the financial burdens of the country, but has produced other evils which every good citizen can but deplore.... It has been negotiated contrary to the terms of the law as understood by the framers and in the method of its negotiation the President assumed to himself powers not only not authorized by law, but contrary to an expressed declaration of the Constitution. And the whole transaction has been conducted in a manner so unusual and informal that, by shameful peculations and misapplications, the loan – as far as at present known – is not likely to realize more than sixty or sixty-five percent of the amount for which, as alleged, the government stand pledged.[9]

Financial difficulties continued to plague the Republic. In 1906 Liberia negotiated a second loan, also through a foreign agent, Sir Harry Johnston, who was agent for the Liberia Development Company – a British firm interested in the development of the rubber industry in Liberia. The loan agreement 'provided for a capital sum to be advanced to the Liberian Government through the Erlanger Company of $500,000 at six percent interest.'[10] Of this amount one hundred and fifty thousand dollars was to redeem the 'floating indebtedness and Treasury Notes of Liberia'.

Two years later, in January 1908, President Barclay informed the Legislature that he had 'indignantly rejected' the proposal made to the Government by Sir Harry Johnston with respect to the purchase by the Government of the Liberia Development Company for the sum of $500,000. In an attempt to resolve the matter the Liberian Government arranged with the Liberia Development and the Erlanger Companies the release of the unused portion of the loan ($150,000) to the Government. The Government later 'severed all connections with the Development Company, making itself responsible for the remainder of the loan directly to the Erlanger group'.[11]

Table 4 *Debt Toll by 1910 – Liberia*

Foreign:	
Loan of 1871, $4\frac{1}{2}\%$, principal and unpaid interest	$443.025
Loan of 1906	464,640
Domestic:	
Funded at 3%, principal and unpaid interest	113,207
Funded at 6%, principal and unpaid interest	30,000
Unfunded non-interest bearing	238,698
Total	$1,289,570

Adapted from Buell, *The Native Problem in Africa* (Frank Cass & Co. Ltd., 1965) p.801

Much of the domestic debt was in the form of Treasury Notes which foreign traders 'had acquired considerably below par'. Still confronted with serious financial crisis, in 1908 the Liberian Government sent a commission to the United States to appeal for help as the experiences with the first two loan agreements (1871 and 1906) with British firms had not proved satisfactory. The British Government later informed the Americans that the 'main risk to the future of Liberia arises from the inefficiency of Liberian administration of their own affairs, especially in matters of finance'.[12] The terms of the 1906 loan provided that the Liberian Customs and Frontier Force be manned and supervised by British officials. Britain had established a strong commercial influence in Liberia. Because of these commercial ties, the British Government informed the Government of the United States 'that it would support any scheme for a loan which would put Liberia's finances in shape, provided that the preferential rights and privileges of British bond-holders of the present Customs loan (ie the 1906 loan) were maintained and that provisions were made in the scheme for the payment of outstanding British claims'.[13] The British Government further expressed the opinion that 'complete control of revenue and expenditure' of the Government of Liberia should 'be placed in the hands of European or American Commissioners'.[14]

The United States Commission

In response to the request from the Government of Liberia appealing for help from the United States, President Taft (1909–1913) of the United States appointed a Commission to proceed to Liberia to investigate the financial affairs of the Republic. On March 4, 1909 the US Congress appropriated funds to enable the Taft Commission to carry out its mandate. The Commission arrived in Monrovia in May 1909, and remained in the country for about a month. The Commission observed that France, due to her own interest in Liberia, 'protested' the presence and participation of British advisers in the management of Liberian affairs. The Commission further stated that 'if Liberia is to be dismembered, France wants a share in it.... It is generally believed in Liberia that Germany has been biding her time till she could undertake with good grace an intervention in Liberian affairs.'[15]

In its report, the Commission proposed the following measures to be taken by the US Government: (1) that the United States extend its aid to Liberia in the prompt settlement of pending boundary disputes; (2) that the United States enable Liberia to refund its debt by assuming as a guarantee for the payment of obligations under such arrangement the control and collection of the Liberian Customs; (3) that the United States lend its assistance to the Liberian Government in the reform of its internal finances; (4) that the United States lend its aid to Liberia in organizing and drilling an adequate constabulary or frontier force; (5) that the United States establish and maintain a research station in Liberia; (6) that the United States should reopen the question of establishing a naval coaling station in Liberia.[16]

President Taft of the United States partially rejected the proposal for an exclusive American control of the Liberian Customs. As an alternative the United States Government arranged a private loan and established control over Liberian finances through the banks.

Rather than an exclusive American control of Liberia's finances as proposed by the US Commission in 1909, an international receivership was established 'with an American as General-Receiver assisted by

French, German and British Receivers'.[17] With all the powers satisfied, Liberia's third foreign loan, financed by American and European financial institutions, was approved. 'The agreement provided for a loan of $1,700,000 at five percent interest to mature within forty years or in 1952'.[18] The purpose of the loan, according to the Agreement, was 'the adjustment of the indebtedness of the Republic and the settlement of claims or concessions, while the eventual balance of the proceeds of the Loan will be used for productive purposes'.[19]

Repayment of the loan of 1871 was made possible in 1912. The principal, including accrued interest, amounted to some $800,000. The 1912 loan, of course, was granted on the condition that Liberia reformulated her fiscal and domestic policies. The Government of the First Republic, either unwilling or lacking the means to institute meaningful fiscal and domestic reforms, made virtually no effort to institute desired changes. Apparently unhappy with the state of affairs in Liberia, the US Secretary of State, Mr Lansing, on April 4, 1917 transmitted a Diplomatic Note to the American Minister in Liberia with the following contents:

> The Department of State has in the past made known to the Government of Liberia through your Office its disappointment in the administration of Liberian affairs, and the time has now arrived when this Government, as next friend of Liberia, must insist upon a radical change of policy. The Government of the United States can no longer be subjected to criticism from other foreign powers as regards the operation of the loan agreement, and can no longer tolerate failure on the part of the Liberian Government to institute and carry out necessary administrative reforms.
>
> Unless the Liberian Government proceeds without delay to act upon the advice and suggestions herewith expressed, this Government will be forced, regretfully, to withdraw the friendly support that historic and other considerations have hitherto prompted it to extend.[20]

It will be recalled that Liberia was in a state of turmoil. President Howard in his Inaugural Address of 1916 admitted that 'all of the officers thus far secured (from the US Government) have been under fire'. Between 1913 and 1916 seven different civil wars had been fought between the native (ie the aboriginal Liberians) and government forces. The First World War was at the same time taking its toll on the economy of a country already devastated by internal strife, mismanagement and, according to President Roberts, 'gross official corruption'.

By 1920, its finances still in a state of chaos, Liberia was in need of yet another loan to revive its badly battered economy.

The Firestone Agreement and forced labor

In May 1922, in an attempt to boost the price of rubber, Britain announced the so-called 'Stevenson Plan'. The objective of the Stevenson Plan was to reduce by 75 percent the production of rubber, an industry monopolized at the time by Britain, and thus to increase the price of the commodity. Britain at the time controlled the production of 80 percent of the world's rubber, while the United States consumed about 70 percent of the total production. Winston Churchill, the then British Colonial Secretary, conceived the Stevenson Plan as an opportunity to settle Britain's World War I indebtedness to the United States.

Mr Harvey S. Firestone, Sr., 'head of a rubber tire company in Akron, Ohio', who was concerned about the British monopoly of the rubber industry, decided to investigate the possibility of offering Britain some competition in that field. Liberia was an ideal choice for the establishment of Mr Firestone's proposed plantation because, prior to World War I, it had been reported that the soil and climate in Liberia were favorable to the rubber industry. This report was partly substantiated by the operation of the Liberia Development Company, the rubber plantation owned by Sir Harry Johnston.

In 1923, Mr Firestone sent a representative to Liberia to establish the authenticity of these earlier reports. Finding the conditions ideal for a rubber plantation, Mr Firestone's representative offered the Liberian Government a proposal for a concession to establish a rubber plantation in Liberia.

The Firestone Company asked for a lease on the Mount Barclay rubber plantation, previously the property of the Liberia Rubber Corporation. It offered to rent this plantation for a dollar an acre for the first year – a total of two thousand dollars – with an option of renewal for ninety-nine years. The object of this concession was to experiment with the soil and the cost of production. In case the experiment proved satisfactory, Firestone proposed to lease for ninety-nine years a million acres at the rate of five cents an acre annually for the first six years, on the understanding that the Liberian Government would give 'reasonable co-operation in securing sufficient labor for the efficient operation of the Plantation'.[21]

The Government rejected the rental rate offered by Firestone for the Mount Barclay Plantation and reduced from one million to five hundred thousand acres the area of land requested for the plantation. The Firestone negotiator, supported by influential Americans anxious to arrest the British monopoly of the rubber industry, was eager to remind the Liberian authorities that the Firestone proposals for 'development' were made 'with the spirit and idea of further strengthening the traditional bonds of friendship and amity that have always existed between the peoples of Liberia and the United States of America'.[22]

On June 19, 1924, Firestone and Liberia reached a tentative agreement in which the previous position of the Government was compromised. In December 1924, when the Legislature assembled to review the Firestone Agreement, President King in his opening address cautioned the Legislature to 'give liberal encouragement to foreign capital'. He advised the lawmakers to '... brush aside the old usual scare, now worn out by age, of "selling the country". Cease looking to foreign Governments for assistance in the shape of loans for the development of our country.... In considering proposals from strong and reliable foreign capitalists, for the development of the economic resources of our country, we should not permit our views to be obscured or warped by narrow and selfish considerations of immediate and direct financial gains accruing to the Government...'[23]

At about the same time as Mr Firestone and his supporters were interested in the establishment of a rubber plantation in Liberia, France had encroached on Liberian territory during the Zinta boundary disputes. At the height of the French threat, United States military aid was requested by the Government of Liberia. In addition to military aid, Liberia was seeking a loan of $5,000,000 to revive her economy. Mr Firestone's offer to provide Liberia with the $5,000,000 loan was refused, as the Liberian Cabinet 'did not want the industrial and financial interest of the country tied up in the hands of one man'.[24]

The Liberian Government, having rejected Mr Firestone's offer to link the industrial and financial interests of Liberia to his proposed rubber concession, instructed the then Secretary of State, Edwin J. Barclay, to proceed to the United States to investigate the possibility of securing a $5,000,000 loan from sources independent of Firestone. The Secretary of State was also instructed to discuss with American officials the military aid requested of the United States by Liberia in relation to the boundary dispute with the French.

While in New York, Secretary Barclay held discussions again with Mr Harvey S. Firestone, Sr., who by now had embarked upon a subtle maneuver. Mr Firestone had organized a financial institution, supposedly independent of Firestone, known as the Financial Corporation of America. Mr Firestone lobbied for, and obtained, the support of some influential members of the United States Congress and the State Department during the negotiations with Liberia. In Mr Firestone's view, 'Liberia offered the best of natural advantages' because of the abundance of 'indigenous labor' considered by Firestone as 'practically inexhaustible'.

Under pressure from the US State Department, Barclay signed the

Agreements with the Firestone Rubber Company on September 16, 1925, including one agreement with the Finance Corporation of America for a $5,000,000 loan at seven percent interest. Mr Harvey S. Firestone later remarked:

> The (Liberian) Government welcomed our proposals and offered most advantageous terms and conditions. Liberians consider themselves more or less a protectorate of America and want American capital to develop the country. They gave us the greatest concession of its kind ever made.[25]

The basic components of the Firestone Agreements signed in 1925 were:

1 Mr Firestone acquires from Government the lease of the Mount Barclay rubber plantation which consists of two thousand acres of tappable rubber trees. The Mount Barclay rubber plantation is leased to Mr Firestone for ninety-nine years at a rent of one dollar an acre or two thousand dollars for the first year and six thousand dollars for the whole plantation annually thereafter.
2 Mr Firestone will lease for a period of ninety-nine years a million acres of land suitable for the production of rubber or other agricultural products, or any lesser area that may be selected by Mr Firestone. All products of the Firestone plantation and all machinery and other supplies for land shall be exempt from customs duties and from any internal tax, except a revenue tax on rubber exports. *But this exemption does not apply to employees nor to laborers.*
3 Mr Firestone will construct and keep in repair the harbor of Monrovia, the Government to repay the construction cost of the harbor at a rate of seven percent per year.

The American Government disclaimed any official support of the Firestone negotiation, especially the American Finance Corporation loan. The US Acting Secretary of State, Mr Castle, admitted only that the US State Department had seen the Firestone Contract and had suggested certain changes. 'The Department took no more part in the loan to Liberia than it does in any foreign loan, and never opposed the Liberian loan. It merely said that from the point of view of National Policy, it had no objection to the loan'.[26]

In the same statement, the State Department denied that the delay by the United States in helping Liberia repel the threat by France over the Zinta boundary dispute had anything to do with the Firestone negotiations. However, immediately following the signing of the Firestone

Agreements, the US State Department was instrumental in sending American marines to Liberia to protect 'American financial investment'.[27] One year after the signing of his concession agreement, Mr Firestone made the following declaration before a Congressional Committee:

> If America is to attain any degree of independence in its source of supply of rubber as well as other materials which are now in the hands of foreign monopoly, our government must give proper encouragement to capital and must assure the industries interested that it will lend it utmost assistance in protecting our investments.[28]

Having induced Liberia to accept the loan from the Finance Corporation of America, a Firestone concern, on the strength of the agreement to construct the harbor at Monrovia, Mr Firestone abandoned the plans for the construction of the harbor 'because of the tremendous expenses which would be involved'.[29]

When Senator Van Pelt denounced the Firestone proposal during a debate in the Legislature, President King threatened to have him impeached 'if he did not confine himself to the truth'. The Senator thereafter supported the Firestone Agreements.

The *Liberian Star* outlined the benefits Liberia was to gain from the Firestone Agreements as follows:

> For Liberia, (a) these leases mean direct increase of public revenue by the payments of rents, commissions and duties by the lessee, (b) construction of ports and harbors, and the development of the interior thereby making Liberia the most important spot in Africa, (c) indirectly the Government will be helped as the company will employ thousands of Liberians, thereby helping to solve the unemployment problem; this means relief to many homes and individuals and an increase in consumption which means larger imports and exports and consequently larger revenues, (d) our people will be encouraged in industry and agriculture as the Representatives of Mr Firestone are open to give advice and assistance to individuals who will plant rubber and other agricultural products.[30]

Though the benefits of the Firestone Agreement as reported in the *Liberian Star* appeared to outweigh the disadvantages, it was never mentioned that under the terms of the agreement the Liberian Government was required to supply 50,000 laborers annually under a 'contract system' to work the Firestone plantation. This was the 'practically inexhaustible indigenous labor' to which Mr Firestone had earlier referred in the early stages of the concession negotiation.

Table 5 Ideal Recruiting Report of Chiefs[31]

Chief	District	Section	Tribe	No of Men	
				Sent	Arrived
CC Kpama Yomo	Kakata	Kpama	Kpelle	15	15
CC Kpabah Gbeles	Kakata	Gbelee	Kpelle	10	7
CC Gbalokai	Kakata	Konoyea	Kpelle	11	11
CC K. Daniel	Kakata	Queline	Kpelle	14	10
CC D. Livingstone	Kakata	Sanoyea	Kpelle	10	18
CC K. Lupu	Kakata	Mekllie	Kpelle	14	14
CC Kpenbah	Kakata	Gbama	Kpelle	11	11
PC B. Zinnah	Bopolu-Suehn	Popolu	Kpelle	24	24
PC Menyongai	Kakata	Gibi	Bassa	42	38
PC Vana Woo	Bopolu-Suehn	Kongba	Gola	13	13
PC Varfee Sirleaf	Bopolu-Suehn	Mecca	Mandingo	9	9
PC Mongru	Sanniquellie	Gborplay	Geh	32	32
PC Mongru	Sanniquellie	Stolay	Geh	21	21
PC Wydordea	Tappita	Messonah	Manp	27	21
PC G. Toweh	Tappita	Boe-Quella	Gio	18	8
PC Wydordea	Tappita	Yarwin	Mano	17	12
PC Weipah Paye	Tappita	Doe	Gio	16	11
PC Segbeh Dahn	Tappita	Gbai-Gblor	Gio	14	6
PC Nyonton Paye	Tappita	Kpiaplay	Krahn	16	16
Total				334	287

Note: 'PC' designates Paramount Chief, leader of a Chiefdom within a District; 'CC' means Clan Chief, leader of a Clan within a Chiefdom; and 'TC' represents Town Chief, leader of a Clan within a town.

The forced labor contract system

In keeping with the agreement to recruit laborers for Firestone, the Liberian Government in 1926 established a Labor Bureau headed by a Commissioner who was appointed by the President of Liberia. The Bureau was part of the Department of the Interior under the control of the Secretary of the Interior. The Labor Bureau performed the task of 'recruiting' by sending out 'requisitions to each Native and District Commissioner who in turn divided up contingents among Chiefs. According to the Commissioner, the Firestone Plantations paid the

Table 6 Tribes as Represented on Firestone's Labor Force[32]

Tribe	Number
Bassa	2,685
Belle	435
Buzzie	4,004
(T) Tcjoem	31
Dey	73
Gbandi	1,594
Gio	3,975
Gizzie	1,969
Gola	766
Grebo	2,585
Kpelle	5,486
Krahn	571
Kru	563
Mandingo	247
Mano	3,666
Mendi	1,197
Vai	259
Total	30,016

Chiefs one cent a day for each boy (laborer) and the same sum to the Government Bureau'.[33] The Labor Bureau was the arm of Government which imposed 'forced labor' upon the 'indigenous people'.

As Liberian officials and chiefs are already accustomed to imposing compulsion whether in securing men for road work or for Fernando Poo, there is no reason to believe that they will employ any different methods in obtaining labor for the Firestone Plantations.

Hundreds of natives are being obliged to work free for the government, and a number of them likewise work almost for nothing upon Liberian farms where some of them are held as pawns.[34]

The recruitment of the laborers for Firestone under the so-called 'contract system' was the principal responsibility of the native chiefs. Villages and towns of chiefs refusing to provide laborers for Firestone or other government officials were often pillaged by soldiers of the Liberia Frontier Force on instructions from 'Higher Authorities in Monrovia'.

As the plantation took form and the work force passed the 30,000 mark, every major tribe in Liberia was represented on the Firestone labor force.

The forced labor system in Liberia, masked as 'contract labor', proved so effective that the price of rubber in the United States had dropped from over $1.40 per pound in 1925 to less than $0.16 cents per pound in 1930, which was far below production cost.[35]

Aided by the Government of Liberia, Mr Firestone exploited the 'indigenous labor' – the natives. The loan of 1926 made available to Liberia by the Finance Corporation of America, a Firestone concern to which its rubber interest was attached, yielded little or no benefits to the majority of the Liberian people. Reflecting on the circumstances leading to the consummation of the Firestone Agreement with Liberia, Mr Buell writes:

> It is impossible for the writer to believe that the State Department of the United States would consciously trade the diplomatic support of this country in return for concessions which, while highly advantageous to American interest, are unfavorable to Liberia and may lead to the organized exploitation of the aboriginal population.[36]

Mr Buell's views were supported by other American observers, as economist J.H. Mower concludes:

> The Firestone Enterprise in Liberia has the elements of the worst of economic exploitation; a large capital investment by a corporation of a powerful nation assuming a dominant position in a weak and backward nation; little or no official restraint or assistance by the powerful nation in these activities; the benefits of the loan going to aid only a minute percentage of the smaller nation's population and these payments attaining only a slight amount of economic progress.[37]

The Firestone Agreement was certainly the most generous of its kind. By the end of the Second World War the financial condition of Liberia had not improved much beyond the conditions of the 1930s. In 1943 a loan was arranged with the United States for the construction of the Free Port of Monrovia. In response to the 'Open Door'[38] policy of President Tubman, several concession agreements, notably for ore mining, were signed between the Liberian Government and foreign firms. By 1950 Liberia had experienced relatively rapid economic growth. Foreign loans (see Appendix 1 for foreign loans negotiated by the Liberian Government 1943–1980) and investment played a significant role in the economic growth and development of the First Republic.

CHAPTER FIVE

The Burden of Forced 'Contract' Labor

Those European industries requiring intensive labor which were established, especially in Africa, in the early 1890s developed largely at the expense of cheap African labor 'recruited' with the aid of Black Slavers – the so-called African élite. Black Slavers aided industrialists in the recruitment of cheap native labor in such places as the then Belgian Congo, Angola, Kenya, Mozambique, the then Portuguese Guinea – Guinea Bissau – and Sao Thomé and Principe. Henry W. Nevison referred to the forced 'contract' labor system as 'Modern Slavery'. Under the so-called 'contract' labor arrangement, the State, through the Department of Native Affairs in Angola for example, supplied laborers for European employers. In the case of Liberia, the Labor Bureau through the Department of the Interior recruited and supplied laborers for Firestone and other foreign employers. Some Liberian officials used the Labor Bureau to forcibly recruit laborers for their private farms.

The system whereby the government recruited laborers for foreign employers inevitably led in most instances to the total 'disorganization of the native village life, a high death rate in labor compounds and depopulation of the villages'.[1] A Portuguese Senior Inspector of Colonies, Captain Henrique Galvao, in a report published clandestinely in 1949, confirmed the observation made by Nevison some forty-one years earlier. Infant mortality in labor compounds and plantations was as high as 60 percent, and Captain Galvao asserted 'that a death rate as high as 40 percent is not rare among workers themselves'.[2]

Denouncing the forced 'contract' labor system, Captain Galvao concluded:

In some ways the situation is worse than simple slavery. Under slavery, after all, the native is bought as an animal; his owner prefers him to remain as fit as a horse or an ox. Yet here the native is not bought – he is hired from the State, although he is called a free man. And his employer cares little if he sickens or dies, once he is working, because when he sickens or dies his employer will simply ask for another.[3]

As early as the 1890s, Europeans regarded Liberia as a reservoir of cheap native labor. In 1890,[4] Frenchmen recruited Liberian laborers to work on the Panama Canal and to serve in the French Colonial Army. Two years later, in a treaty with France, the Liberian Government agreed to facilitate the employment of laborers from the indigenous population. In 1897,[5] a German firm was granted a labor recruiting concession by the Legislature of the Republic of Liberia. Such laborers were to be recruited from the indigenous population of Liberia. As early as 1900[6] the owners of the Spanish Cocoa Plantation at Fernando Poo attempted also to recruit laborers from Liberia. In 1908, the Liberian Legislature passed an Act forbidding the recruitment of laborers, but from Montserrado and Grand Bassa Counties only.

In 1912 the Liberian Government established, by Act of Legislature, a Labor Bureau empowered to 'regulate and supervise the labor situation, to procure laborers and to protect the rights of such laborers engaged by Liberians or foreigners with the Republic'.[7] The Act further stipulated: 'Nothing in this Act shall be construed to compel laborers to engage themselves to work under the provision of this Act....'[8]

Fernando Poo – Liberia's modern slavery

On April 2, 1928, an agreement was entered into between a Spanish syndicate, the Agricola de los Territorios Espanoles del Golfo de Guinea and some prominent citizens of the Republic of Liberia; namely, Messrs Thomas E. Pelham, Robert W. Draper, E.G.W. King, J.C. Johnson, M.A. Bracewell and C. Cooper. These gentlemen were private recruiting agents in Liberia for the Spanish Cocoa Plantation at Fernando Poo and were represented by another Liberian, Mr Sammy A. Ross, as Consul.

The Spanish syndicate managed by Mr Theodomiro Avendano, residing at Santa Isabel, Fernando Poo, was represented by Messrs Barclay and Barclay, attorneys-at-law. Edwin James Barclay, at that time Secretary of State of the Republic of Liberia, was one of the partners of Barclay and Barclay representing the interests of the Spanish Cocoa Plantation. He had been appointed Secretary of State in 1920 by

Charles Dunbar Burgess King, who became President of Liberia in the same year.

Briefly, the terms of the Fernando Poo Agreement were:

1   The Agents will recruit fifteen hundred (1500) boys (laborers) for shipment to Fernando Poo within one year from the date of the signing of the agreement.
2   The boys (laborers) shipped by the Recruiting Agents to Fernando Poo are 'contracted' for the period of two years, one year's salary ($6.00 per month per laborer) to be paid to each laborer in cash at Fernando Poo and the remaining salary to be paid when returning to Liberia.
3   Inhumane punishment not to be inflicted upon the 'contracted' laborers.
4   Living quarters and proper medical care to be provided. (A full text of the Fernando Poo Agreement is reproduced as Appendix 2.)

Though the Fernando Poo Agreement was consummated in 1928, native male laborers had been recruited from the interior of Liberia for the Spanish Cocoa Plantation at Fernando Poo as early as 1920, the year that King and Barclay acceded to their respective offices. Also in 1920, Allen N. Yancy was appointed Superintendent of Maryland County by President King. These two men, in collaboration with a few other Liberian government officials of similar character, exposed the indigenous population of Liberia to the worse forms of savagery and exploitation.

Liberian Frontier Force personnel, by order of President King and his henchmen, pillaged native villages and herded the helpless victims of the raids to the nearest port where Spanish steamers awaited the forcibly 'captured' laborers for shipment to Fernando Poo. In 1928 Mr Yancy became Vice-President to President King.

The bulk of the laborers recruited for Fernando Poo came from three principal regions of Liberia – Maryland and Sinoe Counties and the Tchien (now Grand Gedeh County) area. Mr S.A. Ross, Consul for the Recruiting Agents, was appointed County Superintendent of Sinoe by President King and was assigned to Greenville, Sinoe County. Mr Allen Yancy, the Superintendent of Maryland County, resided in that County, while Mr J.B. Watson, District Commissioner of District No 4, (Tchien District) resided at Zwedru, then District Headquarters.

Forced recruiting in the Tchien area

Especially intensive recruiting of laborers for Fernando Poo was carried out in the Sinoe and Techien areas. In the Tchien area, as was the practice in other areas of the country, District Commissioners received instructions from high government officials in Monrovia to capture as many men as possible for shipment to Fernando Poo. In 1927, Ed H. Blackett, a quartermaster for District Commissioner Watson of District No. 4 (Tchien District) was ordered by Commissioner Watson to capture, with the aid of soldiers, a large number of natives from towns in his section, secure them and deliver them to S.A. (Sammy) Ross at Greenville, Sinoe. Those male natives captured were confined in a special compound reserved for this purpose until a steamer called at the port to carry the men to Fernando Poo. Acting on instruction from President King, Commissioner Watson wrote the following letter to Quartermaster Blackett:[9]

Interior Department
Liberia Hinterland
Tchien H.Q. District No. 4
September 21, 1927

Ref: 'Instruction'

Mr Ed H.A. Blackett
District Quartermaster
District Number Four L.H.

Sir:

You are hereby ordered to proceed immediately with these soldiers upon the receipt of this letter, by the instruction of the Honorable Commissioner General John W. Cooper, of the Liberian Hinterland, R.L. down to Greenville, Sinoe, with as many laborers as you possibly can, not exceeding 250, and there deliver them to the Hon. Samuel A. Ross, for the purpose of being shipped to Fernando Poo, per orders of his Exlcy, the President C.D.B. King; each man is to take with him one hamper of cleaned rice for his ration, and after the shipment, whatever is left you are to sell it out and report the cash here at this office on your return, to assist in paying off the staff.

Fail not: observing the above I remain,

Yours,
Faithfully,
(SGND) J.B. Watson
District Commissioner

P.S. You are to make a general list of the names of the men shipped and from each section they are from.

Forced recruiting in Sinoe County

The recruiting of native laborers for Fernando Poo began as early as 1924 in the Sinoe area. As many as 800 persons were captured by Captain Howard of the Liberia Frontier Force, escorted under armed guard and delivered to Mr Ross, County Superintendent, for shipment to Fernando Poo.

The District Commissioner in the Sikon Section of Sinoe, Mr P.C. Lamandine, reported the matter to the Secretary of the Interior and got no redress. Later, Mr Lamandine also reported the raiding and forcible recruiting of inhabitants of the Sikon area to President King. Mr Lamandine alleges that soon thereafter 'he was recalled from his station (the President appoints all County Superintendents and District Commissioners) and eventually relieved of office'.[10]

In his testimony to the Commission of Inquiry, former Commissioner P.C. Lamandine recalled:

> I was Commissioner in the Sikon District in 1924. During my term of office many boys were sent from the interior by Captain Howard to Mr Ross for shipment to Fernando Poo. They were sent down under military escort with rice and were detained by Mr Ross who placed an armed guard over them till the steamer arrived. I was Commissioner at Sikon near Sinoe at that time and the matter was reported to me. I was one of the oldest Commissioners in the County. I made complaint to the President and to the Secretary of Interior. To these communications I never got any reply, and was shortly afterwards relieved of my post.
>
> Mr Ross was in power (County Superintendent) and he said to me 'you shall regret it. I am going to teach you a lesson.' A large number of boys were sent down under escort to Sinoe during 1924 – 600 to 800 were recruited from my section. I tried as Commissioner to prevent it and to stop the military escort being used, but while I was in one part of the country Mr Ross arranged to send down the boys through another port.[11]

In 1927, one year prior to the signing of the official agreement between the Spanish Cocoa concession at Fernando Poo and the Liberian authorities, the illegal recruitment of laborers for Fernando Poo intensified in the Sinoe area. Secretary of State Barclay granted permission to Mr Ross to recruit laborers for Fernando Poo. Mr Ross' methods of recruiting were so crude that Mr Reginald A. Sherman, then Postmaster-General of Liberia, upon arrival in Greenville, Sinoe County on October 4, 1927, to inspect the local postal service, informed Secretary of State Barclay of the deplorable situation in Greenville in two successive radiograms, both dated October 5, 1927.

In the first message, Mr Sherman petitioned Secretary Barclay to deny the request of Mr Ross to ship '300 boys' to Fernando Poo. He informed Mr Barclay that the 'boys' were decoyed from the hinterland under armed guard and forced aboard Spanish steamers 'just as in the slave days'. Mr Sherman inquired of Secretary Barclay whether it was the policy of the Government of Liberia to use its soldiers to force free men 'out of the country as laborers to build up another country'. Mr Sherman further inquired: 'Shall we whose fathers founded this country to secure liberty for their sons encourage this blighted and cursed practice which is ruining our country?' Finally, Postmaster-General Sherman asked Secretary of State Barclay whether the Government was in fact not a party to the 'slave traffic' practised in the country.

Mr Ross was determined to ship to Fernando Poo the 300 men he had on hand under guard on a German steamer waiting in the port of Greenville. Mr Sherman visited the compound where the men were held and found the conditions indistinguishable from slave traffic. Immediately, Sherman returned aboard the SS *Mesurado*[12] and dispatched the following radiogram[13] to Secretary of State Barclay:

Oct. 5, 1927

To Secretary Barclay, Monrovia

Further to my radiogram concerning shipment of boys to Fernando Poo, have been across the river and have seen the boys. Oh! Secretary Barclay in very truth we have Slave Trade in this place. Boys told me that they chased, caught and forced down here under a purported order from Headquarters. They were flogged and I saw with my own eyes the fresh scars on their backs and the rope marks on their hands. Is it not possible that such practice be ordered stopped by you? The poor creatures are herded up and guarded by Frontier soldiers and messengers. Because some talked to me Station Master Blackett messengers pushed them about and actually slapped them in my presence. My blood boiled and I feel certain that if you had been here you would have dismissed Blackett and ordered the release of the men.

I appeal to you Mr Secretary in the name of all that is sacred, in the name of Justice, Freedom, Liberty and Humanity for God's sake give these poor people their freedom and do not allow them to be snatched from their homes and brutally treated, and order Supt. Grigsby to cause them to be sent back to their homes and oblige.

It is ruining our Hinterland. It will affect the commerce and agriculture of this country and government. It will affect our reputation as a free country. It will be a repetition of the nefarious Slave Trade and will make our Delcaration of Independence a sham.

Ross is asserting broadcast that the leaders of this country are sharing the money he is receiving from this abominable practice and had the audacity to offer me a bribe of (£25) twenty-five pounds to cable you in his behalf. For God's sake do not grant his request for shipment of boys but order them to be returned to their respective homes and oblige.

(Signed) Sherman

Apparently embarrassed by the radio messages from Postmaster-General Sherman, Barclay was forced to cancel the permit issued to Mr Ross to recruit laborers for Fernando Poo. Ross' request to ship the 300 men on hand to Fernando Poo was also denied.

Secretary Barclay's message in response to Postmaster-General Sherman's reads:

Oct. 5, 1927

To Postmaster General Sherman, Sinoe.

Thinking Ross acting *bona fide*, I granted him permit for shipping of 300 laborers. These were supposed to be men voluntarily engaging for service. Your message reveals iniquity. Am cancelling permit. You will instruct Grigsby in my name in the name of the Government to have any man who is involuntarily held released immediately. If necessary have everybody concerned prosecuted. This is preemptory. Blackett must be dismissed.

(Signed) Barclay
Secretary of State

In a message to Mr Ross, Secretary Barclay informed him (that because 'of the iniquitous methods pursued by you in getting laborers for Fernando Poo the permit granted you today is hereby cancelled'.[14] Superintendent Grigsby was instructed by Secretary Barclay to release every person involuntarily held by Mr Ross.

The Attorney General of Liberia instructed the County Attorney of Sinoe, Mr William Witherspoon, to prosecute Sammy A. Ross and Ed Blackett for 'slave trading'. The case was scheduled for the February 1928 Term of Court when Mr Ross, awaiting prosecution for 'slave trading', was appointed Postmaster-General of Liberia by President

King. Ross was to succeed Mr Reginald A. Sherman who was instrumental in arresting, at least momentarily, the forcible recruitment and shipment of Liberians to the Spanish Cocoa Plantations at Fernando Poo. Mr William Witherspoon, the young County Attorney instructed by the Attorney General of Liberia to prosecute Ross and Blackett for 'slave trading', was relieved of his office, as was Superintendent Grigsby.

While in Monrovia as Postmaster-General, Mr Ross continued to recruit 'native boys' in the Suehn area and other parts of Montserrado County for shipment to Fernando Poo. Mr Ross continued this practice in violation of the 1908 Act prohibiting the recruitment of laborers for shipment to a foreign country from Montserrado and Grand Bassa Counties.

Forced recruiting – Maryland County

In the Maryland County area, forcible recruiting of laborers for Fernando Poo was carried out by Mr Allen Yancy, then Superintendent. Mr Yancy imposed excessive fines upon those chiefs refusing to help him recruit laborers for Fernando Poo. Several tribal settlements and villages, including Wedabo and Garroway, were completely decimated because the chiefs of these communities refused to produce men for shipment.

When Superintendent Yancy promised to 'burn' all of the other towns in the Wedabo section if '500 boys' were not provided for shipment to Fernando Poo 'by 7 o'clock' [15] on the morning of December 8, (1924), the people during the night sent messengers to the men who took refuge in the surrounding bushes, begging the 'boys' to come to save their towns from being destroyed. [16] To save their towns from destruction, 316 men surrendered.

On December 8, the Spanish ship *Montserrat* reached Wedabo beach. On board were Superintendent Yancy accompanied by the Spanish Vice-Consul, Mr P.C. Parker. They came from Cape Palmas where they had already picked up 80 'boys'.

When the 316 men from Wedabo were put aboard the Fernando Poo-bound vessel, Mr Yancy, in a letter dated December 8, 1924 sent to the Liberian Secretary of State, Edwin J. Barclay, proudly reported his accomplishments as follows:

I take pleasure to inform you that the Spanish Steamer *Montserrat* arrived here in port about 4 o'clock on the inst. and after shipping 80 boys from this port proceeded to Wedabo at 12 o'clock noon, and laid over until next morning by request of the Chieftain and took on board

316 boys. There was about 200 more to be shipped but the Captain would not wait to take them and left at 12 o'clock noon. The balance of the boys will be shipped from this port ...[17]

Of course Superintendent Yancy made a deliberate misrepresentation to Secretary of State Barclay when he indicated that he and members of his party 'laid over (at Wedabo) at the request of the Chieftain'. What he did not tell Secretary Barclay was that after destroying some towns in the Wedabo section, he had promised to 'burn down' all the other towns in the section if the chiefs failed to give him 500 men for shipment to Fernando Poo by 7 o'clock the following morning. However, since Secretary Barclay was a party to and partner in the 'slave traffic' he certainly understood the contents of Superintendent Yancy's letter. The people of Wedabo continued to suffer the most grievous abuses at the hands of Superintendent Yancy, Secretary of State Barclay and President King.

This 'Sad Song'[18] of the Wedabo women, which evolved from their wailings over the forcible shipment of their husbands, sons and brothers to Fernando Poo, is equally telling:

> We were here when trouble come to our people;
> For this reason Jeh was imprisoned and fined,
> For this reason Yancy come to our country –
> He caught our husbands and our brothers,
> Sail them to 'Nana Poo
> And there they die!
> And there they die!
>
> Tell us
> Yancy, Why?
> Yancy, Why?
> Wedabo women have no husbands,
> Yancy, Why?
> Wedabo women have no brothers,
> Yancy, Why?
> Mothers, fathers, sons have died,
> Waiting for their return
> Yancy, Why? etc.

Jeh, the Chief of the Wedabo section, went to Monrovia and reported the action of Superintendent Yancy to President King. Chief Jeh also petitioned President King to restrain the raids against his subjects.

53

Vexed by the request of Chief Jeh, the irascible King ordered Chief Jeh jailed in Monrovia and imposed on him a fine of '300 pounds'.

In 1928, perhaps as a reward for his inhumane treatment of the people of the interior, Mr Yancy was named Vice-President of the Republic of Liberia.

International Commission of Inquiry

In the spring of 1929[19] the 'contract labor' system as practised in Liberia became the concern of the international community. An American clergyman travelling along the Liberian coast observed a number of Liberian 'boys' herded together upon his ship bound for Fernando Poo. Probably their unhappy looks moved him to investigate, only to learn to his amazement that they were 'contract laborers', the contract being in favor of those who sent them and those who employed them – a disguise so thin as to be easily seen through by a foreigner.

On his return to America, the clergyman informed American officials of his experience on the Liberian Coast. His report was confirmed by French officials who were receiving similar adverse reports from their field representatives. A large number of Liberian natives – especially in south-eastern Liberia, Maryland, Sinoe and Grand Gedeh Counties – fled into the French colony of the Ivory Coast to avoid being shipped to Fernando Poo.

On June 8, 1929, as the embarrassing news caused the world to cast a universal eye on Liberia with smoldering criticism, the American Chargé d'Affaires in Monrovia delivered to the Liberian Government, through Secretary of State Barclay, a Diplomatic Note with the following contents:

I am directed by the (United States) Secretary of State to advise your Excellency that there have come to the attention of the Government of the United States from several sources reports bearing reliable evidence of authenticity which definitely indicate that existing conditions incidental to the so-called 'export' of labor from Liberia to Fernando Poo have resulted in the development of a system which seems hardly distinguishable from organized slave trade, and that in the enforcement of this system the services and influences of certain high Government officials are constantly and systematically used.[20]

Three days later, on June 11, Barclay issued a 'categorical denial' and declared that: 'The Government of the Republic of Liberia will have no objection to this question being investigated on the spot by a competent, impartial and unprejudiced commission'.[21] Liberia's permanent delegate to the League of Nations, following the Secretary's denial and declaration, also addressed the Council of that body claiming that Liberia was the victim of propaganda and inviting the Council to designate a Special Commission of Inquiry.

The League of Nations accepted the invitation from the Government and appointed a Commission known as the International Commission of Inquiry into the Existence of Slavery and Forced Labor in the Republic of Liberia, commonly called the International Commission of Inquiry. The League appointed Dr Cuthbert Christy of England as Chairman of the Commission. America was represented on the Commission by a Negro educator, Dr Charles Spurgeon Johnson, from Fisk University, Tennessee, while Liberia was represented by former President Arthur Barclay, uncle of the Secretary of State, Edwin J. Barclay.

On April 7, 1930, President King formally constituted the Commission at Monrovia and empowered it to ascertain:

a) Whether slavery as defined in the anti-slavery convention in fact exists in the Republic.

b) Whether this system is participated in or encouraged by the Government of the Republic.

c) Whether and what leading citizens of the country participate therein.

d) To what extent compulsory labor exists as a factor in the social and industrial economy of the state, either for public or private purposes, and, if it does exist, in what manner it has been recruited and employed, whether for public or private purposes.

e) Whether shipment of contract laborers to Fernando Poo under the terms of arrangement with Spain, or shipment of such laborers to the Congo or any other foreign ports is associated with slavery, and whether the method employed in recruiting such laborers carries any compulsion.

f) Whether the labor employed for private or privately owned or leased plantations is recruited by voluntary enlistment or is forcibly impressed for this service by the Liberian Government or its authority.

g) Whether the Liberian Government has at any time given sanction or approval to the recruiting of labor with the aid and assistance of the Liberian Frontier Force or other persons holding official position or in Government employ, or private individuals have been implicated in such recruiting with or without the Government's approval.[22]

On September 8, 1930, the Commission completed its task and submitted a rather interesting and provocative report. Based on the Commission's findings the following recommendations were made:

(a) Institution of an 'open door' policy, since the 'closed door' policy which for so long seems to have been favored by the Liberian Government, is not in the best interests of the Republic; that it is, in fact, at the root of the financial and other major difficulties in which the country is now involved. It impedes development by masking maladministration, discouraging research, delaying civilization and education, preventing competition and generally stifling commercial enterprise ...[23]

(b) Extension of education to all alike.

(c) Native policy to be radically reconstructed.

(d) Barrier between civilized and uncivilized to be broken.

(e) Policy of suppression to be abandoned.

(f) Humiliation and degradation of chiefs to cease.

(g) Re-establishment of tribal authority of chiefs.

(h) Complete reorganization of administration of the interior.

(i) Removal of present District Commissioners.

(j) Substitution of European or American Commissioners with Assistant Commissioners.

(k) Institution of some form of Civil Service.

(l) Rearrangement of the political division of the country.

(m) Pawning and domestic slavery to be made illegal as preliminary to total abolition.

(n) Shipment of laborers to Fernando Poo to cease.

(o) Road program to be curtailed.

(p) Much stricter control of Frontier Force soldiers.

(q) Reconsideration of duties of Frontier Force soldiers.

(r) American immigration to be encouraged.[24]

Fearing that the encouragement of black American immigration to Liberia, as recommended by the Commissioner, would pose a threat to the Americo-Liberian oligarchy, President King injected into Article Three, Section Seven of the Constitution an amendment to read:

No person shall be eligible to the Office of President who is not a citizen of this Republic by birth or a naturalized citizen of over twenty-five years' residence and who is not possessed of unencumbered real estate of the value of two thousand and five hundred dollars.

The passage of this constitutional amendment discouraged many American negroes desirous of emigrating to Liberia.

Upon completion of the Commission's task, international public opinion forced the resignation of President King and his Vice-President Allen Yancy. King was succeeded by his young Secretary of State Edwin James Barclay as the 17th President of the Republic of Liberia.

Punitive raids on the natives

When Edwin James Barclay became President of Liberia, following the resignation of President King, the international community, especially the United States, believed that some meaningful changes would take place in the administration and conduct of government in Liberia. It was soon realized that the ailments affecting Liberia were too numerous and grave to be relieved by a mere change of administration.

Though Barclay promised to unify the country, he elected, perhaps deliberately, to ignore the policies recommended for the reconstruction of the country. While international organizations sympathetic towards Liberia sought to arrange much-needed funds to aid the task of reconstruction, malpractices by the Barclay administration resulted in a revolt by the natives residing in the Hinterland. The revolt was led principally by a chain of Kru tribes along the coast of Liberia.

Concerned about developments on the Liberian coast (the Kru War) the British Foreign Office in London, which had not officially recognized the Barclay administration, instructed Constantine Graham, the British Chargé d'Affaires in Monrovia, to protest against the treatment of the inhabitants of the Hinterland by the Liberian Government. An extract from the statement from the British Government to the Liberian authorities reads:

> His Majesty's Government in the United Kingdom is satisfied that the proceedings of the Liberian Frontier Force under the command of Colonel T. Elwood Davis in the country last autumn were tyrannical and high-handed in an inexplicable degree.
>
> According to information which His Majesty's Government cannot disregard, although they equally cannot regard it as confirmed, these proceedings are being repeated at the present time and are exposing the Kru population to personal violence and outrage and the destruction of property.
>
> The Liberian representative denied before the Council of the League on February 6th that these events in any way represented reprisals upon people who had given evidence before the League's Commissions. His Majesty's Government, however, irrespective of the motives underlying the measures which have been taken against the Kru, ask for explicit assurance that such proceedings will be discontinued pending the conclusion of an arrangement between the League, the United States and Liberia for the future administration of the country ...[25]

Equally concerned about the state of affairs in Liberia, the French Government, through its representative in Liberia, presented the Liberian Government with the following communication:

The Government of the French Republic regarding as sufficiently proven the arbitrary and tyrannical activities of the Frontier Force under the command of Colonel Davis since autumn of last year in the Kru country.

According to information which the French Government cannot ignore although it does not consider them as confirmed, those acts are being repeated and exposing the Kru people to abuses, individual violence and the destruction of their property.

The Liberian Government having denied them before the Council of the League, the French Government, without considering the motives which have caused these measures, demand a formal assurance of an immediate end to these acts while awaiting the conclusion of arrangements between the League, the United States and Liberia for the future administration of the country.[26]

From the American Government came also a request for an immediate discontinuation of the atrocities against the Kru population by the Liberian Frontier Force.

The American Government is satisfied that the proceedings of the Liberian Frontier Force under the auspices of Colonel Davis in the Kru country last autumn were tyrannical and high-handed in an inexcusable degree.

According to information which the American Government cannot disregard, although it equally cannot as yet regard it as confirmed, these proceedings have very recently been repeated and are exposing the Kru population to personal violence and outrage and destruction of property.

The Liberian representative denied before the Council of the League of Nations of February 6th that these events in any way represented reprisals upon people who had given evidence before the recent official investigations under international auspices.

The American Government must however irrespective of the motives underlying the measures which have been taken against the Kru ask your government for an explicit assurance that such proceedings will be discontinued immediately . . .[27]

The German Government also registered its regrets and advised the Liberian Government to curtail further acts of 'atrocities committed against the Kru population'. Through its Mission, the German Government issued the following:

I have the honour to advise you that over and over again rumours reached the consulate of atrocities committed against the Kru population down the Coast by the Liberian troops under the command of Colonel Davis.

As quite a number of such cases have been positively confirmed by reliable persons I am obliged in accordance with the instructions which I have received from my government to make representations to the Liberian Government and to remind it emphatically as to the adverse influence which proceedings of that kind must exercise upon the position of Liberia in view of the discussion in the coming session of the Council of the League of Nations ...[28]

After barely four months in office, the Barclay administration was soon subjected to an investigation, initiated by the League of Nations, to ascertain the causes of the disorder which had resulted in another series of massacres of the Kru people by members of the Liberian Frontier Force. With the consent of all parties concerned, D.G. Rydings, the British Vice-Consul at Monrovia was immediately dispatched to the Kru Coast to conduct an impartial investigation.

On April 15, 1932, Mr Rydings, after a brief discription of his journey and entry into the Kru Coast, reported that the natives were reluctant to disclose their plight for fear of reprisals. Mr Rydings further reported:

I am informed that when Colonel Davis arrived at Nana Kru in August, 1931, with a force of about 200 of his soldiers, he caused the arrest of some fifty natives on charges of seditious propaganda, and confined them in the custom house until he left Nana Kru in November in order to proceed to Sasstown. This seditious propaganda consisted in a tendency to discuss the possible intervention of the League of Nations in the administration of Liberia and openly to express preference for white rule. Natives who gave expression of such views were considered to be guilty of seditious practices ...[29]

Upon arrival in Sasstown Mr Rydings reported the following:

The plantation town of Wolokri in Sasstown interior was attacked in the night when the inhabitants were asleep and totally unprepared. The soldiers crept into the banana plantations which surrounded all native villages, and poured volleys into the huts. In the subsequent confusion and flight women and children were ruthlessly shot down and killed. One woman who had that day been delivered of twins was shot in her bed, and the infants perished in flames when the village was fired by the troops. At this town three men, fourteen women and eight children met their death ... Some 12,000 natives, who have been harried and subjected to punitive raids for months past, have taken refuge in the bush, where they are suffering from exposure and malnutrition and are existing under conditions of extreme hardship. The whole Sasstown area has been laid waste and every town, with the exception of New Sasstown, has been burnt and pillaged by the Liberian Frontier Force ... clothing, personal effects and stocks of rice (the principal article of diet in the country) were destroyed in the flames or pillaged by soldiers, and cattles, goats, and poultry killed by the troops for their consumption ...[30]

Despite this impartial investigation and observation by Rydings, confirmed by reliable independent sources,[31] the Barclay administration was obdurate and obstinately insisted that everything was normal, thus deluding itself and the world into assuming that Liberia was heading for prosperity. To regain recognition of his administration by the United States, France and Britain, President Barclay promised 'progressive reforms' in the administration of affairs of state. The reconstruction of the 'Native Policy' recommended by the International Commission of Inquiry in 1930 was never attended to by the Barclay administration. The 'progressive reforms' promised by that administration were also never effected.

CHAPTER SIX

Tubman: Changing the Guard and Guarding the Change

Presidents King and Barclay each ascended to the presidency of Liberia because each possessed the independent means and the requisite family connections necessary at that time for a successful career in politics. The administrations of King and Barclay, spanning a total of twenty-four years (1920–1944), therefore further widened the rift between the so-called Americo-Liberian oligarchy and the indigenous tribal peoples.

In an apparent attempt to restore national unity, incumbent President Barclay decided to bring into the national political arena a relatively unknown politician, William V.S. Tubman, from the 'leeward' county of Maryland. Mr Tubman, then an Associate Justice of the Supreme Court of Liberia, had served as a public school teacher, tax collector and Senator for Maryland County. He practised law through the 'apprenticeship' system.

On May 21, 1942, in their search for a successor to the outgoing President Barclay, 'partisans' of the True Whig Party wrote Mr Tubman a letter informing him of their desire that he should seek the Presidential nomination. The letter reads in part:

On the 5th day of December 1930, when this our ship of State was overcast by the night of political gloom and darkness, when on the international sea the billows rose high and the gale was fierce ... His Excellency, President Edwin Barclay was called upon by the people of this country to take the helm. Firmly has he held it ...

The clock of the years indicates that the hour is fast approaching when, under our Constitution, the watch on the bridge must be changed . . . We have only a few months within which to consider this question.

Certain qualities in you have attracted our attention: Outstanding qualities of leadership.

After mature thought and sober reflection, we the undersigned partisans of the True Whig Party, have decided to ask you for a brief outline of your policy, should the people of Liberia elect you to this high office, also permission to use your name in this connection.[1]

In less than two weeks of the date of the letter, on June 2, 1942, Mr Tubman transmitted to the 'partisans' a detailed outline of the policies to be pursued by his administration under the banner of the True Whig Party, should he be elected President of Liberia. Candidate Tubman promised to improve roads and communications, education, agriculture and the economy in general. Tubman further promised a 'radical' change in the administration of the Interior. Specifically, he promised:

(a) Freedom of the press, of conscience, of speech and of religion;
(b) Equality before the law of all citizens;
(c) Right of trial by jury;
(d) Supremacy of civil over military authority;
(e) Prompt and sacred fulfillment of public and private obligations;
(f) Peace and friendship with all nations.[2]

Regarding the administration of the Interior, Tubman proposed:

Ours would be to strive at educating the population in these regions into citizens who are one people with us all, having equality of rights and privileges, and deriving identical responsibilities, benefits and protection; hence the best possible care that the right kind of training which will graft in them the principles of devotion to Liberia as their only native land, would be given.

The tribal customary laws of the tribes, so far as they are humane, would be religiously adhered to in the administration of the tribes. Due regard for tribal authority would be insisted upon, and malfeasance and misfeasance by officials charged with the administration of the interior, would be dealt with speedily, effectually and rigidly.[3]

Tubman's candidature was supported by Barclay, because Barclay felt his chances of continuing to wield influence and exercise control would be greater in a government headed by the relatively 'little known' and 'non-Monrovia-based' Tubman. The alternative to Tubman was of course C.L. Simpson, Sr, whose qualifying credentials for the Presidency were unmatched by any candidate under consideration by the leadership of the True Whig Party. Simpson came from a family well connected in the Monrovia 'club' of families. Additionally, he served as

Secretary of State, Grand Master of the powerful Masonic Craft and Secretary-General of the True Whig Party.

In view of Simpson's background, Barclay decided to support Tubman as Simpson was unlikely to succumb to manipulation by Barclay. The Tubman-Simpson ticket[4] 'arranged' by Barclay was challenged in the Presidential elections of 1943 by the newly formed Democratic Party headed by James F. Cooper, a wealthy rubber farmer. Cooper's Vice-Presidential candidate on the Democratic Party ticket was R.A. Sherman, Senator of Grand Cape Mount County. It should be remembered that Mr Reginald A. Sherman was relieved of his position as Postmaster-General of Liberia in 1928 by President King when Sherman publicly denounced the Government's policy of forcibly recruiting and shipping Liberians to Fernando Poo as contract laborers.

In the May 4, 1943 election, often described as 'the most partial, unfair and brazenly corrupt,'[5] the 'Barclay-arranged', True Whig Party-sponsored, Tubman–Simpson ticket 'defeated' the Democratic Party challengers.

In what was believed to be an act of appreciation for his support, President-elect Tubman wrote President Barclay the following letter:[6]

Harper, Cape Palmas
May 10, 1943

My dear Mr President,

I confirm my radiogram on the subject of the Election. The Whig candidates were unanimously carried at each of the polls here. As a matter of fact there was no organization of the Democratic Party at this end.

Please allow me to reassure you of my gratitude for the warm support given to my candidacy by you, WITHOUT WHICH THE SUCCESS ATTAINED ON LAST TUESDAY WOULD NOT HAVE BEEN POSSIBLE. I shall be ever grateful and shall look to you for COUNSEL and ADVICE ...

With assurances of my kindest regards and best wishes.

Believe me now and always, Mr President,

Very sincerely yours,
(SGD) Wm. V.S. Tubman

Changing the Guard

In his first Inaugural Address of January 3, 1944, President Tubman declared that 'the spirit of this Administration shall be: *No Reprisals*; *No Pay-backs*; *No Get-Even-With*; *but let the dead past bury the dead.*'[7]

President Tubman further declared, on the same occasion: 'We shall engage in and strive at the assimilation and unification of our various populations composing the body politic. Liberia must be a place for all Liberians to live alike – all to stand equally privileged, responsible and protected by like administration of the law.' [8]

Upon ascending to the Presidency in 1944, Tubman the young politician soon took control as the political wheel began to spin slowly but dependably at his command. In 1946, Mr Tubman took a major step forward in an effort to unify the 'various indigenous populations composing the body politic' – the inhabitants of the Hinterland and the Monrovia-based oligarchy.

Much to the chagrin of the supporters of the status quo, Tubman inducted into the National Legislature members of the tribal 'element' to represent the aboriginal segment of the Liberian population. Several other persons of aboriginal stock were brought nearer the corridors of power by President Tubman. According to the *Liberian Age*, the Government-owned newspaper, this act of President Tubman 'marked for the first time in the history of Liberia the installation of representation of aboriginal Liberians in the Legislature of the Country. It is unique in that never before in Liberia has the aboriginal element been given representation in the Liberian government ...' [9]

Prior to the move by President Tubman, persons of tribal origin interested in observing the proceedings of the National Legislature could do so only upon depositing with the Government in Monrovia the sum of $100. As an observer, a tribal delegate had no voting rights. For no less than a century, the tribal peoples had been taxed to support a Government in which they were never represented.

In the early 1960s, at the urging of President Tubman, the provinces (Eastern, Central and Western) of the Interior were formed into four new counties – Grand Gedeh, Nimba, Bong and Lofa – thus entitling their inhabitants to an equal share in those rights and privileges which had formerly been reserved for the citizens of the original five coastal counties.

Among other changes instituted by President Tubman was the granting of suffrage to Liberian female citizens of twenty-one years of age and over.

The 'Open Door Policy' recommended in 1930 by the International Commission of Inquiry was seriously pursued by Tubman in the mid-1950s. Stimulated by the post-war economic recovery, the Liberian economy under Tubman's leadership experienced rapid growth in the 1950s. In the opinion of the economists [10] the Liberian economy was stimulated primarily by foreign investment in mining and plantation agriculture; dominated and largely directed by expatriate personnel;

fruitful in providing the government with funds for development (directly through tax revenues as well as indirectly through loans and grants); heavily oriented towards production for export; concentrated in a small number of industries; and ineffective in creating internal forces making for structural change in an industrial economy.

In yet another bid to forge national unity, Tubman inaugurated the National Unification and Integration Program. Speaking at the Third Biennial Unification Council held at Kolahun, Lofa County on February 19, 1963, President Tubman reassured the participants of his administration's commitment to effect assimilation and integrity in all parts of Liberia.

> In this great task of uniting and integrating our people we have nothing to fear except the fear that we shall relax our vigilance and determination, that our enthusiasm may become cold and we may lose sight of the purpose and objectives we have set before us. But, knowing that every aspect of our national life has been touched, improved and benefited, we are inspired and encouraged to move forward with greater enthusiasm, vim and courage until unification and integration become part and parcel of every man, every woman, every boy and girl in our country; until all parts of our country are linked by a network of roads and communication; until human creativity and productivity yield us manifold material and spiritual blessings; until we are all one and can march proudly hand in hand in defence of our common country.
>
>   .... When we reflect upon the conditions which existed several years ago and compare them with those we see all around us, we have cause to be proud of our accomplishments. But we can not rest; we must never rest, for to rest is to rust ...[11]

Tubman urged the participants at the Council in particular and the nation in general to 'keep constantly before you a comprehensive picture of a unified Liberia, a happy and prosperous people, and having this picture may you work always towards its realization and eventual enjoyment'.[12]

President Tubman, at the risk of antagonizing the powerful few, issued directives and executive decrees to discontinue certain administrative irregularities never questioned in the past. For instance, Tubman ordered the discontinuation of a policy, generally practised in Government, by which senior Government officials were paid earlier during the month while pay checks for subordinate employees were delayed.

The *Daily Listener*, a Government-subsidized news organ, reports:

> President Tubman is up again with another of his great moves that

have always endeared him to the heart of his people. He has ordered that both *big shots* and low employees of government must be paid at one and the very same time. The Chief Executive, Liberia's Number One Humanitarian, has condemned the selfish practice of certain departmental heads ... Mr Tubman instructed the gentlemen of the Bureau of Audit never to honour any payroll made separate for big shots alone, unless those of the ordinary members of the same Department are included.[13]

When resentment over the abuse of the Government's Foreign Scholarship Program by the 'privileged few' could no longer be ignored, Tubman published an executive decree banning the use of taxpayers' money to sponsor primary school students abroad. The *Listener* reported the incident as follows:

This means ... that the parents of 76 Liberian students of elementary standard now studying abroad will have to reach down into their pockets or vaults or wherever they stack their kudos and finance their children's education ... a check of the list of students abroad by our reporters at the Department of Public Instruction reveals that most of the elementary school children studying abroad on government money have parents who possess the ways and means to take care of their children themselves. In other words the great majority of the children ... come from families in the top bracket of our society ...[14]

While Tubman was committed to effect progressive changes, he was careful to maintain a power base composed primarily of the Monrovia-based oligarchy while building a new foundation to consolidate power in the hands of the indigenous people.

Guarding the change – loyalty to the President

In the process of consolidating power, Mr Tubman 'was careful not to allow elite family cliques, the Party, the Government, the Church, the Hinterland and the Masonry to become more powerful or more influential than himself'.[15] Loyalty to the President was the order of the day. Any opposition, real or imagined, was mercilessly crushed[16] in a manner characteristic of Tubmanism.

Family connections were a powerful determining factor in political upward mobility and consolidation of a force loyal to the President. Families or individuals whose loyalty to the President was questionable were often callously displaced.

A cohort of Public Relations Officers and a chain of Security Agencies – the National Bureau of Investigation (NBI), the Executive

Action Bureau (EAB), the Special Security Service (SSS) and the National Intelligence and Security Service (NISS) – were organized and created to assist the President 'guard the change'. Tubmanism was the doctrine of the era. Any apparent deviation from it resulted in serious consequences for the offender.

One over-zealous pro-Tubmanist placarded the *Liberian Age*, a Government news organ, with the so-called Ten Commandments of Tubmanism:

I am thy President who brought thee from the end of the first to the beginning of the second centuries of our national existence as a result of which the people have been regenerated and rejuvenated to a new way of life and are now breathing the new life of liberty, freedom and happiness . . .

1 Thou shalt have no philosophy whose dogmas are to all intents and purposes diametrically opposed to the sovereign people who are ardent and potent adherents to Tubmanism.

2 Thou shalt not indulge in any kind of malfeasance, misfeasance and nonfeasance, nor conspire with any clique within or without the Republic, for a true Tubmanist will not hold him guiltless who plays the sycophant and the hypocrite.

3 Remember the 29th of November each and every year, so as to celebrate the same, though Tubmanism does not cherish nor favor much gaiety and display of pomp on such day.

4 Honour not only thy father and mother but all those highly placed in Church and State, and in all walks of life, that thy days may be long upon the land which the Lord thy God giveth thee . . .[17]

Tubman was born on November 29, 1895. The Legislature declared November 29 a national holiday in honor of the President.

Though Tubman publicly declared that law and order would be adhered to in his administration, persons accused by Tubman of any offense were publicly condemned by a pro-Tubmanist mob before the matter reached a court of competent jurisdiction. The Press, also unreservedly loyal to Mr Tubman, usually placarded its pages with notices of condemnation of any persons suspected of 'disloyalty' by the President.

The following article, a testimonial by Mr D. Nyeka Chie, appeared in the *Liberian Star* of May 2, 1968, while Ambassador Henry B. Fahnbulleh awaited trial. Mr Fahnbulleh, who served as Liberian Ambassador to Kenya, Uganda and Tanzania, was accused by President Tubman early in January 1968 of 'plotting' to overthrow the Government of Liberia.

Former Ambassador Henry Fahnbulleh, in statements alleged to have been made by him, tried to impress the peoples of the world, that the aborigines of Liberia are dissatisfied with the Administration of President Tubman.

This is entirely false. The exact opposite is true. Let me point out here, however, that under the sun there is no man perfect. Not even Mr Fahnubulleh in his alleged attitude of 'I am holier than thou'.

No matter how strong, powerful and shrewd a leader may be he can never succeed in imposing his will upon his people to continue him in office for twenty-four unbroken years against their will. The fact that Dr William Vacanarat Shadrack Tubman, our dearly beloved President, has enjoyed and shall continue to enjoy this unprecedented privilege unsolicited from his grateful fellow citizens proves conclusively that the overwhelming majority of the electorates of this land are greatly satisfied with his policies, since he took the reins of Government.

A Gift of Providence
In President Tubman we see the Hand of God at work. He is the gift of Providence to Liberia at such a time as this; for no man can do the things he has done, except God be with that man. Name or show me what he has left undone and I will enumerate thousands of things he has accomplished within a relatively short space of time: in governmental, religious, social, fraternal and cultural life of the nation; the physical plant of Liberia, the human and natural resources on land, on the sea and in the air.

For ninety-six years this country was haunted by this very GHOST hoary with age; which caused Liberia to vegetate while other nations were making great strides in national development – those who governed at that time feared that the natives were in the majority and should they acquire equal education, then they might take over the leadership of the nation. Therefore every effort was exerted to discourage mass educational advancement. It resulted in a backward, underdeveloped and sliced nation.

President Tubman did not believe in this school of thought and he did not tread on the trodden path of his predecessors, nor did he keep their cadence. Former Ambassador Henry Fahnbulleh is one of the innumerable fruits of Dr Tubman's bold, unselfish and laudable policies.

Support of all Aborigines
We, the aborigines of Liberia, love President Tubman as we love ourselves, because he first loved us as he loves himself. Mr

Fahnbulleh, his associates, followers and sympathizers should not make any mistake about this. They should not deceive themselves into believing that they can succeed in driving a wedge between the Chief Executive and and the aborigines – his staunch supporters.

We stand solidly behind our indefatigable, great, dynamic and implacable leader, who is everybody's President; no man or group of people have exclusive claim on him – he is a father, brother, cousin, uncle and a friend to all! Even to his bitterest enemies. He has made Liberia one of the quietest and most peaceful spots in our tumultuous, tension-ridden world – an haven of rest.

Can't Afford Violence
While the world around us has run amuck with political tempest raging wildly and human blood is flowing like rivers of water, let us remain calm and unaffected; keeping level heads as befits a politically mature people; remembering all too well that we are numerically weak and therefore we cannot afford violent clashes that might cost us some, if not all of our best brains – it takes a nation a couple of decades or more to replace its lost men and women!

No Scape Goats
If any one has his political axe to grind, let him be a man, come out boldly and appeal to the nation and place his issue before the electorates. Let them stop using us the natives as scape goats to pull their political chestnuts out of the fire. Twenty-four years is a long time enough for any people to understand their leader. During this period, we have had our experience and understand our President and all that he stands for.

We do not need to be told any thing further. If there is any Liberian who misunderstands the Head of this Nation after twenty-four years of his services, that is his business. We do not want to be bothered. We are not in a race to outer space.

A Thankful People
We are a thankful people. We are not ingrates, neither are we hypocrites. We give thanks to Almighty God for President Tubman and his Administration. No matter what the world may think or say about us, we shall stand by our leader and even die if needs be. Let Mr Fahnbulleh and his group redirect their thoughts, forsake their evil ways and foolish plans and ask the Lord to forgive them to be spared His wrath. Let them commend this nation and its future into the Hands of God of our Fathers and our God Who now leads us as He led us in the past.

We are all Liberians now. Americo-Liberianism and Countrymanism are things of the past, dead and buried in the beautiful casket of Unification by President Tubman. To resurrect that ugly GHOST is an unprofitable business and does not serve any useful purpose.

God bless President Tubman and save the State.[18]

Loyalty to President Tubman was manifested in yet another publication – a poem by a supporter of Tubmanism, Delsena Draper, President of a Women's Club in Sinoe – in the May 2, 1968 edition of the *Liberian Star*. Though the accused 'Plotter', Ambassador Fahnbulleh, was never mentioned by name, the poem reveals the extent to which the all-powerful machinery of the Tubman Government and its band of blind loyalists would go in a determined effort to ridicule and destroy anyone suspected of any crime by President Tubman.

Why Liberians Must Love Tubman

Listen! and hear! O hear!
You wicked, jealous, senseless over-ambitious
Selfish and deceitful, handful of Liberian Plotters:
If you love our Liberia glorious land of freedom,
You must love Tubman, the builder, beautiful, up-
Holder of our great heritage.
If you love Liberty, you must love Tubman
Who gave all equal rights.
If you love Prosperity, you must love Tubman
Who unearth our wealth.
If you love Stability, you must love Tubman
Who holds this Country twenty-four unbroken years.
If you love Unity, you must love Tubman
Who has united every Tribe and Clan of ours.
If you love Dignity, you must love Tubman
Who has built Liberia second to none in Africa.

Look! and see!! O see!!
You good for nothing, no vision foolish
Blind, mischief maker, Liberian Plotters.
If you love Paved Streets, you must love Tubman
Who has paved the dirty streets of every city.
If you love modern Buildings, you must love Tubman
The designer of modern Liberia.
If you love flying from county to county,
You must love Tubman who gave us the first
National Airline.

If you love Electricity, Running Water,
Telephone, Television and Radio Systems, you
Must love Tubman the producer of these systems.
If you love Travelling, relaxed in your car,
You must love Tubman who has linked the counties.
Tubman Sinoe Girls, and every sound minded, true,
Loyal, Godfearing Liberian Men, women, girls,
Boys, Young, and old and crippled dearly love and
Honour Tubman because we love Liberia.[19]

Alienation and disillusionment

The high-handed fashion in which the Tubman machinery dealt with potential opponents of the President caused discontent, disillusionment and alienation. At the end of his first eight-year term of office in 1951, President Tubman was challenged by Mr Didwho Twe of the Kru tribe. Mr Twe's United People's Party (UPP) was denied the registration which was required by law to enable it to field a candidate for the 1951 Presidential Election.

When Mr Twe and his supporters petitioned Mr Tubman to arrest what in their opinion was injustice, Tubman wrote Mr Twe a very threatening letter[20] dated April 18, 1951 in response to what he clearly thought was a 'threatening' note from his challengers.

The Executive Mansion
18th April 1951

Mr Twe:

Receipt of your threatening note of April 16, 1951, in the interest of a letter written to me by Thorgues Sie, et al., as representatives of a non-existing political party (UPP), to which I had replied before receiving yours now under reply, is hereby acknowledged.

For the present time, my reply to your note is that you are inherently a traitor to your country, a consummate liar, a senile visionary, a sophisticated bigot and an uncompromising egotist, the truth of which you will be made to realize.

Faithfully yours,
Wm. V.S. Tubman

As promised, supporters of Twe's United People's Party were later arrested and charged with sedition. Twe was obliged to flee to neighboring Sierra Leone on the eve of the 1951 Presidential Election when

Tubman, the incumbent, in his final election speech, alleged that Twe's hands were 'stained with the blood of treason, rebellion and sedition. He had been unfaithful and recreant to his trust as a Liberian citizen'.[21]

Alienated and frustrated, Twe remained in political limbo in Sierra Leone for ten years when he was pardoned and granted immunity from prosecution by President Tubman. Frail and despondent, Twe died shortly after his return to Liberia.

In like manner, when former President Edwin Barclay, who twelve years earlier had hand-picked Tubman to succeed him as President, challenged Tubman in the 1955 Presidential Election by supporting the coalition Independent True Whig and Reformation Parties, Tubman declared Barclay a 'traitor' and renegade.

The 1955 Presidential Election was marred by vicious attacks on personalities instead of addressing issues affecting the whole society.

On August 27, 1954, Edwin Barclay, nominated by the Independent True Whig Party (ITWP) and the Reformation Party coalition to oppose Tubman and the True Whig Party (TWP) in the election, made the following speech:[22]

My Fellow Citizens:

When in 1944 I announced my retirement from public office, that retirement was not intended to be merely a vacation between successive bids for public preferment. I had a sincere desire to be free from the burden which I had to discharge in very serious rational circumstances.

My methods and manner of doing this, Citizens described at that time as successful and satisfactory within the limits of the country's capacities.

I surrendered office all the more gladly because I thought my term of service and my methods of administration had set up an example of decency, honor and honesty in Government which any successor of mine would not only emulate, but would strive to maintain, if not to surpass.

I gave my support to a candidate with whose personal characteristics I was unacquainted, whose real intellectual attitude towards Government was unknown to me, and of whose interpretation of Government's obligation to society I was ignorant. I took him on trust from reports of his friends, and from what, I afterwards learnt, were his hypocritical letters to me.

I have observed with pain, during the past ten years, the structure of public morality, financial integrity and social welfare which I strove with so much labour and sacrifice to found and erect, being ruthlessly torn down and behind a facade of so-called modern developments and purported improvements being replaced by organized corruption, graft and financial irresponsibility.

I saw the welfare of the common people ignored in order that funds might be forthcoming to satisfy the hedonistic appetites of self-appointed leaders. I saw the prosperity of our trading class being sapped because of the corrupt practices of certain foreign traders encouraged and profited from by highly-placed officials.

I saw public servants, contrary to law, ruthlessly deprived of their salaries by being forcibly compelled, notwithstanding their protest, to contribute to the support of the one permitted political party, and submitting to the imposition because they feared to lose their jobs.

I saw municipal areas, such as townships and counties unable to perform their social and legal functions because they are deprived of revenues legally due them, even though the general national income has increased by many hundreds percent.

I saw the highest public offices being profitably commercialized, whilst the common man eked out a miserable existence in a state of semi-starvation.

I saw strenuous and expensive efforts being made to give the foreign public the impression that here in West Africa was a state and an administration which exhibited an example of enlightened liberalism whilst the local population was being ground down in despair at the ever-growing specter of almost universal want, and ever-present fear of unjust and illegal imprisonment.

I heard thousands of our citizens abandoning their homes and fleeing elsewhere, because their complaints against methods of so-called 'enlightened administration' were unheeded and could no longer be borne.

I saw attempts being made to demonstrate how popular the regime was – they claimed 95% popularity – by following the old Roman dodge of granting 'bread and circuses' to a select and very vocal few, whilst the admittedly low standard of living fell lower each day and the cost of living rose to astronomical peaks from the economic point of view of the common man.

I saw totalitarian methods of administration being adopted in public, business and social relations.

I saw the principles of democracy being debased to immoral mob-rule, and the spiritual morale of the people undermined by fear and terror of the President's Gestapo.

I saw the public revenues being squandered for purposes not connected with the public service, but as compensation and reward for personal loyalty to a dictator.

I saw pensions and gratuities being lavishly granted for causes unmerited or for no cause at all, and monuments erected at public expense to commemorate persons of whom nobody had ever heard, and of whose public service there is no record.

I saw those whom people expected to be leaders in the process of maintaining personal liberty and universal freedom reduced to the condition of parasites, time-servers, yes-men and cringing servants to one man's will, content to

'Eke out frustrated fates at bootless tasks,
All manly pride adjured. Their supple spines
Limber with sychophantic oil'

and, anxious to hold a place, however humble and dishonourable,

'Where high-placed brigands rape the common hoard,
And day by day assess their childish wants
Against the people's needs – selling for pelf
What honour should not buy.'

I saw the Hitler technique of the 'Big Lie' become the common tool of Mr Tubman's propaganda. Recently I have seen it dramatized in the comic antics of arousing the military camp at midnight and sending soldiers charging through the town to selected posts on the lying pretext that someone would attempt to assassinate the President. The play, by the way, was amusing since everybody knew that the self-styled 'Master Trickster' was on the prowl. Nobody of any intelligence was fooled and not one of the pretended suspects were disturbed because they were all a-bed sleeping, knowing nothing of what was at foot.

Liberians do not indulge in the practice of political assassination. They rather bring about change by legal means.

I saw liberal foreign aid in the form of trained men and money being frittered away in fruitless official conferences to no substantial public profit.

I saw the lines of demarcation constitutionally fixed between the several powers of Government so obliterated that the process had successfully achieved the dictatorship of one man. The indecent voice of the legislature is stifled. The courts have become obedient to his slightest nod.

I felt the voice of protest silenced for fear of vilification, vituperation or by the fatalistic question – What can one man do?

I saw the whole judicial system's moral independence shattered because of low financial provisions compared with say, the running costs of a single pleasure boat[23] – $87,000 against $125,000.

I myself felt the futility of protest, since the spirit of the old True Whig Party to which the majority of you present belong, seemed dead. The Party originally was a Party of protest, and it continued to be so until, in these later days, a group no longer responsive to the people's will took power.

Then the people became mere puppets of him who dominates the Party Machine.

I was amazed and appalled. I wondered where was the original spirit of protest which, in the past, motivated the actions for the protection of the people's rights and the betterment of their social condition?

Your presence here attests that that spirit still survives. There are a few who do not bow to the Baal of Conformity. There are still a few who wish the people to have a voice in their own Government, as was intended by the framers of the constitution.

I, too, should like to see the trappings of powers taken away from those who have abdicated every claim of constitutional right to occupy their high posts, and handed back to the people.

You, without any solicitation from me, have asked me to be the political Spear-head of this needed reform. I accept the charge and challenge, undeterred by fear, threats or attempts at Tubman's intimidation. We will protest against these evils, and if our protests are unheeded, we will submit them to the arbitrament of an awakened people.

As expected, Tubman won the election but Barclay, alleging foul play, would not concede defeat.

On June 22, 1955, seemingly not content with his election victory which guaranteed him an unprecedented third term of office as President, Tubman's security agents 'uncovered' a plot – the famous, perhaps not so famous, '1955 Assassination Plot' to kill Mr Tubman. Members of the Independent True Whig and the Reformation Parties were skillfully implicated in the 'uncovered' plot by Tubman's agents.

In a fashion typical of Tubman, the accused were duly processed through the Tubman judicial system. In the process of maintaining law and order, security forces pursued S. David Coleman, former National Chairman of the Independent True Whig Party and his son John, and killed them both on June 27, 1955 on a sugarcane farm near Klay, Bomi Territory.

The Tubman political machine swiftly engineered the banning of the Independent True Whig Party and the Reformation Party. The Act by the Legislature to ban these political parties was hurriedly passed on June 28, 1955.

On June 29, confounded and dejected, Edwin Barclay wrote a very touching 'letter of condolence' to S. David Coleman's widow:[24]

Dear Mrs Coleman:

I have no words in which I could attempt to offer you consolation or to assuage your grief for the loss of your husband and eldest son.

In former years, if a man in this country were accused of crime, he was then given the chance of exonerating himself in a public trial by his peers.

In these days, political vindictiveness hides itself behind official pretenses of upholding law and order, and effects its objectives by arranged murder.

I have always held that neither Government, nor political organization, nor private persons should adopt assassination as an instrument for attaining political ends. I have felt that the normal processes of the law should always be followed to establish facts. That men should not be made to suffer in person, property or rights upon mere'unproved assumptions, based upon reports of Tyranny and Usurpation. Men filled with the spirit of Freedom and love of Liberty, will not permit themselves to be reduced to the status of cringing time-serving sycophants. They will fight back to assert and maintain the rights of which it is sought, illegally, to deprive them.

You are a decendant of one of the pioneers of this country who declared that 'THE LOVE OF LIBERTY BROUGHT US HERE'. Coleman and I and Horace led a legal fight to rekindle a fervent desire in the hearts of our fellow-citizens for that LIBERTY. Because of this, the three of us, we understood, were marked down for liquidation.

Coleman is gone; how or in what manner or why, I have no means of knowing. It is likely the other two will soon follow. But among free men the memory of our deaths, motives and aims will be ever treasured as an inspiration never to submit to political, economic or social slavery; and John's name will go down in the annals of these times as the supreme example of filial piety.

I can say nothing more, but leave you to such consolation as God may grant you.

Yours very truly,
Edwin Barclay

Barclay, who led the ITWP, was never arrested.

Of the twenty-four members of the Independent True Whig Party charged with treason in connection with the 1955 'Assassination Plot', only S. Raymond Horace, former 'legal adviser' to the ITWP and

Reformation Party, Thomas N. Botoe, Booker T. Bracewell, S. Othello Coleman (younger son of S. David Coleman), Nete-Sie Brownell and Paul Dunbar were found guilty of treason and sentenced by Circuit Court Judge James A.A. Pierre.[25]

Like Twe, alienated, disgusted and disillusioned, Edwin J. Barclay, the man who 'made' Tubman and later became Tubman's most feared foe, died at the age of seventy-three on November 6, 1955.

End of an era

In 1963 another alleged plot to overthrow the Government of Liberia by force of arms and assassinate Tubman and other officials of the Liberian Government was announced to the Liberian public by Mr Tubman. The alleged 'plotter' this time was Colonel David Y. Thompson of the Armed Forces of Liberia.

On Tubman's orders, Colonel Thompson was court-martialled and 'found guilty of sedition, conspiracy and disloyalty'.[26] Thompson labored under difficult circumstances at the Bele-Yallah prison for more than three years until he was pardoned by Tubman.

The uncoverers of Mr Tubman's 'assassination plot', who often played on the nerves of spineless and sometimes unwillingly subdued citizens, were soon in search of yet another 'plot'. They found it. The year was 1968 and the victim was a learned Ambassador of aboriginal stock.

On January 24, 1968, while serving as Liberia's Ambassador to Kenya, Uganda and Tanzania, Henry B. Fahnbulleh was accused by President Tubman of engaging in treasonable and seditious activities. The Ambassador was arrested on February 13, 1968 and charged with sedition.

The Government charged Ambassador Fahnbulleh with, among other things, having written a book, *Liberia Within Independent Africa*, which criticized the Americo-Liberian domination of the country; and with being the author of a poem of 'an exciting nature' entitled 'Awake, Captain'.[27]

While Mr Fahnbulleh awaited trial in prison, members of the Legislature called upon President Tubman at the Executive Mansion on March 12th 'to assure him of their continuous and unflinching support; and condemned as "diabolical" and "subversive" the acts which Mr Fahnbulleh was alleged to have committed'.[28]

Mass demonstrations were organized against the imprisoned Ambassador. One foreign reporter recorded the following:

On April 30, thousands of members of the True Whig Party, Liberia's sole political party, paraded the streets of Monrovia. Representatives from Grand Bassa, Nimba and Bong Counties and River Cess Territory noisily reaffirmed their loyalty to President Tubman.... According to the *Liberian Star*, the citizens also condemned, deprecated and denounced any diabolical movement or subversion in this country, and reaffirmed their complete faith and confidence in, and irrevocable support of, the President's unification and integration policy.[29]

Meanwhile, every effort by Mr Fahnbulleh to secure a lawyer to represent him proved futile. Four prominent legal firms – Morgan, Grimes and Harmon; Dunbar and Horace; Simpson; and the Barclay Law Firm – refused when contacted to defend Ambassador Fahnbulleh for the following reasons:

The Simpson Law Firm stated it was against their policy to defend treason and sedition cases against the Republic of Liberia, no matter who was involved. Dunbar and Horace cited Rules 26 and 27 of the Code of Moral and Professional Ethics which forbade lawyers to plead cases involving disloyalty to the State. Morgan, Grimes and Harmon referred the court to the law which stated that when a person was unable to retain the service of a lawyer, the defence counsel of the country was there to represent him. The Barclay firm replied, simply but enigmatically, that 'to accept the appointment under the circumstances, would, in our opinion, be doing the defendant a disservice'.[30]

Unable to retain a counsel, and his wife unable to secure employment as she was declared *in forma pauperis*, the Defense Counsel of Montserrado County was appointed to represent Ambassador Fahnbulleh. Embarrassed by the bad image of the Government in this all-important 'Treason Trial' of the century, President Tubman made his displeasure known and shortly thereafter three attorneys offered their services in defense of Ambassador Fahnbulleh.

In addition to imprisoning Ambassador Fahnbulleh's two young children, labelled by Government authorities as 'security risks', several other persons accused of being co-opted by Ambassador Fahnbulleh were imprisoned. An unusual combination of suspects, three of President Tubman's vicegerents – Superintendents Robert Kennedy of Lofa County, James Y. Gbarbea of Bong County and Gabriel Farngalo of Nimba County – were arrested, disrobed and humiliated in connection with the Fahnbulleh case.

Fear became widespread in Liberia as never before. Students of the University of Liberia who frequented the courtroom during the trial to observe the workings of the Liberian democratic process were quickly assembled at a specially convened meeting of the Board of Trustees of the University of Liberia and informed by two of the Board's prominent members – the then Vice-President of Liberia, William R. Tolbert, Jr,[31] and the then Speaker of the House of Representatives, Richard A. Henries[32] – that both they and President Tubman were displeased with the attitude of the students over the Fahnbulleh affair. The students were accused of cheering Mr Fahnbulleh and booing Government officials at the trial, including a chain of 'State-quizzed' witnesses.

Rocheforte Weeks, then President of the University, threatened to expel those students whose behavior he termed 'unpatriotic'. Weeks continued:

> You students have vicarious liability to the University and the Government of Liberia who provide you with the money to get education. Students who continue to reflect discredit on the institution shall be expelled.[33]

Speaker Henries concluded by telling the young people 'that they should give thanks and praise to God for the many opportunities they enjoy under the leadership of President Tubman'.[34]

Fahnbulleh was convicted as charged. The 'jury' took less than half an hour to reach a verdict of guilty.

President Tubman, by making much out of a case believed by many to be a mere 'frame-up', created the very thing he feared most – an opposition. The opposition, as it emerged, 'consisted not only of aborigines, dissatisfied with the slow progress grudgingly allowed them'.[35] The opposition consisted largely of the youth, the future leaders of Liberia, disillusioned and embittered by the cynicism and hypocrisy evidenced by public officials in connection with the trial of Ambassador Fahnbulleh.

In July 1971, at the age of seventy-five, the twenty-seven-year reign of President Tubman came to an abrupt end with his death at an eye clinic in London, England.

CHAPTER SEVEN

Tolbert Years – Expectations and Disappointments

Having served for two decades as Vice-President to President William V.S. Tubman, William R. Tolbert became the 19th President of Liberia on July 23, 1971 following the 'sudden' and 'unexpected' death of Mr Tubman at an eye clinic in London. In addition to his political experience, Mr Tolbert, an ordained Baptist preacher, served as Vice-President of the Baptist World Alliance for Africa and President of the Baptist World Alliance. Locally, he served as President of the Liberia Baptist Missionary and Educational Convention.

With these credentials, William Richard Tolbert at the age of fifty-eight, took over the leadership of Liberia convinced that Liberian society was 'unwholesome'. The primary objective of his administration was to make Liberia a 'Wholesome Functioning Society'. In his first Inaugural Address, Tolbert described his vision of a wholesome functioning Liberian society as 'a society which shall require the total dynamic and individual involvement of every Liberian, and of all within our borders for an ever-spiraling advancement of productivity and achievement'.[1] President Tolbert further declared: 'We seek a Wholesome Functioning Society where merit, not favoritism; productivity, not influence and connection; selflessness, not selfish individualism, form the criteria for real distinction.'

Further defining the concept of a wholesome functioning society, Tolbert declared:

Especially devoted to discipline and order under the law, the Wholesome Functioning Society must express concrete concern for the poor and underprivileged, and must ensure security and protection for its citizens, and their freedom from fear and intimidation. It must guarantee opportunities for all, with the corresponding responsibility that all must be equally dedicated, as a prerequisite, to enjoyment of the benefits to be derived therefrom ...

Waste cannot escape removal; attitudes cannot remain unpurposeful, nor can unnecessary duplication avoid elimination.[2]

Specifically, President Tolbert's goal for Liberia, referred to by him as a stairway to 'Higher Heights', included the following:

1 Mount the Tread of Economy and Honesty in Government, which will entail not only a more vigorous problem of revenue collection, but also an austere administration of self-discipline in Government spending, and an over-all husbanding of its total resources...;
2 Pursue a 'Realistic Appraisal of the Open Door Policy' to attract foreign capital investments;
3 Diversification of the 'Economic Structure';
4 Introduction of 'modern, technologically-oriented agricultural system';
5 Embrace 'Urban Re-Construction and Rural Transformation' for the purpose of accommodating the 'constituents of the Wholesome Functioning Society';
6 Move on a Tread of Education that would re-gear our education system to provide more opportunities for technical, scientific and vocational training...;
7 The enforcement of law and order, to the preservation of the rights of the individual, and to a lasting code of honesty and transparent justice under the Law.[3]

With these objectives, President Tolbert raised the hopes of many Liberians disillusioned by the conduct of Government towards the end of the administration of President Tubman. Tolbert's expressed willingness to purge Liberia of the many 'unwholesome' practices of which he had been a part for twenty years as Liberia's Vice-President was very encouraging at the onset.

President Tolbert declared war on corruption and reorganized the Civil Service, sacking those who carried out no useful function. He placed emphasis on rural development, urban reconstruction and public welfare, with a view to alleviating the tremendous class disparities which existed. He began to involve people all over the country in self-help projects; he launched a National Fund-Raising Rally (commonly known as 'Rally Time') as a means of involving the population in the responsibilities of community national development.[4]

Rally Time

On April 30, 1972, shortly after his accession to the Presidency of Liberia, Mr Tolbert addressed a letter to the Legislature of Liberia proposing the need to organize a National Fund-Raising Rally for the purpose of raising needed funds to implement national development plans. Generally, the concept of 'Rally Time' was not only for fund-raising on a voluntary basis. It was a concept 'forcefully expressing itself in a determined effort on our part as leader of this nation to rouse a people long forlorn to a nobler destiny; to a better and healthier present; and to a greater and more secure future. This necessarily implies a virtual metamorphosis of attitude, a directed revivification of action, a rejuvenation of the national spirit . . .'[5]

As perceived by President Tolbert, Rally Time in Liberia 'must continue to be a time of individual, collective and national awakening from the state of lethargy into which we had fallen; a time for the total reassessment of our moral, social and spiritual values; a time for the regeneration of your thoughts and attitudes to create a wholesome functioning society not only for ourselves and all who reside in or visit our country, but also for posterity'.[6]

It was agreed that of the proposed ten million dollars to be raised, 25 percent would be allocated for the relocation and development of the University of Liberia, while the remaining 75 percent would be divided among the respective political sub-divisions of the country to undertake the following development-oriented projects and programs:

1 *Agriculture:* Extension throughout the nation, with the objective of obtaining our goal of self-sufficiency in our basic food.
2 *Education:* Construction of urgently needed school buildings and procurement of equipment and teaching materials; as well as employment of the necessary professors and teachers to meet the demands of the student-explosion problem.
3 *Transportation:* Construction of roads to various towns and other centers of population, thereby providing for the movement of goods and produce from farm to market and thus bringing the majority of our people into the money economy.
4 *Health:* Building more health centers for the healing of our sick and infirm, and the provision and procurement of the necessary physicians, nurses, drugs and medical equipment to staff and operate same.
5 *Accommodation:* Building of public edifices throughout the nation to house government offices more adequately; and the construction of recreation centers for youth development and social improvement.[7]

In a nationwide broadcast on August 21, 1972, Mr Tolbert officially launched the National Fund-Raising Rally – Rally Time Program – under the general chairmanship of the Vice-President of Liberia, Mr James E. Greene.

Encouraged by this concept, many Liberians at home and abroad as well as foreign residents in Liberia donated voluntarily. Some Liberians were forced to make contributions, though the President had said that contributions would be 'voluntary'.

On May 13, 1973, Tolbert announced that:

We have collected the amount of Four Million Three Hundred Thirty-nine Thousand two Hundred Thirty Dollars and Sixty-eight Cents ($4,449,230.68), not including other amounts to be paid in from the latest activities and contributions, which already have been safely deposited into two local Banking Institutions, the Bank of Liberia and the Bank of Monrovia respectively, under the title of 'National Fund-Raising Rally'.[8]

In thanking those who responded enthusiastically to the 'call for Rally Time', Mr Tolbert said:

I am fully aware of the fact that your enthusiastic response to our call for Rally Time has caused you to make numerous individual and collective sacrifices. I am also aware that a negligible number of our short-sighted, selfish and narrow-minded citizens have adamantly refused to contribute, and have attempted, though without success, to discourage others from doing so.[9]

In keeping the spirit of Rally Time alive, Mr Tolbert formed a permanent national organization known as the Liberian Force for Progress and Development (LFPD) 'headed by a Commander-in-Chief who shall be the President of the Republic'.[10] Other officials of the LEPD included three Lieutenant-Commanders-in-Chief 'to be assisted by nine County Commanders, one from each political sub-division of the country, each of whom shall be assisted in his area by three Lieutenant-Commanders'.[11]

The motto of the Liberian Force for Progress and Development – Faith, Self-reliance, Honesty, Industry and Self-sufficiency – and the national dress or uniform – overalls – were 'suggested' by the Commander-in-Chief.

According to the Commander-in-Chief the 'underlying philosophy of this Force is to quicken the cadence of development of our country as rapidly as possible; and for this purpose, financial and other contributions shall continue to be voluntarily made to the President and

Commander-in-Chief in continuance of the spirit of self-help and self-reliance'.[12]

With the President personally receiving Rally Time contributions, many wayward politicians and favor-seeking opportunists came from far and near to present, personally, to the President of Liberia and Commander-in-Chief of the Force, their 'voluntary' contribution in response to the call for 'Rally Time'.

Until he was removed from office by the People's Redemption Council of the Armed Forces of Liberia on April 12, 1980, President Tolbert continued to receive contributions for 'Rally Time' though he never once reported to the Liberian people the amount he received in contributions. It is also not known by the Liberian people, and now never will be known, the exact amount netted by their efforts in their response to a cause believed to be genuine. These doubts remained because, in reporting to the nation on May 13, 1973, President Tolbert revealed that the amount of $4,339,230.68 had been collected. Mr Tolbert concluded: 'This amount does not include other amounts to be paid in from the latest activities and contributions, already safely deposited in two local Banking Institutions, the Bank of Liberia and the Bank of Monrovia respectively, under the title of "National Fund Raising Rally."'[13]

The amounts deposited in these two banks, one of which – the Bank of Liberia – was co-owned by the Tolberts was never disclosed to the Liberian people. Suspicion soon arose and Mr Tolbert's own credibility, as well as his Government's, became the concern of the citizenry. Despondent and resentful, a freshman student at the University of Liberia wrote and published the following:

Rally Time[14]

When you tell me about rally time
    and of the benefits it'll bring
    of the bridges and roads that are being built
I think of health trips (abroad) and Swiss banks ...

When you tell me about rally time
    and say that I pay part of my monthly income
    to become self-reliant and build a
    wholesome functioning society
I think of ignorance, disease and poverty
    of the need for free education ...

When you tell me about rally time
    and all around me I see

The underfed children and jobless fathers
    and mis-educated students and ignorant mothers
And around me I see
    a class society
The haves and the have-nots
    all living together
With no sense of guilt
    I only see the hyprocrisy
A new scheme to suck the working people
    And I resent it all
In me there's a burning pain,
    a growing desire
To bring this all to an end ...

The youth – the 'precious jewels'

Tolbert referred to the young people of Liberia as his 'precious jewels'. Early in his administration Tolbert 'convened the first youth conference' ever at the Executive Mansion. Believing that young people should be involved in the affairs of government, President Tolbert reduced the voting age from twenty-one to eighteen years. Several youth organizations and movements were formed throughout the country.

Led by the founding of the Federation of Liberian Youth (FLY), several dozen youth movements emerged across the length and breadth of the country. 'Youth Day', simultaneously celebrated in all major political subdivisions of the country, was observed for the first time on October 29, 1973. Local student groups and associations were organized. Youth activities were accentuated nationally and proposed Youth Centers were to be constructed across the country. The first Youth Center building was erected at Zwedru, Grand Gedeh County, in 1974.

In acknowledgement of President Tolbert's avowed policy of engaging the youth of the country in meaningful civic activities, and especially in appreciation of the construction of a Youth Center at Zwedru, the first such structure in Liberia, a local poet, H. Tawile Cooper, described Grand Gedeh in the verses[15] below as 'The Headquarters of Speedy's[16] Precious Jewels'.

Where the honey combs of the busy bees,
Give the fainting hunter a sweet repast,
Where mount Gedeh stands majestically
Over which the sun was born and always aglow,
Where crocodiles are seen along the rushing streams,

This is Grand Gedeh, the Headquarters of Speedy's
    Precious Jewels.

Where mushrooms grow and tortoise creep
And fishes abound in the rivers and creeks,
Where waterfalls are heard afar and near,
Winding their way to the rivers and sea,
Where fishermen gather their meals for the day;
This is Grand Gedeh, the Headquarters of Speedy's
    Precious Jewels.

Where blackgum, oak, and walnut grow,
The mahogany, cedar, and the tall straight pine;
Where raffia is taken from the bamboo tree,
The cabbage is eaten and the wine is drunk,
And the traveler refreshed in the middle of day,
This is Grand Gedeh, the Headquarters of Speedy's
    Precious Jewels.

Where leopards spring on cowardly deer,
Where rats and 'Tabadues' [17] build their homes,
And birds sing happily to the God who cares for them,
Where eagles hunt and feed their young on monkey flesh,
Where grease is taken from 'judu' [18] trees to make a
    palatable meal,
This is Grand Gedeh, the Headquarters of Speedy's
    Precious Jewels.

Where raffia-made skirts were seen in the jungle,
And elephant tusks were found by hunters in the forest,
Where diamonds and gold lay hidden in our fertile soil,
And other minerals undiscovered were also there,
Over which the monkeys leapt from bough to bough,
This is Grand Gedeh, the headquarters of Speedy's
    Precious Jewels.

Where alligators roam to bathe and eat,
And ant-bears trap termites for food,
Where beavers grub for crabs,
Where boa-constrictors swallow their prey,
But yet fearful of deadly ants,
This is Grand Gedeh, the Headquarters of Speedy's
    Precious Jewels.

Where Speedy's dream is being fulfilled,
In the South Eastern region of Liberia free,

Where the women's social and political movement
Assiduously strives to mold Zwedru a second Eden ...

Specially organized political youth groups such as the Youth Organization for the Promotion of the Tolbert Administration (YOPTA) were formed. The hopes of many young people, especially young people in rural areas, were raised regarding speedy reforms in government. Addressing the graduates of St Augustine High School at Bolahun, Lofa County, Mr Tolbert said of the young people:

> ... I am always happy to speak to young people, my precious jewels, particularly those in rural areas who constitute a vital element in our determined efforts to raise the living standard of all our people throughout the nation ... It is important that we pause, periodically, to examine the past, review the present and set new and realistic goals for the future.[19]

In the process of setting 'new and realistic goals for the future', many young people soon found it difficult to reconcile their proclaimed status of 'precious jewels' when opportunities to improve their lot seemed unattainable. Frustration heightened as many young people – the precious jewels – were unable to participate in the affairs of Government by voting because of the 'property ownership' requirement.

Disappointed and disheartened, young Joe Wylie, a junior student at the then Charlotte Tolbert High School in Monrovia (named in honor of President Tolbert's late mother, and since renamed Monrovia Central High School), lamented his status as a 'precious jewel' in poetic fashion.

Am I a Precious Jewel?[20]

When I have to quit the countryside
To come to the city in search of education
Because no attention is paid to my village
In spite of the hut-tax my people pay
From year in to year out,
May I ask one question
Am I a precious jewel?

When education is not free
And books, uniforms, and school fees
Are more than I can afford
And I live in New Kru Town or Old road
And there is no bus to get me to school too,
May I ask you again, Sir;
Is there anything precious about me?

When I have to starve daily because I,
A self-supporting student,
Cannot afford a bag of rice,
When some of my starving brothers get
Jailed and killed because they have
To steal to escape death from starvation,
And you there, with your arms folded,
Saying or doing nothing about it,
Just building huge palaces
While a million bellies go empty
Am I your precious jewel?

When you give me, free of charge,
To Western capitalists
To make their super-profits
Which you share with them,
Making you rich while I,
Whose sweat produces the wealth,
Am impoverished and ignorant,
Think not that I am stupid
I am not a precious jewel!

The changes that never were

President Tolbert took power determined, as he publicly promised, to bring about changes in Liberian society, especially in the conduct of Government and in the guarantee of freedom of the Press, speech and association – all fundamental principles which the Tolbert administration promised to uphold.

Encouraging Liberians to express their views openly on matters of national interest, Mr Tolbert maintained that he did not feel comfortable leading a country when he had 'no idea what the people are thinking', for unless he knew what they thought and wanted it would not be possible to devise policies and programs to suit the needs of the Liberian people.

Taking seriously the President's invitation to discuss national issues in an open forum free of intimidation, some Liberian scholars and laymen advanced the proposition that to enhance national unity it was necessary to review those symbols or laws suggestive of discrimination and divisiveness in Liberian society. Attention quickly focused on the National Motto, *The Love of Liberty Brought Us Here*; the National Flag; the Constitution; and the National Anthem.

At the instigation of Mr Tolbert, the National Legislature, on July 22,

1974, passed 'an Act authorizing the President of Liberia to set up a National Commission to give consideration to possible changes in the National Motto, National Flag, National Anthem and the Constitution of Liberia'.[21] On January 21, 1975 Mr Tolbert issued a Presidential Proclamation setting up a fifty-one member Commission, known as the Commission on National Unity, which was empowered to:

1 Study the Constitution of Liberia, the National Anthem of Liberia and make such recommendations to the President for changes therein as the Commission may consider necessary and proper to depict indivisibility among the people and National Unity.
2 Examine the National Flag of Liberia and recommend to the President such changes as the Commission may consider expedient to reflect our National personality and heritage as an African Nation.[22]

The Commission was chaired by McKinley A. DeShield, Sr, the Postmaster-General of Liberia and Secretary General of the True Whig Party. While the Commission was at work, cosmetic changes such as changing of names and renaming of streets – Front Street was named King Sao Bosso Street in honor of a famous tribal chief, Water Street was renamed 'Total Involvement' Street – were made.

The Commission labored for three years and reported that 'it is clear that the majority of those who have responded are against the changing of the Flag, Anthem, the Motto and the Constitution'.[23]

Tolbert's own perception of the freedom of Press, speech and association was a disappointing contrast to the aspirations of many Liberians whose expectations of a genuine change of attitude toward the Press and general public freedom had been heightened by the public statements of the President. A few examples may suffice.

C. Abayomi Cassell, a historian and former Attorney General of Liberia, told the students at Monrovia College during a graduation ceremony that 'the True Whig Party was beyond reform and so if he could get eighteen fearless men, two from each of the nine counties, he would form a party to provide a sound government'.[24] For reporting Mr Cassell's speech in the *Liberian Star*, the reporter, Mr Rufus Darpoh, was found guilty, according to Government, of 'reporting for public consumption a statement Mr Cassell had made in private to graduating students'[25] and suspended for three months.

Late in 1974, critic Albert Porte, the famous pamphleteer, published an article in which Mr Porte expressed concern about the methods employed by the late Stephen A. Tolbert, Minister of Finance of Liberia, brother of the President of Liberia and owner of the giant Mesurado Group of Companies, to strangle smaller Liberian-owned businesses thus removing any possible competition against the Tolbert-owned Mesurado Group. A libel suit was filed against Mr Porte by Stephen Tolbert. With the entire machinery of Government – the Press, the judges and the jury – siding with the establishment, Albert Porte was found guilty and fined $250,000.

The editor of *Revelation,* a magazine published by students of the University of Liberia, elected to report what was in his view a relatively balanced version of the defamation suit filed against Mr Porte, since no other news organ in the country showed any willingness to inform the public in a non-biased fashion. This angered the Tolbert administration. Publication of *Revelation* magazine was banned by the Government in January 1975 and those individuals connected with the magazine were imprisoned and fined $17,000. Associates and sympathizers, real or imagined, of Albert Porte were harassed by security agents of the Tolbert clan and some alleged sympathizers were arrested and imprisoned.

President Tolbert commissioned his new seventeen-member Cabinet on January 11, 1972. At the inaugural ceremony, Tolbert told the newly-appointed officials that 'honesty, efficiency and integrity must be the order of the day in the performance of (their) duties'. He further advised members of his Cabinet never to let their private or personal interests supercede the national or public interest, adding, 'I will not permit a conflict of interest'. Disconcertingly, however, dishonesty and improbity in the public and private sectors soon became the order of the day. By 1975, barely four years after Mr Tolbert challenged his Cabinet to conduct the affairs of Government in their respective agencies with 'honesty and integrity', the National Force for the Eradication of Corruption was organized to combat official corruption.

The National Force that never eradicated corruption

In an attempt to command public trust, Tolbert established by Executive Order a National Force for the Eradication of Corruption (NFEC). The Force initially consisted of fifty-two personnel and was charged with the following responsibilities:

1 To seek out and discover in Liberia by all legal means corruption, whether in the public or private sector;
2 To be vigilant in protecting the public against all forms of corruption;
3 To collect, check and compile facts and data on any transaction involving corruption, or any organization or persons dealing in corrupt practices;
4 To make available and report direct to the President for attention of

the Ministry of Justice all information, facts, data, articles, and other relevant materials and suspicious cases requiring police probe and prosecution. (See Appendix 3 for text of Executive Order establishing the National Force for the Eradication of Corruption.)

Having publicly announced the intention of his administration to rid Liberian society of all vestiges of social ills and unwholesomeness, Mr Tolbert promised:

> ... We shall not work from the narrow premise of who you are or where you are from. But instead we will act upon the positive basis of what you stand for and what you can do. For we are convinced that sectionalism and tribalism, favouritism and nepotism are cancerous proclivities that can only sap the springs of national vitality and dry the wells of peace and plenty.
> ... We shall not countenance incompetence and inefficiency, corruption in action, dishonesty in practice and anarchy in comportment ...[26]

Dishonesty and corruption in government became widespread and uncontrollable. The National Force for the Eradication of Corruption fell out of use as its functions were usurped by the President and it simply carried out the expressed wishes of the President. Friends and relatives of the President as well as those citizens well connected in society who engaged in dishonest or corrupt practices were seldom prosecuted.

The Force soon became known rather sarcastically as the 'Corruption Bureau' or the 'National Force Encouraging Corruption'.

Corrupt and dishonest practices had become so prevalent and seemingly accepted by society that local newspapers printed lengthy articles describing dishonest practices in the public and private sectors. Moral deterioration in society reached its lowest ebb.

The Liberian society under the leadership of Tolbert suffered such moral deterioration that by 1979 the Government's official news organs carried headlines indicative of a society saddled with the problem of moral decadence. The following are excerpts from a news release headlined in the *Bentol Times*,[27] a government-subsidized newspaper:

HIGHER-UPS EVADING TAXES? . . . .
Justice Ministry to Prosecute

In an effort to improve the national revenue through tax collection, the Ministry of Finance has prepared a list of tax delinquents with the view of forwarding it to the Ministry of Justice for prosecution and, where needs be, to invoke necessary legal statutes to ensure collection from the delinquents.

Reliable sources close to the Ministry of Finance revealed that the list is being headed by several big names in the community, who are least expected to be delinquent in their tax payment.

The sources further revealed that the Minister of Finance, Ellen Johnson Sirleaf, in line with her expressed determination and policy to improve the national revenue collection, plans to crack down on these delinquents no matter their social status or connections. Mrs Sirleaf is believed to have said that nobody is above or should be above the laws of the land and that those laws are meant to be obeyed and adhered to.

However, the question being asked by some observers of the Ministry of Finance is what is going to happen to the 'big shot' delinquents, as in the past several of these names have even been published in the papers and no positive action or results came out of the exercise.

They noted that most of these 'big shots' hide behind the mantle of their social, political or family status to evade tax payment, thereby doing a great disservice to the nation and the national development efforts.

They registered their support for the hard line being taken by the Minister to recover what these delinquents owe the nation and stressed that it is important and necessary for every body to pay their taxes if 'we are not only paying lip-service' to the Administration's national development policy and the policy of Self-Reliance for Self-Sufficiency as preached daily by the Chief Executive, Dr Tolbert . . .

In another investigation into corruption and conflict of interests, *The Sunday People*,[28] an independent weekly newspaper, took the risk of publicly taking Tolbert to task. In bold letters the headline read: 'Is the Fight Against Corruption Real?' In an editorial, the Editor wondered whether the President did indeed condone the acts of dishonesty and official misconduct admitted to by certain officials of Government. The Editor concluded that official misconduct and corruption 'does seem to be rampant, blatant, obvious and institutionalized'. In the same issue of the paper, under the caption 'Corruption at Air Liberia?', the story reads:

Within the last two weeks, startling revelations have been made in the local press regarding alleged gross mismanagement, inefficiency and apparent outright corruption by the Air Liberia management.

In the interest of our readers, we thought it wise to conduct our own investigation about the corporation to ascertain what was indeed happening at Air Liberia. Our reporters have dicovered the following.

It appears that that there is indeed corruption at Air Liberia, but surprisingly enough, it seems that the allegations have been deliberately misdirected, and instead of being laid at the doorstep of the management of the corporation, our investigation reveals that the corruption seems to be centred at the Ministry of Commerce, Industry and Transportation whose Minister is Chairman of the Air Liberia Board of Directors, and which ministry is directly responsible for the overall supervision and direction of the corporation, and apparently the Board of Directors itself.

Item 1. The real reason behind the sustained press campaign against Mr Sirleaf and the corporation's management appears to be based on the fact that he, together with all the senior Liberian management, and British Caledonian, the contractual managing agents, have all objected to the granting of exclusive rights to a newly formed Liberian Corporation called Trans Africa Airlines, whose Chairman just happens to be Hon. A. Benedict Tolbert.

Reliable sources reveal that other top commerce and other high Cabinet level government officials have an interest in other airlines and they are trying to acquire monopolies regarding Liberian air traffic rights which properly belong to Air Liberia, the country's only national airline.

In the next issue of the 'Liberian Inaugural', we will expose the names of the people and the private airlines that they represent in opposition to Air Liberia.

Item 2. BCAL, as part of its management contract, proposed to government that Air Liberia be expanded and offered two Boeing 707 aircrafts to establish air routes for Air Liberia, linking Monrovia on regular scheduled flights to Europe, USA and West Africa. The proposal was approved by the President and referred to the Ministry of Commerce for implementation. Strangely enough, the Ministry of Commerce supposedly responsible for the development of Air Liberia deliberately did nothing, and lo and behold, some six months later, the very same Air Liberia proposal was stolen and resubmitted as an original Trans Africa proposal, using the same planes offered by BCAL, also using BCAL as the managing agents, also proposing the very same airline routes.

The President appointed a committee to review the application (of Trans Africa Airlines) composed of the Minister of Commerce as Chairman, and including Mr Charles Clarke, Minister of State without Portfolio. It is interesting to note that both these Ministers also sit on the Board of Directors of Air Liberia, and also strangely enough these people representing Air Liberia's interest knowingly approved the stolen Air Liberian proposal on behalf of Trans Africa.

To us, it seems a clear conflict of interest, and we cannot but speculate as to whether other considerations influenced their quick

Delivery to (Ministry/Agency)	Invoice to	Ship via		
March 16, 1979 Ministry of Education	Ministry of Finance Republic of Liberia c/o General Services Agency Bureau of Procurement and Supply Monrovia, Liberia			

Item	Quantity ordered	Unit	Description	Unit price	Extension
	4		Wall light living room	35.00	140.00
	4		" " dining "	35.00	140.00
	2		ceiling light "	22.50	45.00
	28		receptacles 110v	1.00	28.00
	4		bedroom wall lights	25.00	100.00
	5		closet ceiling light	8.50	42.50
	2		bathroom light	12.50	25.00
	1		220 v real tech. stove		4.50
	1		220 v " a/c		4.50
	7		2 x 20 w lens fixture	22.50	157.50
	8		braker 30 x 60 A	3.50	28.00
	5		Porch lights	9.50	47.50
	1		garage light	9.50	9.50
	1		door bell		4.50
	30		candle bulbs	.50	15.00
	2		double switch	3.50	7.00
	3		rolls tape	.75	2.25
	4		" 12 - 1 wire	15.00	60.00
					$860.75

For the use of Paynesward School
proforma invoice no...attached

Director of Finance

and speedy approval of the Trans Africa proposal. At this stage, the entire senior Liberian management of Air Liberia, including Mr Sirleaf, Mr Jehu Richardson, General Manager, Air Liberia operations, Mr Abraham T. Simmons, General Engineering Manager, Moses Weefur, Jr, Chief Pilot, Mr Thomas D. Harris, Ground Operations Manager, and Mr Michael C. Jupiter, Manager Fleet 2, wrote the President and informed him that they would immediately resign, if Air Liberia and thereby the entire Liberian people were cheated of their rights by giving away the entire Air Liberian traffic rights to this private company headed by Hon. A. Benedict Tolbert. This seems to have been the beginning of the problems between Air Liberia, the Ministry of Commerce and Air Liberia Board of Directors ...

In the various Ministries and agencies of Government, dishonest practices were equally 'rampant, blatant, obvious and institutionalized'. The appalling degree to which dishonest practices were carried out is reflected in the Purchase Order on page 94, one of several such Purchase Orders, dated March 16, 1979, prepared at the direction of a very senior Minister at the Ministry of Education.

Paynesward School, the institution for which the items on the face of this Purchase Order were supposedly bought, is a small, simple six-classroom rectangular structure. It has no water system, no kitchen, no porch and no garage. It has no bedrooms, no living room nor a single dining room. The building has no closets or bathrooms, except for the one pit toilet (outhouse) in the field behind the building; there are no door bells nor is there a need for candle (light) bulbs as the structure was only recently electrified.

These items, purchased upon the directive of a very senior official of the Ministry of Education from the International Merchantile and Retailing Agency, an Indian-owned building material store in Monrovia, were used in the construction of a private residence for this official. While less than a third of the nation's school-age population can find adequate classroom accommodation, meagre resources set aside to accommodate the expanding student population were being misdirected by high public officials.

Though President Tolbert publicly informed the Liberian people that more than four[29] million dollars of public funds had been embezzled and misappropriated by public officials in 1978, not a single individual was ever prosecuted by the Government.

Publicly, Tolbert stated that 'favoritism and nepotism are cancerous proclivities' capable only of sapping the springs of national vitality and drying the 'wells of peace and plenty'. In the light of this statement, it is interesting to analyze some of the appointments to public offices made by Mr Tolbert.

A sample of the various public offices held by relations of President Tolbert, 1972–1980

Position	Relationship
1 Minister of Finance	Brother
2 President Pro-Tempore of Senate and Senator, Montserrado County	Brother
3 Deputy Auditor-General	Brother
4 Mayoress of the City of Bentol	Sister
5 Assistant Minister of Education/ Supervision	Daughter
6 Deputy Minister of Education/Instruction	Daughter
7 Chairman, House Foreign Relations Committee and Representative, Montserrado County	Son
8 Deputy Minister of State for Presidential Affairs	Nephew
9 Assistant Minister of State for Presidential Affairs	Nephew
10 Agricultural Attaché to FAO, Rome, Italy	Nephew
11 Executive Secretary	Niece
12 Minister of Defense	Son-in-law
13 Minister of National Security	Son-in-law
14 Deputy Minister of State for Presidential Affairs	Son-in-law
15 Commissioner of Immigration	Son-in-law
16 Assistant Minister of Public Works	Son-in-law
17 Mayor, City of Monrovia	Brother-in-law
18 Deputy Governor, National Bank of Liberia	Nephew-in-law
19 Liberian Ambassador to France	Sister-in-law
20 Army Chief of Staff	Nephew-in-law
21 Director, National Security Agency	Nephew-in-law
22 Deputy Director, National Police	Nephew-in-law

Emergence of pressure groups

Liberians young and old, anticipating the social and political reforms promised by President Tolbert, eagerly accepted in good faith his challenge to 'air their criticisms' in a spirit of constitutional democracy. President Tolbert had announced publicly that he had no desire to lead a country where the ideas and thinking of the people were unknown to him, for it is only by knowing what the people think and want that 'he could shape policies to meet their needs'.

The invitation of Tolbert to all Liberians to express their views and thoughts in a democratic fashion led to the initial emergence of social and political organizations, some of which soon became 'organized pressure groups'.

Notable among the pressure groups were the Union of Liberian Associations in the Americas (ULAA), organized in 1974; the Movement for Justice in Africa (MOJA), founded in 1973, and the Progressive Alliance of Liberia (PAL), founded also in 1973.

Both the Union of Liberian Associations in the Americas and the Progressive Alliance of Liberia had their origin in the United States of America where many of the founding members had gone in pursuit of advanced education.

A loosely co-ordinated organization, the Union of Liberian Associations in the Americas comprises a number of smaller and independent chapters of Liberian associations, many of them social clubs, in major American cities such as New York; Washington, D.C.; Atlanta, Georgia; Los Angeles, California; and Minneapolis, Minnesota. The ULAA recently (1978/79) became assertive as a pressure group advocating social and political changes in Liberia by organizing rallies and anti-government demonstrations and petitioning government, in the name of the Union and Liberians residing in America, to change the course of events in Liberia.

The Progressive Alliance of Liberia, founded under the leadership of Gabriel Baccus Matthews and Oscar J. Quiah, was based in New York City until 1978 when its leadership returned to Liberia determined to form a political party to oppose the 110-year-old, single, ruling True Whig Party and mobilize the masses of the Liberian people in the struggle for social and political change. Through *The Revolution*, the official newspaper of the Progressive Alliance of Liberia, PAL informed Liberians at home and abroad of its objectives, plans and the need to 'continue the struggle' for meaningful social and political changes in Liberia.

On January 8, 1980, the Progressive Alliance of Liberia registered, with much difficulty, as a political party named and styled the Progressive People's Party (PPP), making it the first opposition party in the twenty-five years since the Independent True Whig Party was banned by the leadership of the True Whig Party on June 28, 1955.

The Movement for Justice in Africa, on the other hand, emerged originally as a local chapter of the 'continent-wide mass-based Pan-African Organization whose primary objective is to rid Africa of all forms of colonialism and neo-colonialism as well as other forms of social and economic injustice'.[30] The leadership of the MOJA organization in Liberia, which consisted of young academicians, under the protective shield of the international parent organization, artfully maneuvered itself into a position of strength by organizing a Village Development Project (SUSUKU) in south-eastern Liberia in 1977 and providing limited social services to the impoverished. As an international organization, MOJA/Liberia obtained funding for its programs and activities from international donor agencies sympathetic to the cause of the parent Pan-African Movement in support of liberation struggles in Africa. By a proficient use of available resources, MOJA/Liberia soon became a rather virile local organization.

In what might be considered a pitch for political recognition by the ruling True Whig Party, Grand Gedeh County Attorney, David Y. Swengbe, Sr, took the initiative to lead the anti-MOJA/SUSUKU rally in the county. In a letter to President Tolbert, dated April 10, 1978, Mr Swengbe wrote:

Dear Mr President:

The MOVEMENT known as SUSUKU backed by Dr Togba Nah Tipoteh has gone far (of course not too late to apprehend) into Grand Gedeh, and unless the County Officials such as Superintendents, Commissioners and Chiefs are on the lookout, it will be difficult to totally apprehend it. The Chiefs in whose Chiefdoms and Towns this man has established his movement through farming, have actually accepted Mr Tipoteh. His activities in these areas were never questioned by the Government Officials concerned.

The Chiefs received materials and equipments from Mr Tipoteh to operate their farms and in other places they have begone (*sic*) work on the farms. Several lectures have been given by Mr Tipoteh in different conferences held with the Chiefs and the people way back into the villagers (*sic*), and these people have been so impressed that it is difficult to erase the impression he has made around the County.

From my personal observation, many persons are still of the strong opinion that, the SUSUKU MOVEMENT is good and should not be questioned by Government. But, they do not see the intent and effect of this SUSUKU MOVEMENT as it relates to the operation of the Government, and therefore, I think we need strong, sincere and devoted teams of Officials and Loyal Citizens to preach to and teach the villagers the policy of the Government and the simultaneous development programs of our Country.

If I have my own way, Mr President, the Chiefs and Commissioners and other Government Officials who have accepted permitted and supported this SUSUKU MOVEMENT in their areas without reporting to the Government directly or indirectly and have kept such movement as much as possible under cover should be strongly reprimanded if not removed from office. Because it will be difficult for those same Officials of Government to sincerely preach against such SUSUKU MOVEMENT which they have already accepted, permitted and supported to the extent that operation of SUSUKU MOVEMENT have already started (in) some areas.

Mr President, the strength of unity has been the cornerstone of liberty for the Liberian nation, and over (ever) since 1869 the True Whig Party has promoted unity, stability and progress with outstanding zeal and imagination. It has left no doubt that the policies it fosters to embrace and elevate all elements of Society continue to satisfy the aims, aspirations and will of the great and vast majority of the Liberian people.

No person, or persons, or minority, however persistent; no device, however ingenious; nor any false doctrine of whatever attraction, will be permitted to ever penetrate our Society and allure this peaceful nation into disharmony, anarchy and nihilism. We are committed forever to disassociate ourselves from tendencies and practices inimical to the ideal of a free united people.

Over 108 years ago, the True Whig Party has always stood as a symbol of a united people, and one of our surest foundations for achieving a progressive and stable Government. In times like these, when ideologies vary from one form of human emotion to another, and when Governments and other political institutions rise and fall, we the people of Liberia should indeed be proud and grateful to God to know that the True Whig Party still stands majestically as the uncompromising fortress of our national unity, solidarity and stability.

May Good richly bless and guide you and your immediate family.

Kindest regards at RALLY TIME!

> Respectfully yours,
> David Y. Swengbe, Sr.
> COUNTY ATTORNEY, GRAND GEDEH COUNTY, R L.

It probably never occured to Mr Swengbe and his henchmen that perhaps one of the reasons why 'these people have been impressed that it is difficult to erase the impression he (Tipoteh) has made around the Country', was that the True Whig Party, in its 110 years existence as the sole ruling party in Liberia, had never offered a viable alternative for the inhabitants of the country. (Mr Swengbe now claims no association with the True Whig Party and is presently serving as County Attorney for Grand Gedeh County in the Revolutionary Government of the People's Redemption Council. Interestingly, Dr Tipoteh, Swengbe's arch-rival, was the first Minister of Planning and Economic Affairs in the PRC Government.)

Each of the three principal groups mentioned attracted followers of all classes and ages. Before long it was clear that President Tolbert had extended an invitation to all Liberians to 'criticize', and express 'views and thoughts' about, the conduct of government which he was either unable or unwilling to honor. The various leaders, members and associates of every organization whose views on matters of public interest differed from those views expressed by the leadership of True Whig Party – especially MOJA and PPP – became the target of ridicule and harassment by the Government-controlled machinery.

Scandalous leaflets attacking personalities of the leadership of the Movement for Justice in Africa (MOJA/Liberia), and the Progressive Alliance of Liberia (PAL) and the Progressive People's Party (PPP), were often circulated by known public officials and government agents. Witless commentaries, often exaggerating the capabilities of local political organizations, were frequently advertised on national radio while addle-pated editorials placarded the pages of Government-owned newspapers.

CHAPTER EIGHT

The Last Straw –
14 April 1979

For the reasons set out in the foregoing chapters, tension built up over the years to such an extent that some kind of explosion was inevitable. The expected explosion occurred on April 14, 1979. As this event was the 'last straw' which led to the overthrow of the First Liberian Republic, it is necessary to recount briefly the developments leading to April 14, 1979, commonly referred to as the 'Rice Riots' or locally simply as 'April 14'.

In late 1978 the Government announced a proposed increase in the price of rice – the nation's staple food – from $22.00 to a rumored $30.00 per hundred-pound bag. This proposed increase in the price of rice would probably not have enraged the Liberian public so much had the President of Liberia and one of his brothers not been connected with the production, importation and sale of rice.

The Progressive Alliance of Liberia, led by Gabriel Baccus Matthews, through written communications and meetings with President Tolbert and other senior government officials, offered suggestions and alternative measures to try to avoid the proposed price increase. These representations had no effect and, feeling it had done everything possible under the circumstances, the leadership of PAL decided, as a last resort, to stage a mass demonstration against the increase. The Ministry of Justice was asked by PAL to grant a permit to stage a peaceful demonstration, a right guaranteed by the Constitution, but this was refused by the Government.

On March 28, 1979, Gabriel Baccus Matthews took what he described as a four-man 'People's Delegation' to the office of President

Tolbert. At the meeting with Tolbert the rice issue was discussed in detail as each side sought to clarify its position. The issue of the scheduled PAL-organized mass demonstration was also discussed, much to the displeasure of President Tolbert. As far as the threatened demonstration was concerned, President Tolbert declared that any demonstration organized by the Progressive Alliance of Liberia, as a result of the rice issue, would constitute a defiance of the Government's orders banning such demonstrations. The President further maintained that defiant individuals 'would not be allowed to violate the laws with impunity'.[1]

On April 10, 1979, four days before the eventful Saturday morning of April 14, the Progressive Alliance of Liberia made its final offer to the Government in the following letter to President Tolbert:

Mr President: During the meeting with you and the People's Delegation which we carried to the Executive Mansion on March 28, 1979, we raised the query as to whether it is at all possible for Government to help our farmers without increasing the price of rice. You indicated that such a consideration is under study.

As a contribution to the factors for Government's analysis, we wish to offer the following for inclusion and review in your study:

a) According to Minister (of Agriculture) Chenoweth's Annual Report, local farmers produced only 256 metric tons, or 5,688 hundred-pound bags of rice in 1977. (It would seem the figure for 1978 has not yet been determined by her office.) We, therefore, venture the assumption that our farmers will produce 6,500 hundred-pound bags this year.
b) A price increase of $3.00 on locally-produced rice, as had been proposed by Minister Chenoweth, would provide our farmers an addition a profit of $19,500.00.
c) The Progressive Alliance of Liberia wishes to know whether Government would look kindly on the idea of PAL making available the amount of $19,500 for distribution to our farmers at the rate of $3.00 on each bag of rice produced. The price of the rice to the public would therefore remain $22.00 a bag.

Here, Mr. President, is an idea for holding steady the price of rice for at least one year. The farmers would have their additional $3.00 on each bag; there would, or should, no longer be any reason for an increase in the price of rice; we would not have to demonstrate against any such increase; and you would be free from the difficult task of trying to stop a mass demonstration of united citizens who react to a threat to their survival.

What we are here offering is far more than just assistance to both the producers and consumers of rice. We are also offering Government an entire year during which it may work out a reasonable price structure that would not invoke a public outcry or deserve a mass demonstration.

If our proposal is appealing, we would be pleased to discuss the matter in detail with you.

In the cause of the people, the struggle continues!

Progressively, Gabriel Baccus Matthews[2]

By directive of the President, Dr D. Elwood Dunn, Deputy Minister of State for Presidential Affairs and Director of the Cabinet, acknowledged Chairman Matthews' letter as follows:

Dear Mr Matthews: I have been directed by the President to acknowledge your letter of the 10th instant in which you primarily raised the issue of the price of rice which was discussed during your meeting with him on the 28th March, 1979.

First of all, as regards the assertion contained in the first paragraph of your letter that during the meeting, you had raised a query in the interest of rice-producing farmers, the President would have me remind you that your representations related exclusively to consumers, not producers of rice. It was the position of Government, clearly indicated then and reaffirmed here, that on the crucial issue of the price of rice, the interest and welfare of producers and consumers alike must be attended. This is the position, the President adds, while Government is considering the recommendation for possible increase, a recommendation moreover, which has yet to be decided upon, and which is being viewed taking into account all relevant perspectives inclusive of the long-term interests of the masses.

The President would have me thank you for the suggestion which you have advanced in the second paragraph of your letter, and to assure you that consistent with his policy of welcoming views on national issues from any concerned citizen, same will receive objective and meritorious consideration. I am to inform you, however, that that part of your suggestion relating to making available a financial contribution to Government for farmers can obviously not be accepted in the manner advanced, for this is wholly contrary to Government's approach to the solution of national problems.

With reference to your allusions to 'Mass demonstration', the President directs that I again remind you that he has already indicated to you that any such action would serve no positive end, but would, to the contrary, be disruptive of public order. True to his sacred obligation to this country, he emphasizes, no such disruptive activities will be countenanced; neither will Government make a determination on national issues in an atmosphere of emotionalism. And he indicates that Government will never accept alibis for the promotion of lawlessness and the defiance of constituted authority.

The President finally directs that I have you informed that he is under commitment to safeguard the interests of all Liberians without exception, and that this sacred duty he will carry out free from threats and emotionalism from any source. The supreme interest of Liberia, he adds, requires, nothing less. With kindest regards at RALLY TIME! D. Elwood Dunn, Deputy Minister/Director of the Cabinet.[3]

The President's letter acknowledging that of Matthews was urgently delivered at the Monrovia headquarters of the Progressive Alliance of Liberia. Still fearing a mass demonstration, the Government engaged the services of clergymen and other prominent citizens who commanded the respect and trust of the leadership of the Progressive Alliance of Liberia 'to approach PAL and advise the young people' against the planned demonstration.

Also at the request of the President, through Albert Porte, a prominent social reformer, the leadership of PAL agreed to 'call off' the demonstration scheduled for 3.00 pm on Saturday, April 14, 1979 'provided the Government keeps the security forces in the background'[4] so that the PAL leadership might have the opportunity to disperse those individuals gathering at PAL's headquarters for the scheduled demonstration. The Secretary General of PAL, Oscar J. Quiah, gave this assurance to Porte following an Executive Committee meeting of the leadership of the Progressive Alliance of Liberia.

By early Saturday morning on April 14, just as the leadership of PAL was about to defuse the tension, disperse the crowd gathered at its headquarters and 'call off' the demonstration as promised, Government security forces acting the upon orders of the President stormed the headquarters of the Progressive Alliance of Liberia, destroying lives and property.

The Government reacts

By the end of the day, an estimated two hundred persons were dead, hundreds had been injured and property worth millions of dollars had been destroyed. Members of MOJA and PAL, as well as alleged sympathizers of the two organizations, were indiscriminately arrested and charged with treason and sedition. The security forces arrested thousands of young people, alleged PAL and MOJA members, throughout the country and detained them in various prison compounds. Individuals accused of being PAL and MOJA leaders in various parts of the country were brought to Monrovia and imprisoned in the Monrovia Central Prison and other places of detention in the capital.

The Government offered a reward of $5,000 each for information leading to the arrest, dead or alive, of several persons, many of them students, some of whom had not been anywhere near Liberia either before or during 'April 14'. In the weeks that followed, Liberia was in a state of chaos as never before experienced in recent times. The President was, as always, granted emergency powers by the Legislature. Under the Presidential Emergency Powers Act, human rights are disregarded and the writ of habeas corpus is suspended for as long a period as the President shall deem required and necessary.

In a loosely-organized attempt to purge the country of the 'few evil people, criminally-minded and villainous traitors', the Government undertook a massive public relations campaign to restore its credibility. On April 21, 1979, a Government release read:

> This evil thing that happened in Monrovia on Saturday night was the work of some evil people in our midst!
>
> They were not only fighting President Tolbert and the Government, but they were fighting you, too. By breaking up the stores and big business firms, they are out to take jobs away from your sons, husbands and all those who provided you with money to buy rice, fish, palm oil, medicines and all the things you need. Those few evil people are not interested in you. They got plenty of money and are just fooling you.
>
> We must not allow these evil people in our midst to destroy our country. We must join hands with President Tolbert – put our arms around him and rid our country of these evil minded people.

Civil servants as well as government-organized groups of citizens from political sub-divisions of the country delivered resolutions and statements of loyalty and support for the administration of President Tolbert. Every group of citizens pledging its support to the Tolbert administration in a public manner 'vehemently deprecated, denounced and condemned the wicked, satanic, seditious and treasonable acts of lawlessness' perpetrated by an alleged small band of 'criminally minded and villainous traitors'.

On April 24, 1929, the National Legislature passed the following Joint Resolution:

> WHEREAS, the Members of the Legislature of the Republic of Liberia, legal representatives of the people of this great God-fearing Nation, have received the Message of the President reporting the acts of certain wicked, vicious, satanic and diabolical individuals, having

disregard for constituted authority and sheltering behind their so-called objections to recommendation of the Minister of Agriculture for an increase in the price of rice .... an issue which Government was giving due consideration, has resulted in the loss of lives and properties, vandalism, designed primarily to destroy and thwart the progressive and rapid development of this precious and beloved Country, being carried out by our sagacious, dynamic and relentless leader, Dr William Richard Tolbert, Jr., President of the Republic of Liberia; and

WHEREAS, the unparalleled and invaluable achievements of this Nation and its people under the Slogan 'War against the common enemies of mankind: IGNORANCE, DISEASE AND POVERTY', culminating in the individual discovery of himself and his personality; and those wise, farsighted and far-reaching policies and programs enunciated in the first year of his incumbency as Chief of State of this Country and the successful prosecution and implementation of those policies for the betterment of the people of Liberia; and

WHEREAS, in his overall development, the President of Liberia, Dr William Richard Tolbert, Jr., has evenly and meaningfully directed the resources of this Nation to the simultaneous development of all its political subdivisions, which policies continue to receive the fullest approbation and whole-hearted support of the people of this Nation in a manner unprecedented in the history of our beloved Republic; and

WHEREAS, the development growth and progress of this Nation and its people cannot be achieved without national solidarity, stability, respect for the constituted authority and honesty, the core of the Tolbert Administration and which have resulted in the unparalleled development of this Country; and

WHEREAS, the legal representatives of the people of this Nation are determined never to allow a few unpatriotic, treacherous, selfish, self-centered and vicious citizens and aliens to disunite, disrupt and overthrow the lawfully constituted Government of Liberia; and

WHEREAS, the sovereign people of this Nation are overwhelmingly satisfied with and have confidence in the programs and development and the ability and integrity of Dr. William Richard Tolbert, Jr., to implement his program of building a great Nation for the people of Liberia:

NOW, THEREFORE,

It is enacted by the Senate and the House of Representatives of the Republic of Liberia, in Legislature Assembled:

1   That the Senate and House of Representatives Assembled in Joint

Convention in this Fourth Session of the 48th Legislature of the Republic of Liberia, do hereby and in this public Manner vehemently deprecate, denounce and condemn the wicked, satanic, seditious and treasonable acts of lawlessness, disrespect for constituted authority, civil disturbance, rioting, vicious destruction of lives and properties as perpetrated by a small group of vile and wicked persons against the peace, dignity and tranquility of this Nation.

2 The Legislature in its own name and in the sovereign people of Liberia unanimously reaffirms its highest respect and esteem for President William Richard Tolbert, Jr., and endorses to its fullest his leadership and pledges its abiding loyalty to him; its continued confidence in his policies – War against Ignorance, Disease and Poverty, and Mats to Mattresses, Total Involvement, Self-Reliance, and a Wholesome Functioning Society – and his Government; pledging its Wholehearted support, unswerving and unflinching loyalty and solidarity to his Administration; pledging further to unrelentlessly and assiduously work and operate with him in his untiring efforts and desire to raise this Nation to Nobler and Higher Heights, and to restore its image of paradise of Peace and Tranquility.

3 That the Legislature implores Dr William Richard Tolbert, Jr., President of Liberia, by the direction of Almighty God, to employ the powers of his office, the law-enforcing Agencies of this Nation and all other measures at his command to vigorously and strenuously pursue and apprehend and bring to justice those villainous traitors thereby ridding our Nation of a repetition of these acts.

4 That this Joint Resolution be read and presented to the President by the Legislature.

5 This Joint Resolution shall take effect immediately and be published in hand-bills.

In a determined bid 'to vigorously and strenuously pursue and apprehend and bring to justice those villainous traitors' both at home and abroad, 'thereby ridding our Nation of a repetition of these acts', the Government elected to institute legal action against members of the Liberian Student Association in the Americas and other Liberians resident in the United States alleged to be supporters of PAL.

On May 7, 1979, the Chairman of the House Foreign Relations Committee and Chairman of the Propaganda and Publicity Committee of the True Whig Party, A. Benedict Tolbert, requested US Congresswoman Yvonne B. Burke, through her Inglewood, California law office, to 'institute legal action' against the Liberian Student Association 'for defaming the impeccable track-record of Liberia, and seditiously trying to destroy the trust and confidence which many nations of the world have in us'. The letter reads as follows:

Dear Mrs Burke:
I guess by now you may have already heard of the horrible and fatal occurrence of April 14th in Monrovia, in which several persons lost their lives and major businesses as well as Government property up to the tune of $100,000,000.00 (ONE HUNDRED MILLION DOLLARS) were destroyed and looted.

This act precipitated from a handful of reckless, irresponsible and diabolical persons in our midst, calling themselves the Progressive Alliance of Liberia (PAL). We are of the opinion that this demonstration, backed by their foreign friends, was an attempt to overthrow the Liberian Government, destroy our democratic and Free Enterprise Systems, and replace same with an oppressive form of Government.

There is an organization in the United States referred to as the Liberian Students Association, based in New York City, that have organized themselves in support of this illegal act, by attempting to mare (*sic*) the long held reputation and integrity of Liberia. It is in this light that I call upon you, through your Law Offices to institute legal action against this Association for defaming the impeccable track-record of Liberia, and seditiously trying to destroy the trust and confidence which many nations of the world have in us.

This Association have charged to the Government of Liberia of massacring more than 200 unarmed civilians. They charged the National True Whig Party of Liberia as being 'characterized by systematic and consistent blood-bath, oppression and police brutality'. They accused the President, Dr William R. Tolbert, Jr., of authorizing 'his blood-thirsty police and secret agents to shoot at 30,000 demonstrators who were marching peaceably only to dramatize their disapproval of rice price being increased by the Government'.

We categorically deny all these fictitious and malicious fabrications levied against the Government of Liberia by these diehard and satanical innuendos, whose prime concern is to breathe in disunity, disharmony and discord amongst our people.

From explanations given *supra*, you will realize that the increase in the price of rice was used only as an alibi in fostering their proposed illegal plan. As a matter of fact, there was never an increase in the price of rice. They misconstru(ed) the issue and failed to come to grasp the truth that it was a PROPOSED increase in the price of rice. There were two groups to petition Government to demonstrate for and against the proposed increase in the rice price. Knowing the mentality of her people, Government put a ban on both demonstrations. Despite the ban, the Progressive Alliance of Liberia, still persistent in going ahead with their plan, incited the people to demonstrate under the pretext that it was the problem of the increase in the price of rice.

Predicated upon the above, we request you to use all legal means to bring to justice all persons connected with this Association. They can be reached at the following address:

Mr Kolue Panye
President, The Liberian Students Association
Office of the President
525 West 158th Suite 1C
New York, N.Y. 10032
Telephone – 212/795-2723

I have today addressed a letter to President Tolbert, requesting him to kindly give his approval for the Liberian Government to employ the services of your Law Firm, to bring to justice any and all such persons whose intention would be to mare (*sic*) the good name and reputation of Liberia.

> Best regards,
> Sincerely yours,
> A. Benedict Tolbert

The credibility of the administration was further marred when the Government, in its official account of the events of 'April 14', revealed that 'forty young Liberians are dead, more than five hundred have been injured and seventy-eight remained hospitalized as of this writing. More than $35 million worth of property has been destroyed...'[5] Every sane Liberian was aware that the death toll resulting from the 'April 14' incident exceeded forty while the number of 'reported injuries' was in excess of seven hundred.

On April 25, 1979, Gabriel Baccus Matthews, Chairman of PAL, who was accused of 'planning and master-minding' the 'April 14' demonstration in Monrovia, wrote from his maximum security prison cell a rather interesting letter of repentance to President Tolbert. In the letter which the authorities 'permitted' Matthews to write the President, he appealed for 'fatherly consideration to permit us to utilize our energies in helping to carry out a meaningful program of national reconstruction, to heal the wounds, under your direct supervision'.[6] The letter continues:

I plead that you constitute all of us into a Special Committee for National Reconstruction. Its duties may include, as you see fit, the awakening of public spirit for the OAU Conference; promoting a nation-wide 'All Liberians Are One' campaign; reassuring business houses that the events of April 14 are behind us and will not be repeated; and, with assistance of our associates abroad, a well-ordered public relations campaign to raise high again our country's image abroad.[7]

Tolbert replied to Matthews on the same date assuring him that his appeal would be given 'timely consideration'. On May 5, 1979, one week later, Tolbert delivered an unusually lengthy policy speech to the nation. In the speech, Tolbert addressed such vexing national issues as the Government's response to 'April 14'; the Government's foreign scholarship program; the closure of the University of Liberia; embezzlement of public funds; development in Bentol City; and the presence of Guinean troops in Liberia.

Towards national reconstruction

In announcing the constitution of a Special Commission of the kind referred to by Matthews in his letter of April 25, Tolbert declared:

We remain continuingly open to new approaches. I have no monopoly over ideas; let us all join to build the new Liberia. This is why as we undertake to assess fully the implications of the events of April 14, we have decided to constitute a Commission charged with the responsibility of *receiving* and *analyzing* suggestions from concerned citizens for the reconstruction of Liberia, and submitting recommendations for the attention of Government, and I assure you they will be given speedy attention by Government.[8] (See Appendix 4 for full text of Address.)

The Commission of thirty-one members chaired by Counsellor Nete Sie Brownell, former Attorney General of Liberia, was known as the Commission on National Reconstruction. The Commission viewed the civil disturbance of April 14, 1979, as a 'manifestation of serious social, economic and political problems with deep roots in our national society'.[9] In its report submitted June 12, 1979, the Commission made several recommendations. In addition to recommending the reopening of the University of Liberia, the Commission recommended that students be awarded scholarships on the basis of merit, regardless of social status or family connections.

Some recommendations advanced by the Commission included the following:

1 On the crucial rice issue the Commission recommends the dissolution of the Rice Committee and that all interested parties be given the opportunity to import rice. This would lower the price of rice to less than the artificial official price a bag. Government's role should be to maintain standards, safety, supply, security and control of pricing in such a way that it would be compatible with the minimum wage. Government should also ensure by all forms of encouragement the domestic production of rice.

2 Over eighty percent of the letters received and the people we talked to expressed concern not only for those imprisoned in connection with the April 14 incident but also about those directly responsible for the death by shooting of unarmed citizens. The Commission therefore recommends that general amnesty be granted those arrested. Such a step would help tremendously to bind the nation's wounds, promote the national image, defuse tension, and render more conducive the atmosphere for national reconstruction.

3 The people have suggested that the members of the Cabinet and other officials who through their official conduct directly or indirectly contributed to the events of April 14, especially to Director of Police and the Ministers of Justice, Agriculture, Defense and Finance, stand indicted in the public eye. To restore full CREDIBILITY to the Executive Government, the Commission recommends that their official conduct in relation to the causes leading to April 14 be investigated.

4 With reference to serious conflict of interest involving Public Officials to the detriment of the struggling masses, the Commission recommends that the President appoint a Committee of well-considered persons to prepare a *Code of Conduct*. Elements to be included in such a Code should be:

   a That all principal Government Officials shall be required to declare their total property and cash assets before taking office and shall be fully audited before they are removed from office.

   b With reference to the appointment of Commissioned officials of the executive and judiciary branches, Government will take the necessary measures to ensure a meaningful effectuation of the principle of advise and consent of the Senate.[10]

The Commission's Report is very revealing as it attempts seriously to address relevant social and political issues of the time. Appendix 5 is a full text of the Commission's Report.

On June 26, two weeks following the submission of the Commission on National Reconstruction, Tolbert granted a general amnesty to all persons detained in connection with the April 14 events. Tension lessened and the Liberian Government hosted the 16th Ordinary Session of the Organization of African Unity in July 1979.

In what appeared to be an honest attempt to implement some of the recommendations and address other key issues raised by the Commission on National Reconstruction, President Tolbert appointed in August 1979 a seven-member Committee chaired by J. Rudolph Grimes, former Secretary of State in both the Tubman and Tolbert administrations, to devise a code of conduct for public officials.

The Code of Conduct Committee identified the 'three principal kinds of misconduct of Government employees/officials which should, as far as possible, be avoided or prevented', as follows:

1 Government employees/officials should not be permitted to use Government to their special advantage or to the special advantage of any entity on the outside in which they have a personal economic interest.

2 Government employees/officials should not be permitted to assist individuals or entities on the outside where the latter are seeking to move or influence Government action to their special advantage against the public interest.

3 Government employees/officials should not be allowed to use their position/office as a source of power or of confidential information for purposes of advancing their personal economic interest.[11]

The Committee recommended the enactment, by the Legislature, of a statute to deal with the problems of conflict of interest. The Committee strongly emphasized the need to enforce fairly all laws created to minimize dishonesty, official misconduct and conflict of interest in Government. A detailed fourteen-point proposal was submitted by the Committee to Tolbert for consideration for implementation. (See Appendix 6 for a full text of the Report of the Committee to Devise a Code of Conduct for Public Officials.)

Conflict of interest is a serious problem in this society. It is common practice for senior public officials, including members of the Legislature, to serve as lawyers for concessions and business houses doing business with the Government. Government projects are often 'contracted out' to private firms owned by or represented by senior public officials. Consequently, many projects undertaken by Government are seldom completed, if indeed they are ever started.

On the issue of the price of imported and locally produced rice, a conflict of interest which involved the President himself as the largest single local producer and seller of rice, President Tolbert issued a five-point Executive Ordinance on February 27, 1980, to regulate the importation of rice into the country. The Ordinance ordered:

1   The immediate dissolution of the Rice Committee established June 1979. A Rice Monitoring Committee, chaired by the Minister of Commerce, Industry and Transportation and composed of the following membership – Minister of Agriculture; Planning and Economic Affairs; a representative each from the Chamber of Commerce and Agricultural Concessions – was established.

The Ordinance further specified the quality of rice and the procedures by which the Committee was to regulate the pricing of imported rice as follows:

2   That the present fixed price of $20.00 (Twenty Dollars) per 100 lb. bag shall be applied to that quality of rice which is known as the US Parboiled Rice No. 5 with maximum 50% brokens or its equivalent and the importation of this rice shall be restricted to the Liberian Produce Marketing Corporation (LPMC) and to Liberian importers on the following basis:
a) The monitoring Committee shall invite, from the LPMC and Liberian importers through public announcements, tenders for up to three-month supply for this quality of rice and the bidder with the lowest offers shall be permitted to import the rice.
b) Liberian importers shall be considered to be those Liberians whose businesses are duly registered with the Ministry of Commerce, Industry and Transportation and can demonstrate their contact (s) with rice exporters abroad by submitting offers when a tender is called by the Monitoring Committee.
c) Should the lowest offer be made by a Liberian who is not in the position to open the required Letter of Credit, the LPMC shall open the Letter of Credit; in consideration of which fifty percent of the rice upon arrival, will be for the account of the LPMC. Payment for the consignment shall be shared equally by the importer and the LPMC.
d) Should the LPMC itself make the lowest offer, then the LPMC would be required to make available for the account of the other Liberian importers involved in the tendering a minimum of 50 (fifty) percent of the rice, upon arrival. Payment for the consignment shall be shared equally by the LPMC and the other Liberian importers involved in the tender.
e) Should a Liberian importer make the lowest offer and is in the position to open the Letter of Credit, a minimum of 50 (fifty) percent

of the rice shall be made available for the account of the other Liberians who participated in the tender.

f) The importer will, in all cases, exercise his discretion in terms of the distribution among Liberian importers who participated in the tender under the control of the Monitoring Committee.

3 That all other foreign rice will be imported and/or sold in the local market freely by all, including foreigners; due regard being given to minimum standards of nutritional value.

4 That the price of locally produced rice will be kept at TWENTY ($20.00) DOLLARS per 100 lbs. bag and Government will devise a programme whereby assistance may be provided to local farmers so that they do not produce at a loss.

5 The Monitoring Committee will monitor the importation and distribution of rice within the country to assure that the marketing of rice in Liberia is fully Liberianized and widely dispersed to permit the free flow of all rice to all segments of the population, and ensure against bottlenecks in the availability of rice to all Liberians at all times.[12]

The last bout

Between April 14, 1979 and March 1980, public trust in the Government was the gravest of Tolbert's problems. The newly registered Progressive People's Party seized the opportunity to demand the immediate resignation of Tolbert and his Vice President, Bennie D. Warner. The PPP's 'Declaration of Intent of the Liberian People' reads:

DECLARATION OF INTENT OF THE LIBERIAN PEOPLE
'The end of the institution, maintenance, and the administration of Government, is to secure the existence of the body politic, to protect it, and to furnish the individuals who compose it, with the power of enjoying in safety and tranquility, their natural rights, and the blessings of life, and whenever these great objects are not obtained, the people have a right to alter the government, and to take measures necessary for their safety, prosperity and happiness.' (*Article I, Declaration of Rights, Constitution of the Republic of Liberia*)

At the advent of Dr William R. Tolbert, Jr. to the Presidency of Liberia, he enunciated to the Liberian People a number of wide-ranging promises, none of which he had any desire or will to fulfil, as circumstances have confirmed, following almost ten years of his incumbency. Those promises included, *inter alia*, 'From Mat to Mattress; Self-Reliance; Self-Sufficiency in Food Production; Reduction of International Credit on the part of Liberia; the War on

Ignorance, Disease and Poverty; Simultaneous Rural Development and Urban Reconstruction; Liberianization; and the Eradication of Corruption.'

Apart from his failure to deliver on his promises, which constitutes gross acts of omission, his Administration embarked on a dangerous and unprecedented course of action, characteristically lacking in judgment, thus making him the only President in the history of Liberia whose stay in office has led to political instability, labor unrest, and civil disturbances resulting in the loss of the precious lives of very many of our fellow citizens. These results, in themselves, are manifestations of the breach of his OATH of office and an indication of his contravention of the organic laws of the Republic of Liberia.

We, the Sovereign People of the Republic of Liberia, have observed that, apart from Dr Tolbert's acts of omission and commission, there now exists a drastic decline in previously existing government services, for example:

EDUCATION

In recent years, there has occasioned a decline in the provision of educational facilities in Liberia. Basic classroom needs, such as textbooks as are available, are generally obtained from street peddlers. The Ministry of Education has publicly indicated that textbooks are not readily available and those that are, are too expensive for the Liberian public.

In the wake of the Liberianization Program, which calls for technical skills that can only be obtained abroad, the Tolbert Administration has inconsiderably suspended the Foreign Scholarship Program.

HEALTH

As funds are now being expended on prestige-conscious projects such as an artificial lake, a statue, financing unprofitable public corporations, etc., the Tolbert Administration contends that there is an insufficiency of funds to operate an effective health delivery system. As Dr Tolbert and members of his family secure their medical attention abroad, he lacks even a personal reason for improving the quality of health services at home.

AGRICULTURE

Dr Tolbert's agricultural promises, based on the Utopian objective of 'No imported rice after 1980', ended, unfulfilled, in April, 1979.

UNEMPLOYMENT

The best that can be said about the Tolbert Administration's efforts to combat unemployment is that no employment policy exists. Worse, labor laws are designed to protect the interest of management, and the efforts of workers to secure their rightful interests have constantly been met with threats emanating from the Tolbert Administration.

115

SOCIAL INJUSTICE

Public confidence in government, secured by law, has been substantially eroded by the Administration's deliberate violations of the basic tenets of our social structure to the point that social injustice is highly prevalent; illegal search and seizure, false arrests, illegal detention, denial of the right to bail, lack of speedy trial and general due process of law, are the order of the day.

RAMPANT CORRUPTION

One of the major ironies of the Tolbert Administration is that, as its fight against corruption has existed only in words, corruption is today more rampant than ever. The Administration's treatment of corrupt officials has bordered on condonation. Usually, corrupt officials are only temporarily dismissed to be re-employed to positions of greater responsibility.

Furthermore, gross conflicts of interests have been the hallmark of the Tolbert Administration. Dr Tolbert and members of his family are exerting both political and wide-ranging economic control over the country, in violation of both law and public policy. This has contributed largely to the Administration's inability to curtail high prices and to employ other regulatory measures to control business activities in the country. One of the cogent factors which have strongly contributed to the erosion of public confidence in Government is the Tolbert Administration's repeated collection of irregular and extra-legal taxes, particularly in the rural areas.

CONCLUSION

In view of the foregoing, it is therefore resolved that the only means by which public confidence in government can be restored and the stability of the state preserved is for the Tolbert Administration to immediately resign. And we, the sovereign people of the Republic of Liberia, do hereby call on Dr William R. Tolbert, Jr. and Vice President Bennie D. Warner to immediately resign and turn over the Executive functions of Government to a coalition of the political parties.

As a manifestation of the people's will, a nationwide general strike is hereby called, and it will last for as long, and only as long, as it shall take the Tolbert Administration to resign and the provisional administration to assume its responsibilities.

LET IT BE KNOWN, AND LET IT BE DONE!!!

Done in the City of Monrovia, Montserrado County, Republic of Liberia this 7th day of March, A.D. 1980, in a MASS MEETING Under the auspices of the

PROGRESSIVE PEOPLE'S PARTY (PPP)

for the Sovereign People of the Republic of Liberia.

Signed:
Gabriel Baccus Matthews, Chairman, PPP
Oscar J. Quiah, Secretary General, PPP
Richard Gaye, Treasurer, PPP

Sixty-seven thousand seemingly genuine signatures were attached to the original document. On Saturday, March 8, 1980, Monrovia was again in a state of chaos. The nationwide tension intensified as Government rounded up the leadership and members as well as alleged members and sympathizers of the Progressive People's Party. The crime supposedly committed by those arrested was treason and sedition. In addition to the many persons arrested and detained in prison in various regions of the county in connection with the March 7, 1980 Declaration of the Progressive People's Party, some five hundred young people, accused by the Government of forming the core of the PPP leadership, were detained at the Monrovia Central Prison and the Military Post Stockade (maximum security prison) at the Barclay Training Center in Monrovia.

On March 10, 1980, Tolbert informed the nation that attempts had been made by the Progressive People's Party to overthrow the Government of the Republic of Liberia. In a special message to the First Session of the 49th Legislature, Tolbert reported:

Despite our pronouncements, and in brazen defiance of our laws and total disregard for the imperatives of public peace and security, members of a recently organized political party, known as the Progressive People's Party (PPP), led by Mr Gabriel Baccus Matthews, conspired to overthrow the legally constituted Government of the Republic of Liberia.

In their attempt to implement their diabolical and treasonable design, this group of lawless and criminal-minded citizens, joined by hooligans, came out under the cover of darkness on Monday, March 3, 1980, and the morning of (Saturday) March 8, 1980, during the period of our absence from the Capital on an official tour of development activities in Nimba County, to destabilize the Government of Liberia, enthrone anarchy and deprive the Sovereign People of Liberia of their inalienable rights and cherished tradition of choosing their leaders through the electoral process, as dictated by the Constitution and Laws of the Republic.

But for the Grace of Almighty God, the unity and solidarity of our people, and the vigilance of our Security Forces, their sinister designs might have materialized.

It was only a few yards from the Executive Mansion and within the vicinity of the Ministry of Information, Cultural Affairs and Tourism, a strategic Government installation, that their movement was timely intercepted; and when questioned as to the reasons for their action, Mr G. Baccus Matthews, Leader of PPP and Spokesman of the group, declared that they had converged to meet with officials of Government to express what he referred to as their 'Grievances'.[13]

Commenting on the issue of the PPP 'Declaration of Intent', Tolbert said:

While the investigation was yet under way, this newly organized political party, the Progressive People's Party, held a public meeting during which time a document impersonating the sovereign people of Liberia, was circulated, calling for a nation-wide general strike which, they claim, must be sustained until Government was destabilized and replaced by a provisional administration.

Intelligence reports reveal that the Progressive People's Party had designed a plan to execute an armed insurrection with intent to overthrow the duly constituted Government of the Republic ...

Road blocks were mounted at some strategic points in and around the city, and attempts were made to burn down the Telecommunications Building, destroy the Gabriel J. Tucker Bridge, and seize the information services of the Liberian Government, all with the apparent intent to sever vital communications links between the Capital and other parts of Liberia, and also to isolate the nation from the rest of the world ...

All of these operations were to be co-ordinated in such a manner that Mr Matthews and his associates would have forcibly seized and occupied the Executive Mansion and criminally, illegally and illegitimately installed themselves in power.[14]

In conclusion, Tolbert assured the Liberian people that the accused would be speedily and fairly tried and that 'the full force of the law' would be carried out 'without mercy' against all violators. Finally, Tolbert assured the nation 'that the situation is well in hand and the nation is secured'. He reiterated his promise that 'those who violate the laws will bear the full consequences of their action (this permit me to repeat with emphasis: Verily, those who violate the laws will bear the full consequences of their action). This is the time for extreme rigidity and, in the supreme interest of the people, no flexibility whatsoever can, or will, be exercised by us.'[15]

As the first anniversary of 'April 14' neared, Monrovia was alive with reports that the trial of those arrested in connection with the PPP Declaration was scheduled for the eventful date of April 14. It was also revealed that plans were being speedily concluded by the Tolbert Government, for the execution of key leaders of the Progressive People's Party, including some sympathizers and alleged collaborators.

On April 12, 1980, barely a month after reassuring the nation 'that the situation is well in hand and the nation is secured', Tolbert's régime was brought to an end by a People's Revolution led by a military People's Redemption Council of the Armed Forces of Liberia.

CHAPTER NINE

The Deeds of
the True Whig Party

'... We will protest against these evils (of the True Whig Party), and if our protests are unheeded, we will submit them to the arbitrament of an awakened people.'
   Edwin J. Barclay, August 1954

'If these views are representative of those held by most of our people (the probability of which is highly likely due to their startling similarity), then, in spite of its past glories and achievements, and its present advantageous position as the incumbent and only legitimate political party in Liberia, the True Whig Party is in danger of imminent collapse and disintegration.'
   Report of the Special Task Force on Party Reform, October 1979

The motto of the True Whig Party, Liberia's sole political party until April 12, 1980, reads: 'Deeds not words'. It was in protest against the 'deeds' of the True Whig Party that its former Standard-Bearer, Edwin J. Barclay, accepted nomination by the Independent True Whig Party (ITWP) to oppose the True Whig Party in the 1955 Presidential Elections. Ironically, it was also the 'deeds' of the True Whig Party which led to its ultimate overthrow on April 12, 1980 by seventeen enlisted men, non-commissioned officers, of the Armed Forces of Liberia.

Formed in 1869 to oppose the Republican Party which had previously maintained a caste-like system by permitting only mulattoes or those colonists of lighter complexion to occupy elected or high public positions, the True Whig Party won the election of 1869 and saw the inauguration of the first full-blooded Negro, Edwin James Roye,[1] as President of the Republic of Liberia.

Forced out of office barely a year after his inauguration, Roye and the

Whigs lost power to the Republicans. In 1877 the True Whig Party regained power, supposedly 'to protect and promote the rights of every citizen'. After that, the True Whig Party did indeed employ every means to protect and promote its existence as the sole political party in Liberia.

A nation of Whigs

Except for a very few truly brave and self-assured Liberians, every Liberian, especially those in the employ of Government, was assumed to belong to the True Whig Party and behaved as such. 'Every officer in government, whether a judge or administrator, must belong to the True Whig Party before he can secure an appointment.'[2] At ordinary court trials 'only Whigs are appointed as jurors'.[3]

Every Representative or Senator 'elected' to the National Legislature was a Whig, as no other political party was allowed to exist, let alone field a candidate. Every gainfully employed citizen 'contributed' a portion of his earnings to the True Whig Party, and Party rules required each executive official of the Party to pay a percentage of his annual salary into the treasury of the Party to be used as 'campaign funds.'

Only members or assumed members of the True Whig Party were appointed judges in the various courts within the Judiciary. With the executive, judicial and legislative branches of Government controlled by partisans of the True Whig Party, any opposition, imagined or real, was systematically crushed in a style characteristic of the Whigs.

Control of the electoral system

Control of the electoral mechanism kept the True Whig Party in power. The Constitution (Article I Section II) provided that 'all elections shall be by ballot, and every citizen of twenty-one years of age possessing real estate shall have the right of suffrage'.[4]

Since all officials of Government, including those responsible for the conduct of public elections, were members of the True Whig Party, it was understandable that the Whig partisans would try to rig elections in their own favor. To meet the property requirement to vote 'it was the practice of the Government, before 1905, to urge chiefs holding a collective title to land register and vote as a unit the members of their tribe'. That practice was latter prohibited by Act of Legislature because it 'led to so many abuses'.

It used to be the responsibility of judges of local courts to open election polls at the request of voters in their respective localities. This practice was also abused, and in 1910 that law too was repealed by the Legislature.

The President took control of the electoral system when the Legislature in 1923 empowered President King 'to open additional voting polls by proclamation'. The People's Party, supported by former True Whig Party Standard-Bearer President Daniel E. Howard (1912–1920), protested against this act of the Legislature as it would completely destroy the 'voice and power of an intelligent electorate'.

To ensure his re-election against the People's Party in 1923, President King 'opened three new precincts in remote spots – Kakata, Mount Coffee and Cheesemanburg – which rolled up tremendous majorities for the incumbent administration'.[5]

Another method employed by the True Whig Party to ensure victory at the polls was described by Buell[6] as follows:

To register as a voter, a Liberian need not register personally. If in the good graces of the Whig Party, a man may bring to the registrar a list containing, say, one hundred and fifty names, together with deeds purporting to show that the men listed own property and hence are entitled to vote. The clerk thereupon registers the list. On election day the man who registered the list of one hundred and fifty men brings around, say fifty boys to answer to the names on the list; after casting his ballot, a boy is said to go to the end of the line, sometimes changing his clothes, to vote again when another name is called.

Stuffing ballot boxes was another fraudulent means employed by the True Whig Party to maintain power. In 1923, the number of property owners eligible to vote in Liberia was about six thousand. 'But in this election a total of fifty-one thousand votes were cast, of which President King, the incumbent, received forty-five thousand.'[7]

Again in the Presidential Election of 1927, the People's Party lost to the Whigs (Mr King was re-elected for a third term) by an 'unprecedented majority' of one hundred and twenty-five thousand votes. Regarding President King's 1927 victory over the People's Party, a Liberian correspondent wrote:

Irrespective of their expressions, these natives were forced, under the direction of Secretary of Interior, John Lewis Morris, to appear at the polls on election day and there with soldiers at their backs place ballots in the boxes, ballots which they were unable to read, and practically all of which were marked with King's name. In some places the chiefs refused to force their men to vote but most yielded when they were threatened with imprisonment.

There had been no legal registration in the interior. Pseudo names were entered in registration books and the practice was to vote as many men could be secured over and over again until the lists were exhausted. This was practised throughout the Republic. In some cases legal voting was thwarted and legal voters driven from the polls.[8]

Former Presidents before King had employed similar fraudulent means to win elections. In 1903, the *Liberian Recorder* reported that the election of President Arthur Barclay (1904–1912) 'was due to wrong and unrighteous measures which throws quite a shadow over the success achieved'.[9] It was further reported that 'the evils are growing to alarming proportions'.[10]

Interestingly, fifty-one years later in 1954, Edwin J. Barclay – himself a former President of Liberia (1930–1944) and Standard-Bearer of the True Whig Party, nephew of Arthur Barclay, a former Liberian President (1904–1912) and True Whig partisan – in accepting his nomination by the Independent True Whig Party to oppose his former Party, said: 'We shall protest against these evils (of the True Whig Party), and if our protests are unheeded, we will submit them to the arbitrament of an awakened people.'[11]

The reputation of the True Whig Party did not alter much during the twenty-seven year reign of President Tubman. Under the system, Tubman only had to identify a potential opponent and then, working through the Legislature and Judiciary, adroitly silence him.

When Twe's United People's Party opposed Tubman and the True Whig Party in the 1951 Presidential Elections, Tubman simply dismissed Twe as one whose hands were 'stained with the blood of treason, rebellion and sedition'. Tubman alleged that Twe 'had been unfaithful and recreant to his trust as a Liberian citizen'.[12] On the eve of the elections Twe was obliged to flee to neighboring Sierra Leone where he remained for ten years until he was granted immunity from prosecution by President Tubman.

The opposition to the True Whig Party by the coalition Independent True Whig and Reformation Parties following the 1955 elections was shortlived, as the two parties were banned by an Act of the True Whig Party-controlled Legislature, passed on June 28, 1955 at the request of President Tubman.

The 'awakened people' of whom Edwin Barclay spoke in 1954 were not to be heard for another quarter of a century.

TWP – the final tests

By 1978 it was evident that the True Whig Party had to contend with a generation of Liberians convinced that the True Whig Party was 'out of step' with the new Liberia. Under the protective cloak of the continent-wide Movement for Justice in Africa (MOJA), officers of the local chapter – MOJA/Liberia – challenged the True Whig Party by launching a Village Development Project in south-eastern Liberia with assistance principally from foreign donors. The selection of Penoken in Putu Chiefdom, Grand Gedeh County as the site of the Village Development Project by the leadership of MOJA/Liberia was calculated to provide the MOJA organization with mass support in its opposition to the True Whig Party. In justifying their selection of Putu Chiefdom, one of the poorest areas in south-eastern Liberia, for the Village Development Co-operative scheme, a MOJA-published brochure described the area as follows:

... In Putu Chiefdom itself, about 4273 persons live in 17 different villages. Putu is blessed with huge natural resources. There is the great Putu mountain filled with iron ore which is soon to be dug out by a foreign mining company. There is the rich forest filled with lumber which is rapidly being cut down by Liberian and foreign logging companies. And there are the people – strong, hard-working and intelligent.

Yet, the people of Putu are poor. 95 percent of them are engaged in upland rice farming, using the slash and burn method. Tools in use are still the simple hoe, axe, cutlass and knife. As may be expected, the work is hard, and the returns are low. Most of what is produced is eaten, with a little sold to obtain cash payment of taxes.

Only about 10 percent of the people of Putu can read and write. Some 300 students are jammed-packed into four make-shift buildings. The school stops at the elementary level. Last year (1977) at least 650 students were not admitted into the school because there was no space available.[13]

In an attempt to counter MOJA's activities in Putu, the True Whig Party embarked upon the construction of a school building as a 'Party project' intended to win the hearts of the people. The school building was never completed and was subsequently abandoned by the True Whig Party.

The students, the most uneasy of the new generation of Liberians, were equally vocal in testing the spirit of the True Whig Party.

A third pressure group which further compounded the problems of the True Whig Party was the Progressive Alliance of Liberia. Early in 1978, PAL launched a massive mobilization campaign and a nationwide membership drive. Following the events of April 14, 1979, PAL decided to register a political party – the Progressive People's Party – in opposition to the True Whig Party.

The True Whig Party-controlled courts were either undecided about, or unwilling to allow, the registration of an opposition party. By early September 1979 the stage was set for what might have been a potentially

Penoken Public School. This make-shift structure is the only educational facility available to hundreds of school-age pupils.

Penoken school building 'project' undertaken by the True Whig Party and later suddenly abandoned.

violent confrontation between the Government and the leadership of the Progressive Alliance of Liberia. Believing that such confrontation would serve no useful purpose, the leadership of PAL circulated the following on September 27, 1979:

> The Progressive Alliance of Liberia wishes to inform the Liberian people that the Government presided over by the Chairman of the True Whig Party has panicked over the decision of the Liberian people to go to court tomorrow and register the Progressive People's Party.
>
> Exactly who is running the show here? First, someone decided that the Probate Court be ordered closed, and an announcement was made on the radio this morning. Later, someone else decided that the court will, in fact, be opened.
>
> It is our information that soldiers and security forces have been given 'shoot to kill orders' effective tomorrow. For unknown reasons, some soldiers were last night stationed all along the beach from the Barracks to the Executive Mansion. We have also been informed, and many persons have noticed, contingents of combat troops arriving in Monrovia from Todee, Schiefflin, etc.
>
> Security forces are all over the neighbourhood of PAL's headquarters. Last night, some began firing shots thereby alarming residents in the area ...
>
> Citizens all over Monrovia have indicated that they have a right to visit courts of law, and they are going to exercise that right tomorrow. Groups of them have made it quite clear that, if they are shot upon, they will not engage in any looting, but, from Sinkor to New Kru Town, from West Point to Paynesward, they will burn the city down. Liberian people are serious these days; we prefer not to underestimate them.
>
> In view of all of these factors, we wish to reflect the sense of responsibility and maturity which does not seem to be coming from the True Whig Party and its Government at this time.
>
> Let it be known that, in the interest of the peace and harmony of our country, and in order to avoid the loss of human lives, we have decided to quietly go to the Probate Court one day next week. The public will be notified thereafter.
>
> Calm down. Sleep well. Have a nice weekend.[14]

Testing the electoral process

In what could be termed the most serious test yet of the 'will' of the True Whig Party, Dr Amos Sawyer, professor of political science at the University of Liberia and Chairman of MOJA's Committee on Membership and Vigilance as well as Director of MOJA's Special Projects, decided early in 1979 to test the True Whig Party-controlled electoral process by announcing his candidacy, as an Independent, for the Monrovia mayoral election slated for November 1979. As expected, the True Whig Party made every effort to discourage and sometimes embarrass him.

While the True Whig Party gave every support to its mayoral nominee, incumbent Edward David, the Independent candidate Sawyer was refused the use of the Monrovia City Hall, a public facility, for an organized rally in support of his candidacy. Stating his purpose in joining the Monrovia mayoral contest, Dr Sawyer remarked:

... I also enter the race for another important reason. My candidacy for Mayor is meant to call attention to a political situation which stands in need of remedy. It is my intention to test the electoral process, to appeal to our political system to return to meaningful and lawful electoral politics so as to ensure that there is an opportunity for popular participation in the political life of this country. You see, April 14 taught all of us a lesson. We now find a greater capacity for violence in all quarters of our society. This is a dangerous development and one which cannot be stopped unless we undertake genuine reconstruction of our national institutions and practices. I see my entry into the race for Mayor as a modest contribution toward political reconstruction generally and the reconstruction of electoral politics particularly.[15]

Explaining how his candidacy for Mayor would make a contribution to the reconstruction of electoral politics in Liberia, Sawyer said:

.... you do realize that I am running to be mayor as an Independent. This means that I am not only challenging Edward David the current mayor, I am opposing Edward David, the candidate of the True Whig Party or whoever the True Whig Party may choose to put forward as mayor. In the last thirty years, we have not seen elections in which individuals or groups have posed serious challenges to the TWP and have reached the polls; as a result, there has been no need to count votes properly, carefully watch the polls, etc. These are very important activities in a functioning democracy. If we are to ensure peaceful change in Liberia, our people have to get exposed to the effective use of the electoral process. My candidacy as an Independent will try to ensure that greater respect is shown for our electoral laws, that we promote voters' registration, proper supervision of voting, and proper counting of the votes. All of these things are specified in the election laws of this country. These laws should be respected. I am trying to make a small contribution toward this end.[16]

After attempting unsuccessfully to obstruct Sawyer's campaign, the leadership of the True Whig Party changed candidates in the heat of the election, replacing Edward David with a Monrovia banker, Francis Horton. Mayor David was appointed Deputy Minister at the Ministry of Local Government, Rural Development and Urban Reconstruction. Sawyer's candidacy in the meantime had been endorsed by diverse groups of Monrovia residents.

In October, 1979, President Tolbert cancelled the mayoral election set for November 13, 1979 and postponed it until June, 1980.

Introspection – TWP style

Feeling that the Party was under pressure and needed to examine itself, the President and Standard-Bearer of the True Whig Party, on October 13, 1979, convened a special meeting at Bentol to which senior and middle-level public officials as well as civil servants were invited. The invitation was carefully written to convey the impression that each invitee would meet the President personally. Of course the purpose of the meeting was never mentioned in the invitation. The plan was to gather together as many persons as possible for what seemed an attempt to revive a virtually disintegrated True Whig Party.

Upon arrival at the meeting hall President Tolbert ordered that the seating arrangements be made informal 'so that we can all be on the same level'. He directed those officials who accompanied him to spread out and sit at a table with a group of invitees.

The President took a seat at one of the tables already occupied by a few young public officials, including Mr Momolu V.K. Sackor Sirleaf, Deputy Managing Director of Air Liberia and Dr George S. Boley, Assistant Minister of Education. Hon. Frank E. Tolbert, elder brother of the President, Senior Senator of Montserrado County and President *pro tempore* of the Senate, elected to sit at an adjoining table with another group of young people including Mr E.K. Sherman, Assistant Minister at the Ministry of Local Government.

It would appear that the invitees at the meeting were carefully chosen because the audience was relatively youthful. When those officials who accompanied President Tolbert were comfortably seated, the President told his audience that the purpose of the meeting 'is for us to critically but constructively examine the True Whig Party. How does the Party see itself in the light of the new thrust?'

Tolbert admitted that 'much had been taken for granted by the Party'. 'In view of the further challenges thrust upon the Party now by time and circumstances', Tolbert continued, 'we need to know the members of the True Whig Party.' Though Tolbert never mentioned the PAL and

MOJA organizations by name, it was clear that 'challenges thrust upon the Party' came principally from these two camps.

The word 'Whig', Tolbert said, 'means "We Hope In God"'. Since its founding in 1869, the True Whig Party had come a long way. 'In the face of the nation's many daunting socio-political problems, it served as the rallying force for a common, spontaneous inner enthusiasm and psychological staying power for survival.'[17] Continuing his remarks, Tolbert said: 'Nations and institutions, like the people who constitute them must, in time, arrive at a stage of renewal where a confrontation with new realities occurs and objectives are re-appraised.'[18] President Tolbert referred to the True Whig Party as the 'People's United Democratic Party', with no left and no right, but 'one strong force moving together'.

The Standard-Bearer admitted that the True Whig Party 'is highly centralized' and 'decentralization within the party is long overdue. There must be justice in the party', Tolbert concluded.

Finally, President Tolbert requested members of the True Whig Party in the audience to stand up to be identified. Almost everyone in the hall stood up, some confidently, others hesitantly, except for three individuals; namely, Mr H. Carey Thomas (who later died of heart failure while in protective custody in April 1980 following the military coup in which President Tolbert was assassinated), Mr E.K. Sherman and Dr George S. Boley.

Mr H. Carey Thomas argued that, as Chairman of the National Elections Commission, he must remain neutral (though he was in attendance at the meeting which he must have known was a political partisan meeting.) Senator Frank E. Tolbert was enraged when Mr E.K. Sherman, seated at the same table with him, did not stand up to be identified as a member of the True Whig Party. The infuriated Senator loudly remonstrated with Mr Sherman and publicly requested his brother, President Tolbert, to order him out of the meeting hall and immediately relieve him of his assistant ministerial post at the Ministry of Local Government. Of course, President Tolbert did not grant his brother's request, at least not then and there.

Surprisingly, Dr Boley was never asked to explain his motives for remaining seated. Other officials of the TWP seated at the table with Dr Boley, in addition to President Tolbert, were Robert I.E. Bright, Secretary-General of the True Whig Party; A.B. Tolbert, Chairman of the TWP Publicity Committee; and T. Siafa Sherman, Deputy Minister of Foreign Affairs and Recording Secretary at the Bentol meeting.

Encouraged by the critical observations made in the opening remarks by the Standard-Bearer, several young partisans of the True Whig Party, speaking for several hours, criticized the policies of the party and called for immediate reform. Closing the meeting, President Tolbert expressed concern that the True Whig Party 'had taken the Liberian people for granted' for a long time. In response to the petition for immediate reform within the Party, a twenty-seven member Special Task Force on Party Reform, chaired by Emmanuel L. Shaw II, was constituted by President Tolbert.

The Committee was given a mandate to advance recommendations to reform the Party 'for timely consideration' by the Party at its First Quadrennial Congress on October 24–26, 1979, at Buchanan, Grand Bassa county. The original text of the Report of the Special Task Force on Party Reform is found in Appendix 7.

TWP – beyond redemption

In anticipation of reforming the True Whig Party, many Liberians were hopeful that some positive changes would be made to improve the national body politic. The Report of the Special Task Force on Party Reform, described by high True Whig Party officials as a 'national bombshell', was submitted to the leadership of the True Whig Party at its First Quadrennial Congress. In considering the Report, several committees were appointed by the Standard-Bearer to review pertinent recommendations made by the Task Force that would effect the desired reforms within the True Whig Party.

It was the consensus of the General Congress that the rules and regulations governing the operation of the Party were in dire need of revision as recommended by the Special Task Force on Party Reform. The committee charged with revising Party rules and regulations included Grand Bassa Senator Joseph Findley, Senator Albert T. White of Grand Gedeh County, Montserrado County Representative Ijoma Flemister and former Justice Minister and the aspiring Secretary General of the True Whig Party, C.L. Simpson, Jr, among others. Dr George S. Boley was appointed to the 'Rules and Regulations Committee' as representative of the Special Task Force on Party Reform. As the True Whig Party was often labelled the 'Montserrado (County) Club' or 'Monrovia Club', the Rules Committee took care to ensure that Party rules which permitted domination of Party leadership by a 'few elder statesmen' resident in Montserrado County or Monrovia were revised to provide opportunities for participation in party leadership by partisans who were not resident in either location.

On the recommendation of the 'Rules Committee', the Congress unanimously adopted a new rule stating that not more than two persons from each county (there are nine counties and six territories in Liberia; Bomi, Gibi and Marshall Territories form part of Montserrado County while Kru Coast, Sasstown and Rivercess Territories each form part of

Maryland, Sinoe and Grand Bassa Counties respectively) should be elected to positions of leadership at the national level within the Party. It was also argued by the delegates at the Party's First Quadrennial Congress that if the Party was to adopt reform at this Special Congress, the National Standard-Bearer or high ranking Party official must respect the electoral process and the rights of party members at succeeding elections to choose the candidates of their choice.

Disconcertingly, the leadership of the True Whig Party did not have the political will to accept the reforms and play the game by the rules approved by the Congress. Firstly, the President of Liberia and National Standard-Bearer of the TWP influenced the election of C.L. Simpson, Jr. as Secretary General of the Party, although some delegates at the Congress would have preferred to cast their votes for Robert I.E. Bright, the incumbent Secretary General. The National Standard-Bearer, through an intermediary, Jackson F. Doe, informed each delegation of his personal choice of candidate and the required votes were obtained to 'elect' Mr Simpson. Secondly, having elected E. Reginald Townsend and C.L. Simpson, both of Montserrado County, to the respective positions of National Chairman and Secretary General of the Party, Tolbert decided to retain P. Clarence Parker, also of Montserrado County, as the National Treasurer of the Party. (E. Reginald Townsend and P. Clarence Parker were subsequently executed, along with eleven other True Whig Party members and officials of the Tolbert Government, by firing squad on April 22, 1980 following the military coup of April 12, 1980.) To accommodate his desire, Tolbert, in consultation with Simpson, the Secretary-General-elect and Richard A. Henries, Legal Counsel for the True Whig Party, simply altered the rule which limited to two the number of persons to be 'elected' from each county to serve the party at the national level. Interestingly, not a single member of the True Whig Party present at the Congress found the courage to enquire of the President and Standard-Bearer the purpose of altering a rule specifically designed and adopted by the entire Congress to provide fairly equal opportunities for all partisans in the national leadership of the Party. When Dr George S. Boley, an observer and member of the Task Force and 'Rules Committee', raised the issue of the change of rule unilaterally by the President and Standard-Bearer, Dr Boley was later privately 'advised' by Speaker Richard Henries to avoid raising issues 'that could embarrass the President'. When the votes were counted, Parker received 715 votes, compared with 15 votes for his opponent, Major Clemens. (All the delegates at the Party's First Quadrennial Congress cast their votes by standing up to be counted as there was no secret balloting. Consequently, all the officers elected were those for whom the National Standard-Bearer cast his personal vote.)

Later, following the 'election' of Party officials, Mr Edward P.

Massaquoi, Director of the Special Security Service and Chief Security Officer to the President, informed Dr Boley that his query about the unilateral change of rule by the Standard-Bearer was a good point. However, Massaquoi quickly cautioned Dr Boley against the need for any 'confrontation with the President'. Though unexpected, the kind words of 'caution' offered Dr Boley by the President's Chief Security Officer were taken in good faith. (Upon his release from protective custody following the April 12, 1980 military coup in which President Tolbert was assassinated, Edward P. Massaquoi was, 'in the spirit of reconciliation' appointed co-ordinator of Joint Security Operations July 1982 by the Head of State and Chairman of the People's Redemption Council.)

Richard A. Henries, Speaker of the House of Representatives and a fourth member of the 'old guard' of the Party, was the only person of consequence who refused to be nominated for 're-election' as Legal Counsel for the True Whig Party, a post he had 'occupied with distinction for thirty-two years'. Senator Joseph Findley of Grand Bassa County was 'elected' to replace Speaker Henries.

The positions of First, Second and Third Assistant General Secretary were created to form a part of the Secretariat of the True Whig Party. Mrs Delsena Draper of Sinoe County, Trohoe Kparghai of Grand Gedeh County and Scott G. Toweh of Nimba County were 'elected' First, Second and Third Assistant General Secretary respectively.

The Congress had not yet adjourned when the partisans realized that the exercise to reform the True Whig Party was a futile one. At the adjournment of the Congress, almost all of the delegates departed from Buchanan disheartened, disgruntled and visibly demoralized.

TWP accepts an Opposition

After the banning by the TWP of the Reformation Party in 1951 and the Independent True Whig Party in 1955, there was no serious opposition to the True Whig Party. The registration of the Progressive People's Party as an opposition party on January 8, 1980, was therefore interpreted by political observers that the True Whig party was 'breaking with tradition'.

But the True Whig Party soon returned to 'tradition'. On March 8, 1980, two months after its registration as a political party, the Progressive People's Party published what it termed a 'Declaration of Intent of the Liberian People' demanding the resignation of President Tolbert. The True Whig Party responded by effecting mass arrests of alleged members and sympathizers of the Progressive People's Party.

Supporters of the True Whig Party further petitioned President Tolbert and the Liberian government to ban the Progressive People's

Party. Campaigning to ban the Progressive People's Party, the True Whig Party circulated the following interesting leaflet:

'TRUTH CRUSHED TO THE EARTH SHALL RISE AGAIN'
PPP DEFEATS HERSELF

March 1980

Fellow Liberians:

The wicked intention of the Progressive People's Party (PPP) to undermine the dynamic and progressive administration of President Tolbert, discredit the Grand Old True Whig Party, and also disturb the peace and tranquility of our beloved country (the Israel of Africa), has finally been made clear to all Liberians, foreign residents and the world as a whole. These people have shown us all that their intentions are wicked and destructive. 'By their fruits ye shall know them.'

Let it be reiterated that President Tolbert has exercised all principles of democracy in allowing the Progressive People's Party the right to exercise their political franchise.

To enumerate, the Government of Liberia granted PAL (PPP) the permission to order and sell rice at $9.00 a bag, since they proclaimed that they had the solution, and because they used this as a pretext on April 14, to defy Government's ban on demonstrations of any sort. It was further learned that PAL (PPP) was expecting rice from a donor organization and was trying to dupe the Government of Liberia. Until this day, the rice has not yet arrived.

The Liberian Government is presently subsidizing rice at the rate of $5.00 a bag which makes rice on the Liberian market the cheapest commodity in the whole of Africa.

In addition, a leading member of PAL was appointed to a very important position in Government; Director of Price Control, and do you all know what happened? He colluded with the merchants to increase prices and also he received every imaginable bribe.

With all such privileges, the leaders of the Progressive People's Party could do nothing else but exhibit their innermost intentions to destabilize the legitimate Government of Liberia and plunge our country into chaos.

Fellow Liberians, how many times must we get burned before getting wiser: are we going to give these nefarious elements another chance? We all know that Liberians are not stupid. 'We were only giving the fish sufficient rope.'

In view of the above, let us all now, more than ever, stand behind our leader, Dr William Richard Tolbert, in exterminating this atrocious monster, the Progressive People's Party by banning it!

Joint the TWP Band Wagon!
Join the National Standard Bearer
And the entire Leadership of the TWP
For many more peaceful years of *Stability* and *Progress*!

LONG LIVE LIBERIA! LONG LIVE PRESIDENT TOLBERT! LONG LIVE TWP!

This propaganda leaflet is most revealing of the disposition of the True Whig Party as a political organization.

Finally, the True Whig Party-controlled Legislature was 'convinced beyond doubt that the Progressive People's Party has departed diametrically from the prescribed purpose of a political party under the law in Liberia', and, on March 28, 1980, passed an Act banning it.

WHEREAS under the general provisions of the Election Law of the Republic of Liberia, an 'Organized Political Party' means any group of eligible voters of not less than three hundred persons organized, probated and registered in the Probate Court of any County as a political party associated under a special name and style '*for the purpose of canvassing and nominating any person or group of persons for election to any position to be filled at any general election*'; and

WHEREAS it has come to the attention of the Legislature that a group of persons under the leadership of Gabriel Baccus Matthews organized themselves into a political party under the name and style of the Progressive People's Party; but

WHEREAS the citizens of the Republic of Liberia from each and all of the political subdivisions of this County have come and petitioned the Senate and House of Representatives sitting in its First Session of the Forty-Ninth Legislature, complaining of the churlish, dangerous, treacherous, unpatriotic, unconstitutional, illegal, diabolical, conscienceless and satanic acts committed by the Progressive People's Party throughout the Republic of Liberia, causing and inciting fear and panic among the people of Liberia and other residents mainly to create instability; and

WHEREAS, the Legislature is convinced beyond doubt that the Progressive People's Party has departed diametrically from the prescribed purpose of a political party under the law in Liberia i.e. is not 'canvassing and nominating any person or group of persons for election to any elective position to be filled at any General Election' but engaging itself in a series of violent activities, illegal demonstrations, inciting public fear and unrest, both covert and overt, to subvert and overthrow the authority of the Government of the Republic of Liberia and the autonomy of the State:

NOW, THEREFORE,

It is enacted by the Senate and House of Representatives of the Republic of Liberia, in Legislature Assembled:

Section 1   That from and immediately after the passage of this Act, the said Progressive People's Party because of its dangerous, treacherous, unpatriotic, unconstitutional, illegal, diabolical, conscienceless and satanic acts is hereby dissolved, outlawed, banned and thereby prohibited and restrained from functioning or operating in any manner or form within the Republic of Liberia as a political party.

Section 2   Any person or persons who, directly or indirectly, after the passage of this Bill into law, participate in any act or acts designed to perpetuate or to continue or revive the operation, administration and/or functioning of the Progressive People's Party, in violation of this Act, shall be guilty of a felony and punished by imprisonment for not less than ten years or more than fifteen years and fined in the sum of not less than $10,000.00 or more than $25,000.00 ...

The passage of this Act leaves the Progressive People's Party with the dubious distinction of being the shortest-lived (eighty days) political party in the history of the First Liberian Republic. Such were the 'deeds' of the True Whig Party.

Heedless of the alarms sounded by various prominent well-intentioned citizens and re-echoed by the findings of the Special Task Force on Party Reform, the True Whig Party as a political organization had disintegrated to such an extent that it was totally beyond redemption. The 'alternatives' were clear and the 'options' well defined. The True Whig Party and its leadership somehow never 'found the wisdom and the courage' to face the stark realities of the times. Characterized by 'narrowmindedness' and 'short-sightedness', the True Whig Party invited its own eventual destruction and brought to an end many years of the kind of 'peace, stability and progress' best known to itself and its leadership.

Appendixes

Appendix 1 Foreign Loans Obtained by the Government of Liberia, 1943–1980

	Name of Loan	Agreement Amount	Agreement Date	Purpose of Loan	Interest Rate	Grace Period	Estimated Yearly Repayment	Maturity Year
1	U.S. Gol/Port of Monrovia	$18,922,682.39	Dec. 31, 1943	Construction of Monrovia Port	Left Open	23 years after first disbursement	$482,592.00	1999
2	Eximbank 489/GOL Various	$5,000,000.00	Feb. 21, 1951	Improvement and maintenance of Highway Project	$3\frac{1}{2}\%$ per annum	12 years	–	1976
3	Eximbank 479/	$1,350,000.00	July 7, 1951	Construction of water and sewer system for Monrovia	$3\frac{1}{2}\%$ per annum	1 year after first disbursement	–	1975
4	Eximbank 596/GOL Various	$15,000,000.00	Feb. 9, 1955	Construction of highway and acquisition of related facilities	$4\frac{3}{4}\%$ per annum	$2\frac{1}{2}$ years	$906,300.00	1980
5	Eximbank 1072/GOL Various	$7,265,000.00	June 12, 1957	Power project	$5\frac{3}{4}\%$ per annum	3 years	–	1974
6	Eximbank 1560/GOL Various	$4,750,000.00	Oct. 27, 1961	Improvement and expansion of electric power system in the Monrovia area	$5\frac{3}{4}\%$ per annum	2 years after first disbursement	$190,000.00	1976
7	U.S.A. Govt. Loan PL 480	$658,695.00	April 12, 1962	To expand trade in agricultural commodities	4% per annum	1 year after	$38,447.29	1977
8	Moche Alon/Bassa-Sinoe	$2,610,247.50	June 4, 1962	For the construction of road projects in Buchanan and Greenville-Sinoe County	$6\frac{1}{2}\%$ per annum	5 years	$124,841.00	1977

No.	Name	Amount	Date	Purpose	Interest	Term	Amount	Year
9	Buccimazza Industrial Works	$2,303,000.00	Dec. 12, 1962	Construction of telecommunications building and warehouse; Construction of telephone exchange satellite station	9% per annum and 6½% thereafter	1 year	$160,000.00	1977
10	USAID Loan 669-H-005	$24,300,000.00	Sept. 16, 1963	Mount Coffee Hydro Project	¾ of 1% per annum	10 years after first disbursement	$724,207.00	2004
11	Eximbank R-5 GOL Various	$13,250,000.00	Oct. 10, 1963	Project credits	5¾% per annum	6 years	$1,325,000.00	–
12	USAID Loan 669-H-006A	$1,700,000.00	Oct. 28, 1963	Construction and equipment of Monrovia Junior & Senior High School	¾ of 1% per annum	12 years after first disbursement	$49,802.73	2006
13	RCA Victor/	$1,388,000.00	Oct. 29, 1963	Export Credits Insurance Corporation	6% per annum	2 years after first disbursement	$50,000.00	1977
14	USAID Loan 669-H-004A	$5,300,000.00	Dec. 5, 1963	Construction of National Medical Centre	1% per annum for 10 years and 2½% thereafter	13 years after first disbursement	$156,141.26	2006
15	IBRD 368/1st Highway Project	$3,250,000.00	Jan. 8, 1964	Construction of Clay Pujehun & between Schiefelin-Robertsfield Roads	5½% per annum	8 years	$415,000.00	1982
16	USAID Loan	$7,000,000.00	Aug. 27, 1964	For the construction & equipping of an expanded water system for Monrovia Area	¾ of 1% per annum & 2% per annum thereafter	10 years	–.-	–

Name of Loan	Agreement Amount	Agreement Date	Purpose of Loan	Interest Rate	Grace Period	Estimated Yearly Repayment	Maturity Year
17 USAID Loan 669-H-006B	$400,000.00	June 17, 1965	First Amendment to loan 006A (Monrovia Jr. & Sr. High School) and increase total loan to $2,100,000.00	1% per annum for 10 years and $2\frac{1}{2}\%$ thereafter	10 years	–	–
18 USAID Loan 669-H-007A	$150,000.00	June 17, 1965	First Amendment to loan 007A and to increase total amount to $500,000.00	1% per annum for 10 years and $2\frac{1}{2}\%$ thereafter	10 years	$5,141.00	2006
19 USAID Loan 669-H-007B	$150,000.00	June 17, 1965	Ministry of Education; Monrovia Elementary School project	$\frac{3}{4}$ of 1% per annum	$9\frac{1}{2}$ years	–	2004
20 U.K. Export Credit	$24,757.50	1965	Road equipment.	Rescheduled	10 years	–	1989
21 USAID Loan 669-H-009	$7,200,000.00	1965	To extend Monrovia Systems.	1% per annum for 10 years and $2\frac{1}{2}\%$ thereafter	10 years	$246,704.00	2006
22 U.S. GOV'T Loan PL480	$813,207.02	Jan. 18, 1966	Purchase and sale of U.S. Rice	1% per annum up to April 28, 1968 and 2% per annum thereafter	2 years	$42,800.37	1986
23 USAID 669-H-010	$1,324,689.00	Feb. 18, 1966	For foreign exchange and local costs of commodities and services project	1% for the first 10 years and $2\frac{1}{2}\%$ therefore	10 years	–	1976

24	KFW 65-65-261/Capital By-Pass	$960,662.00	Dec. 5, 1966	For the construction within Monrovia, of the Capital By-Pass Project	2% per annum	8 years	$27,292.00	1991
25	KRED-AL-328	$960,667.00	Dec. 7, 1966	Construction of Capital By-Pass	$\frac{1}{4}$% per annum on disbursed amount; and 3% per annum on disbursed amount	8 years	–	1991
26	USAID Loan 669-H-012	$550,000.00	April 25, 1967	Technical assistance for commodities and services	1% per annum 10 years and 2$\frac{1}{2}$% thereafter	10 years	$18,961.00	2004
27	USAID Loan 669-H-013/Commerce–RIA	$270,000.00	April 25, 1967	Improvement of Roberts International Airport's landing area, air traffic control systems, navigational aids and supporting facilities	1% per annum for 10 years & 2$\frac{1}{2}$% per annum thereafter	9$\frac{1}{2}$ years	$8,940.96	2016
28	USAID Loan 669-H-014	$850,000.00	Aug. 10, 1967	Airborne geographical survey of Liberia mineral resources	1% per annum for 10 years and 2$\frac{1}{2}$% thereafter	10 years	$29,223.00	2007
29	US GOV'T Loan PL 480	$812,000.00	Oct. 23, 1967	For sales of agricultural commodities	1% per annum up to 1970 and 2$\frac{1}{2}$% thereafter	3 years	$42,718.92	1988
30	USAID Loan 669-H-015	$525,000.00	March 17, 1968	Technical assistance projects	2% per annum	10 years	–	2009
31	Rediffusion Overseas/GOL	$1,000,000.00	June 27, 1968	To operate and manage ELBC	6$\frac{1}{2}$% per annum	–	–	1989

Name of Loan	Agreement Amount	Agreement Date	Purpose of Loan	Interest Rate	Grace Period	Estimated Yearly Repayment	Maturity Year
32 USAID Loan 669-H-004B	$1,510,000.00	Aug. 13, 1968	Costs of equipment, commodities and services	1% per annum for 10 years and 2½% thereafter	–	–	2006
33 Pan American/ Spriggs Payne Airfield	$500,000.00	Aug. 28, 1968	Development, management and operation of the Spriggs Payne Airfield.	6% per annum	2 years	$55,000.00	1980
34 IBRD 617/Port Port Dredging Project	$3,600,000.00	1969	Financing of a port dredging project	6½% per annum	2 years	–	1984
35 Eximbank 126/ GOL	$5,297,230.00	April 23, 1969	To facilitate export exchange of commodities between U.S. and Liberia	6% per annum	–	–	–
36 USAID Loan 669-H-016	$975,000.00	Nov. 18, 1969	Construction of two rural access roads (Kolahun-Kamatahun and Zwedru-Ziah town)	2% per annum	10 years	$33,408.52	2010
37 USAID Loan 669-H-017B	$4,000,000.00	Dec. 18, 1969	Construction, supervisory and engineering services for the improvements to Roberts International Airport	2% per annum for 10 years, and 3% thereafter	10 years	$139,602.90	2011
38 IBRD/PUA 684 LBR	$7,400,000.00	June 4, 1970	Loan agreement for PUA	7% per annum	5 years	$237,000.00	1990
39 U.S. GOV'T Loan PL 480	$862,653.14	June 24, 1970	For sales of agricultural commodities	2% per annum up to 1972 and 3% thereafter	2 years	$45,402.80	1990

No.	Loan/Project	Amount	Date	Purpose	Interest	Term		Year
40	USAID Loan 669-H-019/ (Pleebo-Sanniquellie Project.)	$3,400,000.00	1972	Cost of goods and services required for construction of two rural access roads. (Pleebo-Barclayville and Saclepea-Gbahn-Sanniquellie).	2% per annum for 10 years and 3% thereafter	10 years	$118,540.56	2012
41	USAID 669-H-017A	$3,500,000.00	1972	First Amendment to loan #017 (Roberts International Airport) and provide additional funds	2% per annum for 10 years and 3% thereafter	10 years	$116,667.00	2013
42	U.S. GOV'T Loan PL 480	$1,281,000.00	April 26, 1972	For sales of agricultural commodities	2% per annum up to 1974 and 3% thereafter	2 years	$67,421.05	1992
43	IDA 305 Education Project	$7,200,000.00	May 17, 1972	Construction, furnishing and equipping of two new Multilateral High Schools; one new College of Agriculture and Forestry	$\frac{1}{2}$ of 1% per annum	10 years	–	2022
44	IBRD 839/ LBIDA	$6,000,000.00	June 26, 1972	Forestry Development Authority	$7\frac{1}{4}$% per annum	3 years	$25,000.00	1990
45	A/S Edelbetong Co. #1	$2,750,000.00	Jan. 24, 1973	Implementation of low cost housing project	8% per annum	–	–	–
46	USAID 669-H-020/Road Maintenance Equipment	$4,400,000.00	Feb. 26, 1973	For the purchase of road maintenance equipment	2% per annum for 10 years, 3% thereafter	10 years	–	–
47	IBRD 907	$3,000,000.00	June 13,1973	2nd Highways Project	3% per annum	5 years	$70,000.00	1997
48	ADB-001 Sierra Leone-Liberia	$1,106,713.00	Dec. 5, 1973	Sierra Leone-Liberia Road Link	6% per annum	3 years	$31,165.00	1991

Name of Loan	Agreement Amount	Agreement Date	Purpose of Loan	Interest Rate	Grace Period	Estimated Yearly Repayment	Maturity Year
49 Eximbank 5059/Presidential Jet	$1,462,500.00	1974	Presidential jet	6% per annum	3 years	–	1979
50 KFW AL – 688	$2,247,191.00	Feb. 11, 1974	For the purchase of equipment for Greenville Harbour	2% per annum	10 years	–	2004
51 Morgan Grenfell #2	$8,807,540.00	April 24, 1974	Equipment for tele-communications	8% per annum	–	–	1979
52 National Port Authority/GOL Various	$2,500,000.00	1957	–	3% per annum	1 year	$250,000.00	1981
53 Italian Loan/ Monrovia Street Drainage	$9,360,000.00	Feb. 28, 1975	To implement the Monrovia road project-sewerage, construction and paving	$8\frac{1}{2}$% per annum	2 years	–	1981
54 USAID Loan 669-H-023/ MPW	$4,000,000.00	Aug. 1975	Five-year road maintenance and development project	2% per annum for 10 years and 3% thereafter	$9\frac{1}{2}$ years	$59,872.76	2024
55 IDA 577	$6,000,000.00	Aug. 1, 1975	Lofa County agricultural development project	$\frac{1}{2}$ of 1% per annum	10 years	–	2025
56 IBRD #1150	$1,800,000.00	Aug. 1, 1975	Loan Agreement	4% per annum	1 year	–	1981
57 IBRD #1156	$27,500,000.00	Aug. 28, 1975	Highway projects	$\frac{3}{4}$ of 1% per annum	5 years	$910,000.00	2000
58 IBRD #1156	$6,000,000.00	Aug. 28, 1975	Third Highway projects	$8\frac{1}{2}$% per annum	5 years	$655,000.00	2000

No.	Project	Amount	Date	Purpose	Interest	Duration		Year
59	IBRD #1156 3rd Highway Project	$27,500,000.00	Aug. 28, 1975	Construction of a two lane bridge (about 1,400 ft.) across the Mesurado River in Monrovia	$\frac{3}{4}$ of 1% per annum and $8\frac{1}{2}$% per annum	5 years	–	2000
60	ADB/005 – Totota-Ganta Highway	$6,073,550.00	Sept. 8, 1975	Construction of two lanes bitumen standard of approximately 40 miles of the Ganta portion of the Totota – Ganta road project	6% per annum	4 years	–	1997
61	USAID 669-	$5,000,000.00	Nov. 10, 1975	Rural development in Lofa County involving improvement of upland agricultural project	2% per annum for 10 years and 3% thereafter	$9\frac{1}{2}$ years	–	2024
62	ADB-003/ LEC PUA	–	Dec. 31, 1975	To improve and increase water supply systems in Monrovia	6% per annum	3 years	–	1988
63	IBRD/2nd Educational Project	$4,000,000.00	June 7, 1976	To design, construction, furnishing and equipping of about 100 primary school units in about 50 villages in the counties of Bong, Lofa, Bassa, Cape Mount, Nimba and Montserrado. Improvement and expansion of a primary Teacher Training Institute at Zorzor	$6\frac{1}{2}$% per annum	–	–	1989
64	U.S. Department of Defense (Federal Financing Bank) FFB	$1,700,000.00	June 30, 1976	For the purchase of defense articles	–	1 year	$170,000.00	1982

	Name of Loan	Agreement Amount	Agreement Date	Purpose of Loan	Interest Rate	Grace Period	Estimated Yearly Repayment	Maturity Year
65	U.S. Military Assistance 761	$1,700,000.00	June 30, 1976	For the purchase of defense articles	–	1 year	$170,000.00	1982
66	KFW/Buchanan Water Supply	$3,000,000.00	July 6, 1976	Buchanan Water Supply	(To be determined)	10 years	–	2009
67	Chase Manhattan Limited (London)	$30,000,000.00	Jan. 11, 1977	Proceeds to be provided to Liberian Public Corporations for use by them for general corporate purposes	–	2 years	$5,454,556.00	1984
68	ADB-007/4th Educational Project	$4,342,860.00	May 5, 1977	South Western Liberia Educational Project	4% per annum	5 years	$931,430.50	2001
69	KFW/Water Supply	$8,235,294.00	May 25, 1977	Water supplies for the towns of Voinjama, Sanniquellie and Gbarnga	(To be determined)	6 years	–	2007
70	IBRD 1417/	$6,300,000.00	May 26, 1977	3rd Educational Project	8.02% per annum	5 years	$150,000.00	1997
71	Eurodollar Credit Agreement	$1,010,000.00	Aug. 27, 1977	Loan Agreement	2% per annum	2 years	$167,372.00	1982
72	Grindlay & Caravelle & Samas Glory Maritime Corporation	$5,500,000.00	Sept. 15, 1977	To assist: Grindlay Limited to refinance other short term loans; Caravelle and Samas to repay the principal amounts outstanding	$1\frac{3}{4}$% per annum	$1\frac{1}{2}$ years	$550,000.00	–

No.	Name/ID	Amount	Date	Purpose	Interest	Term		Year
73	ADB-008/ Tubman Bridge Bomi Hills Road	$6,073,500.00	Sept. 16, 1977	Construction of the Tubman Bridge – Bomi Hills road	7% per annum	4 years	–	1996
74	IDA 700	$7,000,000.00	Dec. 29, 1977	Bong County Agricultural development project	$\frac{1}{2}$% of 1% per annum	10 years	–	2026
75	USAID 669-T-025	$6,600,000.00	1978	Upper Bong County integrated rural development	2% per annum	$9\frac{1}{2}$ years	–	2027
76	ADB-009/Monrovia Water Supply	$2,612,841.21	Jan. 23, 1978	For a 15,000 ft. 36 inches gravity raw water main to be laid from Mount Coffee Hydroelectric Power Dam to the existing treatment works of Monrovia Supply at White Plains	7% per annum	3 years	–	1993
77	IBRD-1544/ LRDU	$7,000,000.00	April 21, 1978	For Rubber Development Project	$7\frac{1}{2}$% per annum	5 years	$235,000.00	1997
78	IBRD-786	$6,000,000.00	April 21, 1978	Rubber Development Unit	$\frac{1}{4}$ of 1% per annum up to 1998 and $1\frac{1}{2}$% thereafter	10 years	–	2028
79	IBRD-1544/ LBR	$7,000,000.00	April 21, 1978	Additional financial assistance	$7\frac{1}{2}$% per annum	5 years	$235,000.00	1998
80	Citibank/ AGRIMECO	$7,800,000.00	May 31, 1978	Loan Agreement	$1\frac{3}{4}$% per annum	2 years	$100,000.00	1985

Name of Loan	Agreement Amount	Agreement Date	Purpose of Loan	Interest Rate	Grace Period	Estimated Yearly Repayment	Maturity Year
81 IBRD-1573/4th Power Project (LEC)	$13,800,000.00	June 2, 1978	The construction and improvement of the Paynesville-Totota road (about 71 miles) and reconstruction of the Paynesville-Robertsfield road (about 28 miles)	$\frac{3}{4}$ of 1% per annum	4 years	$460,000.00	1998
82 IBRD-1573 4th Power Project (LEC)	$13,800,000.00	June 2, 1978	4th Highway project	7% per annum	5 years	$270,090.00	1998
83 IBRD-1573/ LBR	$13,800,000.00	June 2, 1978	To assist in financing part of the project on the terms and conditions set forth in the Kuwait Fund loan agreement.	$7\frac{1}{2}$% per annum	5 years	$460,000.00	1998
84 Commonwealth Development Corporation/ Rubber Development Project	$7,128,275.00	June 9, 1978	Rubber Development Unit	$7\frac{1}{4}$% per annum	6 years	–	1997
85 Saudi Fund/ Tubman Bridge Bomi Hills roads Project	$9,000,000.00	June 12, 1978	Tubman Bridge, Bomi Hills roads and St. Paul Bridge project	2% per annum	5 years	–	1997
86 BADEA/ LIFZA	$3,200,000.00	June 14, 1978	For the financing of the Industrial Freezone Project	–	–	$577,192.00	1984

No.	Source	Amount	Date	Purpose	Interest	Term		Maturity
87	Eximbank 6449/Citibank Boeing 737	$11,543,850.00	June 30, 1978	To purchase New 737 Boeing Aircraft and spare parts	$8\frac{5}{8}\%$ per annum	–	$577,192.00	1984
88	KFW-65-231/FDA	$4,975,124.00	June 30, 1978	Wood Processing and Training Centre for Bomi Hills Project	6% per annum	5 years	–	2009
89	KFW-Greenville Harbour	$5,814,799.00	July 1978	Rehabilitation and extension of the Greenville Harbor	2% per annum	8 years	–	2005
90	Republic of China/GOL	$23,000,000.00	July 1, 1978	Developing national economy	Free	10 years	–	2000
91	IBRD #1600	$10,000,000.00	July 7, 1978	4th Power Project (LEC)	–	5 years	–	1997
92	Kuwait Fund/Road Rehabilitation	$7,500,000.00	July 18, 1978	Reconstruction and improvement of the Paynesville-Totota road (about 71 miles) and reconstruction and improvement of the Robertsfield road (about 18 miles)	$3\frac{1}{2}\%$ per annum	4 years	–	1996
93	IDA-839/FDA	$6,000,000.00	July 28, 1978	The first phase part A: Institutional support for FDA. Part B: Industrial trail Plantation, Part C: Training	$\frac{3}{4}$ of 1% per annum	10 years	–	2028
94	Eurodollar Credit Agreement	$60,000,000.00	August 2, 1978	Credit agreement	$1\frac{3}{4}\%$ per annum	2 years	–	1985
95	Chemical Bank/LPRC	$15,000,000.00	Aug. 9, 1978	Finance the acquisition and improvement by LPRC of the assets of a refinery	$3\frac{1}{4}\%$ per annum and $2\frac{1}{4}\%$ thereafter	2 years	$100,000.00	1985

Name of Loan	Agreement Amount	Agreement Date	Purpose of Loan	Interest Rate	Grace Period	Estimated Yearly Repayment	Maturity Year
96 KFW-78-65 575/OAU 79	$4,696,150,00	Sept. 4, 1978	Procurement of goods and services which are required for the holding of the Summit Conference of the OAU	2% per annum	10 years	–	2008
97 U.S. Miltary Assistance	$500,000.00	Sept. 19, 1978	To purchase defense articles.	–	1 year	$50,000.00	1984
98 ADB-010-FDA	$5,101,782.00	Sept. 27, 1978	To finance part of the foreign exchange costs of the Forestry Project	7% per annum	5 years	–	1998
99 DG Bank/GOL #LB01	$5,000,000.00	Nov. 24, 1978	Development project in Liberia.	$10\frac{3}{8}\%$ per annum for 5 years and 12% thereafter	4 years	$357,142.86	1986
100 KFW/LEC 77-65-357	$3,118,017.00	Nov. 30, 1978	Import costs of the extension of power distribution system, Monrovia II project	6% per annum	3 years	–	2008
101 Republic of Liberia/ LBIDI	$5,000,000.00	Dec. 4, 1978	Financial development project in Liberia.	$10\frac{3}{8}\%$ per annum	5 years	$30,000.00	1993
102 OPEC Fund TBRI Bomi	$3,000,000.00	Dec. 19, 1978	For the construction of a two-lane Tubman Bridges and Bomi Hills road.	4% per annum	5 years	$93,000.00	1998
103 Amman and Whitney Engineers USAID-669-T-024	$5,200,000.00	Dec. 22, 1978	Consulting services for rural road III for the Belle Yella-Kolahun Road.	2% per annum for 10 years	11 years	–	1999

No.	Borrower	Amount	Date	Purpose	Interest	Term	Balance	Year
104	CITIBANK N.A./MATADI	$10,000,000.00	Dec. 31, 1978	Construction of the Matadi Housing project.	$1\frac{3}{4}\%$ per annum	1 year	$100,000.00	1985
105	LWSC #859	$8,000,000.00	Jan. 8, 1979	Loan agreement.	$\frac{1}{2}$ of 1% per annum up to 1998 and $1\frac{1}{2}\%$ thereafter	10 years	–	2028
106	Eurodollar Credit Agreement	$300,000.00	Feb. 1, 1979	Loan agreement	$1\frac{3}{4}\%$ per annum	2 years	$167,372.00	1982
107	Japan/OECF Federal Roads	$20,000,000.00	March 30, 1979	Loan agreement.	4% per annum	1 year	–	1981
108	LWSC-AL 73-66-230	$1,568,629.00	April 2, 1979	For water supply for Zwedru town.	2% per annum	10 years	–	2009
109	IBRD #1664 Feeder Roads Project	$10,700,000.00	April 4, 1979	Construction, improvement and subsequent maintenance of feeder roads.	$\frac{3}{4}$ of 1% per annum and 7% thereafter	5 years	–	1998
110	Taiyo Kobe Bank	$30,000,000.00	April 23, 1979	The proceeds of this loan is to be used towards the financing of the local cost requirements of various development projects.	From 1979–1985 $= 8\%$ and from 1985–1989 $= 8.06\%$ per annum	4 years	$2,076,923.04	1989
111	P.K. Bank/GOL	$950,000.00	June 20, 1974	Purchase of three coast-guard cutters.	6% per annum	1 year	$50,699.00	1990
112	L.B.D.I.-DG/GOL	$5,000,000.00	June 28, 1979	To finance development projects within the Republic of Liberia.	$10\frac{3}{8}\%$ per annum	5 years	–	1987
113	Commonwealth Development/GOL.	$2,000,000.00	Aug. 14, 1979	Liberia Water and Sewer Corporation	$8\frac{1}{2}\%$ per annum	5 years	–	1998

Name of Loan	Agreement Amount	Agreement Date	Purpose of Loan	Interest Rate	Grace Period	Estimated Yearly Repayment	Maturity Year
114 KFW/GOL 65-346 Commodity Aid	$277,839.00	Oct. 4, 1979	For the payment of foreign exchange and goods & services and water supply systems of Harper & Greenville.	2% per annum	11 years	–	2009
115 KFW-79-65-270/Kakata Water Supply	$427,321.00	Oct. 4, 1979	The project is for test drilling including evaluation of the findings and further planning work for the water supply scheme of Kakata.	2% per annum	11 years	–	2009
116 A.D.B./011	$7,978,580.00	Nov. 16, 1979	Financing of the Decoris Oil Palm project.	7% per annum	5 years	–	1999
117 IBRD 1765/DOPC	$12,000,000.00	Dec. 21, 1979	Decoris Oil Palm project.	8% per annum	6 years	$400,000.00	1999
118 IDA/WP # L-1092-A	$3,380,000.00	1980	To assist in the financing and development of SME's Investment Enterprises through grants or sub-Loan	$\frac{1}{2}$ of 1% each instal; and $1\frac{1}{2}$% thereafter	10 years	–	2030
119 Eximbank/ # 6736 Hydro	$2,125,000.00	March 10, 1980	For the completion of a feasibility study for the St Paul hydroelectric power project	$\frac{1}{2}$ of 1% per annum	–	–	–
120 U.S. Department of Defense (Federal Finance Bank) FFB.	$1,400,000.00	Aug. 11, 1980	For the purchase of defense items.	–	1 year	$140,000.00	1986

No.	Name	Amount	Interest	Term	Purpose	Date		Year
121	OPEC Fund #205 P	$5,000,000.00	4% per annum	4 years	Bushrod Power Expansion	Oct. 24, 1980	$156,200.00	2000
122	IBRD #1907/ GOL	$5,000,000.00	9¼% per annum	6 years	Exploration for hydrocarbon resources in Liberia.	Nov. 21, 1980	$165,000.00	2000
123	Norweign Loan #1.	$3,000,000.00	8% per annum	5 years before first instalment	Commercial credits granted to Liberia.	Dec. 19, 1980	–	1985
124	Norweign Loan #2.	$8,317,056.00	8% per annum	5 years final instalment	Commercial credits granted to Liberia.	Dec. 19, 1980	–	1989
125	KFW/LEC	$3,118,017.00	6% per annum	3 years	Distribution of power to Monrovia.	Feb. 11, 1974	–	2004
126	Gov't of Liberia Telecommunications	$6,500,000.00	3½% per annum	2 years	Improvement and expansion of telecommunications operations.	Jan. 20, 1977	$590,910.00	1984

Appendix 2 Fernando Poo Labour Agreement of 1928

This indenture of agreement made and entered into this 2nd day of April in the year of our Lord nineteen hundred and twenty-eight (A.D. 1928) in the City of Monrovia and the Republic of Liberia by Messrs. Barclay & Barclay, attorneys-at-law under special power of attorney to act for and on behalf of Theodomiro Avendano, president of the Syndicato Agricola de los Territorios Espanoles del Golfo de Guinea, residing at Santa Isabel, Fernando Poo, hereinafter referred to as the Syndicate, of the first part, and Thomas E. Pelham, Robert W. Draper, E.G.W. King, J.C. Johnson, M.A. Bracewell, and C. Cooper, citizens of the Republic of Liberia, recruiting agents now represented by S.A. Ross, of counsel for the recruiting agents, hereinafter referred to as the Recruiting Agents, party of the second part.

That the party of the first part agrees to pay to the party of the second part nine pounds sterling to cover headmoney, taxes, advances, compensation and food; in other words, including all expenses (except passage to Fernando Poo), which is to be borne by the party of the first part, exclusive of the nine pounds sterling above mentioned. The party of the first part requests the party of the second part to recruit and ship fifteen hundred boys to the Spanish authorities at Fernando Poo in accordance with the laws and regulations of Liberia government shipment of labourers.

On arrival of these boys at Fernando Poo to the Curadoo, the Curadoo and the Liberian Consul shall engage these boys to the Syndicate, which the Syndicate undertakes to see done according to Spanish Law, the Liberian Consul being present and superintending the engagement of said boys as per the law of the colony.

The fifteen hundred boys above mentioned should be shipped within one calendar year from the date of the signing of this agreement, and the party of the second part should do their level best to have these boys shipped.

The boys shipped by the Recruiting Agents are contracted for the period of two years, one year's salary to be paid each boy in cash at Fernando and the remaining salary to be paid each boy when returning to Liberia, by cheque on the Bank of British West Africa, Ltd., in Monrovia, or the agency in Sinoe or Cape Palmas.

The party of the first part agrees and faithfully promises not to inflict any inhumane punishment upon these boys but to treat them kindly and feed them properly, furnishing quarters for said boys, and in case of sickness to give said boys proper medical treatment.

The party of the first part empowers the party of the second part to make advances to each boy in the sum not exceeding three pounds sterling, which is allocated within the nine pounds sterling above mentioned, and will be the only sum chargeable to the boy. All other sums within the nine pounds sterling is free to the boy and paid by the party of the first part.

The party of the first part further agrees to pay to the head man of each gang of 25 boys the sum of $10.00 money of the colony in cash per month; and to each common labourer the sum of $6.00 money of the colony in cash per month; and, at the expiration of the period contracted for, the boys are to be returned to the place from whence they were shipped in Liberia.

Should any of the boys die, whatever amount may be due said boy at the time of his death will be paid over to the Liberian Consul. The party of the first part and their assignee further agree that at any time that the Liberian Consul desires to visit any of the farms where these boys are engaged for the purpose of inspecting and looking after the welfare as well as the interests of said boys he shall be permitted to do so without any objection on the part of the party of the first part, or their assignee.

The party of the first part further agrees to remit the sum of nine pounds sterling through the Bank of British West Africa, Ltd., as agreed upon to the party of the second part on each boy on return to the steamer conveying these boys to Fernando Poo without failure, said cheque to be drawn in the same of S.A. Ross, counsel for the party of the second part.

The party of the first part agrees and will pay to the counsel of the party of the second part the sum of one thousand pounds sterling as a bonus at the signing of this agreement; and further agrees to pay another sum of a thousand pounds sterling in British coin, to the party of the second part for every additional fifteen hundred boys shipped to the party of the first part.

In consideration of the above stipulations above mentioned, the party of the second part promises and agrees to recruit and ship to the Curadoo at Fernando Poo, fifteen hundred labourers and more if possible, under the laws of Liberia made and provided for, as long as there be no intervention on part of the Government to prohibit the recruiting of boys to Fernando Poo, said boys should be shipped within one calendar year from date.

The party of the second part further agrees and accepts from the party of the first part the sum of nine pounds sterling to be sent through the Bank of British West Africa, Ltd., to the party of the second part as full expenses on each boy so recruited and shipped to Fernando Poo.

The party of the second part further agrees and accepts from the party of the first part the sum of one thousand pounds sterling as a bonus on the fifteen hundred boys to be shipped, on the signing of this agreement; and also further agrees to accept from the party of the first part another sum of a thousand pounds sterling on a further additional shipment of fifteen hundred whenever shipped as stipulated on the above agreement.

The party of the second part further agrees to recruit boys and ship same to the Curadoo at Fernando Poo within the space of two calendar years, providing there be no objection on the part of the government of Liberia.

After two years, either party being dissatisfied may serve notice on the other party as to their intention of serving this agreement, said notice to be in writing.

And should there be any indebtedness to the party of the second part by the party of the first part at the terminus of this agreement same shall be paid, and all indebtedness on part of the party of the second part to the party of the first part shall also be refunded.

It is further agreed, and the party of the second part so requires, that the party of the first part not presenting any authorization showing their status, before signing this agreement, shall be guaranteed by the Spanish Consul duly accredited to the Liberian government at Monrovia.

It is duly agreed that the party of the first part shall cause the Spanish steamer to call at the Ports of Greenville and Harper or any other port with the Sinoe and Maryland Counties, the party of the second part furnishing port charts, where these boys may be recruited according to the laws of Liberia, monthly, and that no delay should be occasioned on the part of the party of the first part by said Spanish steamers not calling.

All inconveniences and expenses which the party of the second part may be exposed by such steamer not calling shall be chargeable to the party of the first part, and the party of the first part hereby agrees to pay all damages incurred on account of delay of steamer, such damages and delays to be settled by arbitrations. (Arbitrators to be appointed in the usual legal way.)

It is mutually agreed between the parties that the party of the second part shall also operate within the County of Maryland, either in person or by appointment or subsidiary agencies in Maryland County, to carry out the intention of this agreement, and will do all in their power to recruit and ship to Fernando Poo fifteen hundred boys or more, making a grand total of three thousand boys under the laws of Liberia made and provided so long as the government of Liberia places no obstruction in the way.

The party of the first part further agrees to pay to the party of the second part the sum of nine pounds sterling per boy for all expenses incurred on labourers from Maryland County as above stated and further to pay the sum of one thousand pounds sterling, gold or silver coin, as a bonus for this privilege, making a total of two thousand pounds sterling to be paid at the signing of this agreement.

In witness whereof the parties hereto and hereunto have set their hands and seals this 2nd Day of April, A.D. 1928.

For the Syndicato Agricola of Fernando Poo:
(Sgd.) Barclay and Barclay
Party of the first part.

For the Recruiting Agents:
(Sgd.) S.A. Ross,
Party of the second part.

Witnesses:
J.A. Dougan
J.W. Howard
E.A. Monger

Appendix 3 Executive Order Establishing the National Force for the Eradication of Corruption (NFEC)

WHEREAS, it has been discovered that efforts undertaken to improve the general condition of all of our people are being impeded and frustrated by the adverse effects of corruption, practised by selfish, unpatriotic members of our society; and

WHEREAS, it has become evident that unless timely action is taken to assist the people in the fight against corruption, this monstrous evil could get out of hand; and

WHEREAS, in our attack against this evil it is necessary to combat and root out any and every form of corruption from our society in order to ensure that our efforts in building this nation and improving the social and economic status of all of our people will continue to be fruitful and beneficial to all; and

WHEREAS, to accomplish this objective, it is desirable and necessary to establish a National Force for the Eradication of Corruption;

NOW, THEREFORE, it is hereby ordered that there shall be established the NATIONAL FORCE FOR THE ERADICATION OF CORRUPTION from our Country.

The Force shall be created in the Office of the President, and shall be headed by a Director to be appointed by the President, by and with the consent of the Senate. The President shall also appoint, by and with the consent of the Senate, a Deputy Director who shall be the principal assistant to the Director.

The National Force for the Eradication of Corruption shall be organized in such manner as shall be determined by the Director, subject to the approval of the President. The composition of the Force shall be, as follows:

1 Director
2 Deputy Director
3 Fifty-two (52) personnel, of whom four (4) shall be in each County, except Montserrado in which there shall be eight (8) and two (2) in each Territory.

The principal functions of the National Force for the Eradication of Corruption shall be, as follows:

(a) To seek out and discover in Liberia by all legal means corruption whether in the public or private sector;
(b) To be vigilant in protecting the public against all forms of corruption;
(c) To collect, check and compile facts and data on any transaction involving corruption, or any organization or person dealing in corrupt practices;
(d) To make available and report direct to the President for attention of the Ministry of Justice all information, facts, data, articles, and other relevant materials collected on acts of corruption and suspicious cases requiring police probe and prosecution.

Given under my hand this twenty-sixth day of August, A.D. 1975

(*Sgd.*) William R. Tolbert, Jr.

Appendix 4   An Address to the Nation by Dr William R. Tolbert, Jr. President of the Republic of Liberia Centennial Memorial Pavilion, Saturday, May 5, 1979

My Fellow Citizens,
Members of the True Whig Party,
Friends Throughout the Length and
Breadth of the Republic of Liberia and
Throughout the World:

Three weeks have passed since we witnessed the horrible tragedy of April 14, 1979.

As government intensifies its efforts to heal the wounds, lift the national spirit and advance the task of reconstruction, I consider it most propitious and incumbent upon me to come to this sacred national shrine, the Centennial Memorial Pavilion, where I took the Oath of Office on January 3, 1972, seven years and four months ago, to speak to the Nation from the very depths of my heart.

Since the violent Civil Disturbances which disrupted our peace and threatened our economy and our progress, I have had cause to speak to you on various occasions – through your chosen representatives and the mass media. A number of other Official Statements and press releases have been made on that dastardly event including the upheaval. We have also released a small pamphlet portraying an Official Account of the events of that day.

It should now be clear to all that that occurrence was a direct result of an illegal demonstration in defiance of Law and was designed and executed by a group of misguided persons calling themselves the Progressive Alliance of Liberia, aided and abetted by its internal and external collaborators, using the rice-price issue as an alibi. As I see it, the true objective of the illegal and diabolical action was to create a civil disturbance so as to adversely affect our economy and destabilize our government.

Thanks to the protective shield of Almighty God who has guided this Nation throughout these 132 years of its history, and the vigilant action of a united people, their design was frustrated. However, our hearts are pained and our heads are bowed over the loss of precious human lives, the destruction of millions of dollars of valuable property and the disrepute brought upon our cherished image of stability and peaceful existence. May Almighty God grant to the souls of those departed, a blissful repose, and comfort the hearts of all bereaved ones.

I have not therefore come merely to reiterate the gory details of what transpired on that day; nor have I come to narrate Government's immediate responses, for this is amply revealed in the Official Account which has been released.

Instead, I have come, My Fellow Citizens and Friends, to pour out to you my spirit. I have come to speak to you frankly and candidly about our national promise and prospects. In so doing, I consider it vital and significant that I call to your remembrance the vision which I saw for our Republic as conveyed in my First Inaugural Address delivered from this hallowed shrine on January 3, 1972. And I quote:

I view this nation as an energized Republic, totally involved in reconstruction and development. With an accent on youth and speed,

159

and on competence and effectiveness, I see a dynamic nation propelled by forces of measured movements and lasting results. With undiminishing faith, I see shrinking areas of rural underdevelopment and, rising in their place, I watch the emergence of an increasing consortium of wholesome urbanization and resilient industry.

As I gaze across the horizon, I catch the rewarding glimpse of my people, and of foreigners alike, totally involved in the participatory industrialization of our progressive nation.

Dimly before my eyes, I see a vision of the children of this land quenching their thirst for knowledge with cooling drafts of the waters of greater enlightenment, in order that the blights of ignorance may be obliterated, and the brilliance of their future unfolded before them.

Releasing themselves from the shackles of a primitive existence, I see a people industrious and strong, reaching into the very depths of their soul, to seize the motivating sparks of courage that would elevate them onto a plateau of creativeness, productiveness, and *true self-respect*.

And then I read in the skies above, that it is our compelling mission to achieve these things, and to bring grace, love and humility to the tenor of human life: for the fate of mankind is our greatest challenge

Translation of a vision

This then, My Fellow Citizens and Friends, represents the vision which we faithfully conveyed to you as we embarked upon our national stewardship. With reconstructed attitudes of self-reliance and concerted will for total involvement in our thrust toward Higher Heights, we have endeavoured to translate that vision into tangible achievements for our common upliftment as a nation and for the enrichment of humanity. All of you stand as living witnesses to the measure of success which we have thus far achieved, by the Grace of Almighty God.

The fact is well known that our accession to the Presidency coincided with the period when the whole world was experiencing disquieting economic uncertainties, a situation whose consequences have been most difficult for both developed and developing countries. Galloping inflation attained double-digit levels worldwide and a major recession in the demand of primary commodities, including our two principal primary exports, iron ore and rubber, resulted in serious setbacks to our economy.

Aggravated by a worsening world currency crisis, an almost constant fall in the value of the US dollar, upon which our economy is based, imposed further hardship for us as we were faced with rising import prices, due mainly to the upward spiralling increases in the price of oil, that vital commodity to national progress. And even now we continue to grapple with further increases in the price of oil.

Amidst this situation of global economic recession and stagnation, we were also faced on the domestic scene with a reduction in the growth performance of our gross domestic product, compounded by administrative short-comings in our revenue generating program, thus causing serious setbacks in Government's expenditure-control measures.

We endeavoured to meet that challenge by inspiring into action the resourcefulness of the Liberian People. In so doing we have activated a greater sense of dedication, achievement and enterprise as vital prerequisites in the pursuit of material self-sufficiency through self-reliance and international co-operation.

The results of this collective effort by a united and purposeful people have reflected some degree of encouragement. Revenue and receipts have increased from $77.5 million in 1972 to $185.5 million in 1978, an average annual growth rate of over 15 percent. With the enactment of the 1977, Revenue and Finance Law, the regressive 'austerity' tax was abolished, and the income tax structure was made more progressive. As a consequence of tariff harmonization under the Mano River Customs Union, a higher tariff has been imposed on luxury goods; and lower income groups have found relief through exemption and the lowering of taxes on 'necessity' commodities.

Insofar as the public debt is concerned, outstanding debt (excluding undisbursed) has steadily decreased in relationship to our gross domestic product, accounting for an average annual 4.2 percent between 1971 and 1977, compared with an average annual eight percent in previous years. We are receiving statistics for 1978–1979 which will be released accordingly.

Although our economy is based on the free enterprise system in which prices are determined by market forces, the spiralling inflationary trends of the 70s have caused Government to institute measures to minimize the effects of this economic crisis on the average Liberian consumer. Executive Order No. 2, issued in 1973, authorizes the Ministry of Commerce, Industry and Transportation to fix prices at which imported as well as locally manufactured and agricultural commodities are sold. We constituted a special High-Cost-of-Living Commission which visited a number of West African Countries to compare prices and determine how best a successful price reduction program could be implemented to ease the burden on the masses of our citizens. Although the Commission found the prices of commodities in Liberia to be much lower than in the Countries they visited, we have not relented in our efforts to control the prices of essential commodities in the interest of our people.

Moreover, we realize that any development in Liberia which fails to give attention to agriculture in which is engaged more than three-fourths of our population, can hardly be self-sustaining. Thus, we have enunciated programs of action which would give this sector its deserving role in the economy.

In pursuance of this Policy, we invested over One Million Dollars in 1972 in a wholly Government-owned mechanized Agricultural Company (AGRIMECO), to spear-head land clearance and development of vast areas to cope with the proliferation of agricultural co-operatives which we have encouraged, nurtured and provided with agricultural extension and technical services.

Further diversifying this sector, we have organized crash programs to enable Liberian farmers to move into the cash economy. Along this line, two public corporations have been established to maximize the production of oil palm, cocoa, and coffee.

Already, the impact of the revolution in three crop production is being generally felt throughout the country, more especially in Lofa, Bong, Grand Gedeh and Maryland Counties and the Territories of Sasstown and Kru Coast.

Our commitment to the indispensable development of our human resources has led us to open the doors of all Government elementary and high schools free to all our school age pupils, and we are subsidizing up to fifty percent tuition, books and board for all College and University students throughout the country. Despite our financial limitations we have extended the benefit of free education to vast areas of our rural population. We certainly have plans to extend same to all parts of our country, and when our resources permit, we will have free education throughout the land.

Parallel with this, we have instituted strategic reforms to improve teacher training and incentives, physical facilities, curricula and instructional materials, school administration and supervision.

Increasingly have we placed emphasis on technical and vocational education and training to supply the nation's manpower needs in this vital area. The Booker Washington Institute has been remodeled and is being fully staffed and equipped; and the W.V.S. Tubman Technical College in Maryland County has opened its doors in furtherance of the vocational dimensions of our educational program.

Another area of service which we have increasingly improved is our Health and Social Welfare Program. Deeply concerned about the high infant mortality rate, we have expanded our health facilities to include free medical care to prenatal mothers and infants up to two years, and effected appreciable budgetary increases in support of this and related activities. These increases have resulted in the development and expansion of health services within the country, especially in the rural areas where the need is greatest. And we hope, by the Grace of God, when our resources permit us, to even extend free medical care throughout the length and breadth of the Republic.

We have reorganized and made more rational and equitable conditions in the Civil Service, and have effectuated three successive salary increments since 1972, with a national fringe benefit scheme for both senior and junior civil servants.

Vigorously pursuing our policy of Liberianization in the private sector, steady progress is being made in the provision of higher wages, better housing and medical facilities, and greater opportunities for self-fulfillment for our working class.

Continuingly being guided by the vision which we held out for the nation, we have sought to ensure an atmosphere where the fruits of our collective labor can be enjoyed with equity and where the dignity of man and respect for fundamental human rights would permeate our thoughts and guide our actions.

My Fellow Citizens and Friends, I have here endeavoured to capsule our humble endeavors, though moderate they may be, to enable all conscientious individuals, citizens and foreigners alike, void of prejudice and bias, to determine for themselves whether we have not tried to keep the faith with you. We have earnestly and honestly marshalled all our energies even at the expense of my health and my very life to get resources to translate our vision into concrete achievements for the nation and for all our people.

What in 1972 we solemnly promised by the inspiration of Almighty God, we have tried to deliver in a democratic way in our democratic society. While fully realizing the inevitability of change, we have labored to build on the achievement of the past. Espousing continuity and change alike in our policies, we have remained ever conscious of the fact that in order to avoid any semblance of violent change, our policies have been fully accommodative of such peaceful changes as would be consistent and promotive of the aspirations of our people.

We have never rested on our oars, and we cannot; for, our experience and conviction continuingly lead us to a full appreciation of the dynamics of our socio-political culture and intervening circumstances of our contemporary world. But our point of reference continues to be the vision which we held out for the nation as we assumed national leadership. That vision encompassed, as you will no doubt agree, a recognition of the inevitability of change, as well as a commitment to the unassailable ideals which form the very bedrock of this Republic.

My Fellow Citizens and Friends, all that I have done conscientiously and with the fear of Almighty God before me, and looking seriously at what occurred on April 14, I am led to ask: '*What lack I yet?*'

I realize my imperfections and my limitations for I am but mortal. I have been searching my soul for the answer, and certainly I can only imagine that the answer is: Continue to give the best within you, and even more sacrificially and faithfully serve the people of Liberia, Africa and mankind throughout our One World. This I am committed to do; So help me God!

Interruption of our progress

In the midst of our efforts to translate into reality what we envisaged for the nation; in the midst of our implementation of the social need for orientation of our policies; in the midst of our democratic policy of dialogue with our people on matters of legitimate national concern, came the violent Civil Disturbances of April 14, 1979.

We now know that the agitation was fomented by covert and overt opponents to our policies specifically conceived, designed for, and being faithfully executed in the interest of the masses, that great majority of our citizens who have been long neglected. We now know that a number of those involved in the illegal demonstration were misled and incited by motives of a subversive and treasonable character. We now know that conspirators and those who aided and abetted the Civil Disturbances include a few inordinate individuals unappreciative of our chosen course for the masses. We also know that there are still others who have sought every means of defeating our program for social cohesion, the building of mutual confidence and the virtue of patience.

At any rate, I am speaking according to my conviction, I am persuaded that as one whose faith is firmly rooted in God Almighty, He has permitted the occurrence of April 14th for a purpose. He permitted it not to destroy Liberia, but to enable us to pause and reexamine ourselves as a people. Are we moving to higher heights together, if not, why? Are we true and sincere to each other, if not, why? Are we loyal, patriotic and respectful of legally and legitimately constituted authority, if not why? Are we not convinced that all avenues to peaceful change are being effectually opened to us all alike? Why would we contemplate and perpetrate lawlessness, destruction and wholly un-Liberian activities?

My Fellow Citizens, I call upon each and every one of you to first undertake an objective self-examination, as I am doing, and then join with us as we embark upon a national self-examination so that we can reconstruct our Country.

Government's response to April 14

As we have already indicated since the awful and shocking events of April 14, Government will, as already begun, uphold the letter and spirit of the Constitution and the laws of the Republic, as well as the Universal Declaration of Human Rights to which we have unreservedly subscribed. We do this because we have always held the conviction, and we continue to do so now, that nothing in the life of the nation can be pursued in an atmosphere of lawlessness and disregard for constituted authority.

Our chief concern has been to ensure a full clarification of the entire situation and its attendant circumstances. In this regard, we are still in the process of isolating the hard-core conspirators from those who were innocently caught in the melée as it progressed, and who seized upon the occasion to satisfy their greed and corrupt habits.

Government will persist in doing what is right and just. We call upon our people to continue to give us their full understanding and to have faith in us. Since the establishment of this Republic, it has always been our way of political development to continuously improve upon our system of Government, while accepting the realities of our situation at every stage. In this, we have stood for peaceful relevant change. We have demonstrated this by the nature of the programs and policies which we have advanced.

We remain continuingly open to new approaches. I have no monopoly over ideas; let us all join to build the new Liberia. This is why as we undertake to assess fully the implications of the events of April 14, we have decided to constitute a Commission charged with the responsibility of *receiving* and *analyzing* suggestions from concerned citizens for the reconstruction of Liberia, and submitting recommendations for the attention of Government, and I assure you they will be given speedy attention by Government.

The Commission of Thirty-one which is chaired by one of the nation's Elder Statesmen, Counsellor Nete Sie Brownell, includes the following:

2	Honourable Momolu Dukuly	Member
3	Honourable Henry Ford Cooper	–
4	Honourable J. Dudley Lawrence	–
5	Honourable Roland Cooper	–
6	Honourable Albert T. White	–
7	Honourable Lawrence Morgan	–
8	Dr Christian Baker	–
9	Mr Richmond Draper	–
10	Counsellor Toye C. Bernard	–

11	Dr Flomo Stevens	Member
12	Mrs Corina Van Ee	–
13	Dr Patrick L.N. Seyon	–
14	Bishop George D. Browne	–
15	Mrs Sophie Dunbar	–
16	General Benyan Kesselly	–
17	Father Edward G.W. King	–
18	Honourable Nathaniel Baker	–
19	Professor Abraham James	–
20	Counsellor Robert Azango	–
21	Honourable Elizabeth Collins	–
22	Honourable Luvenia Ash-Thompson	–
23	Mr John Scotland	–
24	Honourable George F. Sherman	–
25	Honourable Ellen J. Sirleaf	–
26	Honourable David Farhat	–
27	Honourable Samuel Greene	–
28	Dr Stephen Yekeson	–
29	Mr Roland Dahn	–
30	Miss Massa Crayton	–
31	Dr D. Elwood Dunn	Secretary

Within thirty days as of Monday, May 7, 1979, Government will expect to receive the report of the Commission's findings. If you submit it within one week, I will act on it.

Government scholarship program

My Dear Friends, we stand for a Government of human dignity, equity, equal opportunity for, and justice to, all without exception. We fully adhere to this approach in our Foreign Scholarship Program. The basic objective of that program remains that of responding to the national manpower needs in those areas where satisfactory academic and specialized training is not currently available in Liberia. The bases, strictly adhered to, for the granting of scholarships to deserving Liberians include:

1 Priority field already determined by Government.
2 Indications provided by manpower studies.
3 Needs expressed by institutions and agencies of Government.
4 Availability of the candidate's chosen field and level of study in Liberia.
5 Availability of funds for a given year.
6 Preparedness of candidate for proposed field of study.

To aid in the execution of this important program, from which I divorced myself completely, early in our administration we appointed an Ad Hoc Foreign Scholarship Committee which now is composed as follows:

1	Professor Agnes Cooper Dennis	Chairman
2	Dr J. Bernard Blamo	Chairman Ex-Officio
3	Honourable Bismarck Kuyon	Member
4	Dr D. Elwood Dunn	–
5	Mrs Isabel Karnga	–
6	Honourable James E. Bass	–
7	Dr Flomo Stevens	–
8	Honourable Lawrence V. Sherman	–
9	Honourable Luvenia Ash-Thompson	–

These were given terms of reference and are continually expected to act in the best interest of Government and for the benefit of all our people, giving all of them equal opportunity.

Closure of the University of Liberia

Because of the subversive actions of some individuals associated with the University of Liberia and their link with PAL, the group styling themselves as the Progressive Alliance of Liberia, it became necessary to close that institution on a temporary basis in order to avoid any eventuality consequent upon the tense conditions occasioned by the defiance of Government's authority. The institution as such is not being charged; neither have all the students, but we know that there are certain lawless elements within its fold.

As soon as the latter have been sufficiently identified and Government judges the unlikelihood of any further campus disturbance, timely consideration will be given to reopening the institution so that such meaningful education will be pursued as would instill patriotism and respect for constituted Authority. We are indeed hopeful that it will not be long before the institution is re-opened, for I am anxious to see young people return to their classes.

Embezzlement of public funds

The Policy of this Government in respect to those who embezzle public funds is never to shield or protect them from justice. On the contrary, once they have been discovered through the vigilance of our auditing system and the National Force for the Eradication of Corruption, they are turned over to the Courts for prosecution in strict accordance with the law. It is the courts that must do their duties and see that punishments are meted out to those who have done injustice to the Republic of Liberia.

Development in Bentol City

When by legislative enactment Bentol City was made the Capital of Montserrado County, appropriate steps were taken to give the new Capital a face-lift which would make it representative of the County. The Legislature authorized this. Accordingly, roads were built and an Administrative Building and Superintendent's residence were constructed at a cost of nearly two and quarter million dollars.

Also undertaken were the construction of a market house, experimental low-cost houses, a Youth Center and the expansion of the school facilities, raising the Junior High School to the level of a Senior High School, all at a total cost of $1,809,567.20.

Finding the natural scenic beauty of the area to be attractive for tourists, plans along this line were concluded and implemented for an artificial lake at a total cost of $235,000.00. In this public lake fish will be cultivated for the people.

Some of the citizens of the area, in response to our call to return to their homes and assist in its development, have thus gone to Bentol and are making their contributions to the development effort.

Our own modest endeavor to improve what we personally possess has been of absolutely no cost to Government; the Ministry of Public Works can bear this out. For in all sincerity, we would not attempt to betray our sacred trust, and God stands as our righteous judge.

The Guinea troops

With reference to the Guinean troops currently in Liberia, let me make it clear that we made the decision after much agonizing. My Fellow Citizens, you do not know what I went through that night but God knows. We accepted the brotherly offer of President Ahmed Sékou Touré during what appeared to have been one of our darkest hours, and at a trying moment when we were convinced that the action would help save precious human lives and property, and assist in restoring peace and order.

Nevertheless, it was only after consultation with the leaders of state in the Legislature, the National Security Council and the Chief of Staff, that we considered it in the best interest of the security of the state to accept the assistance offered. The troops came under the umbrella of our Mutual Defense Pact, and have been available; but they have never been involved in any incident. I now feel convinced that there is no further need for their presence. Accordingly, they will be returning home within the next few days.

Within the framework of the fraternal relations between Guinea and Liberia, and on the basis of an understanding between my Brother, President Touré and myself, a Contingent of our Army will before long be making a friendly visit to the Republic of Guinea and will participate in military exercises with them as well.

My Fellow Citizens, as your Captain at the helm of the Ship of State on April 14, we saw a huge iceberg, as it were, and decided to direct the course of our sailing in this manner to avoid collision. We consequently took what in our best judgement and under God's guidance, were the necessary measures, to safeguard the security of the State. I take the full responsibility for the action, under the sure conviction that it was in the best interest of the Republic of Liberia.

On balance, I am pleased to state that the Liberian Army has proved itself loyal, patriotic and in a great measure, effective. Whatever deviation that occurred on that occasion is being thoroughly investigated and appropriate action will be taken in the premises. We have had several meetings with high ranking officers of the Army as well as with non-commissioned officers and some enlisted men and many facts have been revealed of which we had no previous knowledge. We will give immediate attention to problems as we find them existing so as to occasion the needed efficiency, discipline and effectiveness in the Army and thus improve its services at all levels.

But no matter how well the Army performs its duty to the State, the fact remains that it is the people as a whole – the entire citizenry – that must defend and protect our country and the Government. I therefore call upon you, My Fellow Citizens, to shoulder this fundamental and patriotic duty of defending and preserving this our sacred heritage given to us by Almighty God.

Decision now to be made

There are a few decisions which we consider necessary to make at this time. They are as follows:

1   While we will continue to guarantee to all of our people and all persons within our borders the enjoyment of their human rights and fundamental freedom, including the Freedom of the Press, we will demand, as the occasion requires, that no one commit any infringement upon the rights of others and abuse the rights accorded them. Neither will we at any time countenance a disregard

for constituted authority, and flagrant and irresponsible defiance of law and order.

2 Government will take firm and swift action against any group or individual who, by sowing seeds of discord, disharmony and divisiveness in our Country, disturb our peace and adversely affect our development and progress.

3 Our city remains overcrowded with vagrants, citizens and aliens alike. In accordance with our vagrancy laws, immediate action will be taken to clear our city of all such persons. Those who are not citizens and who are not gainfully employed will be required to return to their homes, because we know that on that occasion, the greatest amount of the looting and destruction of property was done by foreigners and not Liberians.

4 While Government will shortly embark on measures to facilitate the entry of *bona fide* businessmen, tourists and other visiting friends, stringent measures will be taken to check illegal entrants.

5 All wayward youths of our city will shortly be removed from our streets and placed in corrective institutions. Arrangements are currently being made with Episcopal Bishop George D. Browne for the use of the Episcopal School building at Dodokeh near Pleebo in Maryland County to complement the National Center for Care, Correction and Rehabilitation of Juvenile Delinquents soon to be constructed in Careysburg. In the interim, we will endeavor to find other locations to accommodate their removal from our streets and I call upon all of our people to operate together with us in this national enterprise.

6 Government, through the Ministers of Finance, Planning and Economic Affairs and Commerce, Industry and Transportation, in collaboration with Bankers and other financiers, is studying the effects of the events of April 14 on the national economy, and in the next fortnight the public will be duly informed of our actions in the premises. I have received reliable information that the insurance companies will honour their legitimate obligations, growing out of the events of April 14. In the meanwhile, Government is determined now, more than ever before, to operate on the strictest economy.

7 I call upon Ministers of the Gospel to preach the word of God in truth and sincerity and not use the Pulpit or their sacred commission to sow seeds of disunity, disharmony, discord, confusion and divisiveness among the children of God – the People of Liberia.

8 So that high virtues and morality may be inculcated among students, I direct that the Holy Bible, the Holy Koran and such other religious codes of conduct as would be compatible with our national culture, be introduced and made required subjects to be

taught in all Public Schools; Freedom of Religion being granted to all, in their choice of religious study, in keeping with our Constitution.

9   I further direct that civics and ethics be made compulsory subjects taught in all schools – both public and private, so that patriotism and moral conduct and sound principles in living may be inculcated in the minds of our youth.

10 I direct that rigid discipline be introduced and enforced in all schools throughout the land, and all persons, students as well as professors, be prohibited from engaging in any and all activities in our institutions of learning that would tend to promote tribalism and sectionalism and cause disunity, disharmony, and divisiveness among the students and the people of Liberia.

When I spoke to the Legislature, I said there will be hard decisions to take. I am taking those decisions and as I take even harder decisions, the people of this Country will be notified.

Conclusion

My Fellow Citizens and Friends, my experience in Government has caused me to reach the unmistakable conclusion that the problems of Liberia are socio-economic in nature. Upon my assumption of the Presidency, I entertained the strong feeling that the masses of the people are anxious for more schools, roads, clinics, hospitals and such basic infrastructural facilities as water system, electricity and communication. As we faced these imperatives, these social needs indispensable to the Wholesome Functioning Society which we envisaged, we did so against the cruel realities of economic restraints.

Our complex problems can evidently not be solved by agitation but by continuing commitment, patience and perseverence and working together. Through our policy of self-reliant development the people have enthusiastically responded in an effort to minimize the restraints. We renew to them Government's appreciation for this great national service, and appeal to them not to relent in our task of nation-building. Liberia must be built by all of us so that all of us can enjoy it.

To all of the political sub-divisions of our Country, to the National Legislature, our Grand Old True Whig Party, the Militia and other men in arms, Students, Women's Organizations, Trade Unions and to all our law-abiding people at home and abroad, we gratefully and humbly acknowledge your statements and messages affirmative of your faith and confidence in our national stewardship. With such heartening, strengthening and uplifting indications and demonstrations of support, and solidarity, I invite you, all of you, the sovereign people of the Republic of Liberia, to join hands with me as we, totally involved, undertake the sacred task of national reconstruction. Let us always bear in mind the motto of the True Whig Party, 'Deeds, not Words'.

A pre-requisite to this imperative, however, is national introspection. We must examine ourselves and our entities of interaction. We must examine the structures for the implementation of policy. There must be a veritable SPIRITUAL RECONSTRUCTION, if the PHYSICAL RECONSTRUCTION is to be enduring, as it must.

All employees of the Government, at all levels, must comport themselves in a manner reflective of true and faithful servants, remembering at all times that as trustees, we are continuingly accountable to the people. Let us prove ourselves worthy servants indeed.

My Fellow Citizens, the tendency has developed among some of our people to indulge in the habit of disseminating false and misleading information about individuals in our society. This evil practice, adverse to a Wholesome Functioning Society, often takes the form of writing anonymous letters and employing fictitious names rather than patriotically reporting action or activities inimical to the national interest.

Many times people write me and sign, 'Concerned Citizen'. If you are indeed concerned, sign your authentic name.

I invite, in this public manner, responsibly-signed information on any known irregularities in the operation of Government. And I am sincere. If anyone knows something, write and sign your name and send it to me. You will see what will happen thereafter. I assure you that as much as possible confidentiality will be protected, but thorough investigation will precede any action so that there may be no violation of human rights and the innocent may be safeguarded. I cannot go out, My Fellow Citizens and Friends, and take action against anyone except there are evidences that that individual had done something worthy of such action.

Finally, the events of April 14, have indeed occasioned 'stringent tests of our faith, exacting measures of our courage; searching scrutinies of our purpose'. In availing ourselves equal to the challenge, let us fully ensure that our total response provides 'rigid determination of the dynamic strength of our will to achieve'.

Let us, therefore, in full assurance that our cause is just, calm our fears and restore confidence in ourselves and our institutions; for I remain firm in the conviction that a stronger Liberia with an even more united people will emerge from the tragedy just experienced.

Let us fervently and repentantly beseech Almighty God mercifully to forgive us individually and collectively of all and every sin we have committed, and with thanksgiving for His bountiful blessings vouchsafed unto us as a nation, and for His deliverance, rise to a newness of life.

Now, as never before, is the time for unity, cohesiveness and peace. I accordingly call upon our people to abandon hate, selfishness, greed and corruption, and let us as a united people, genuinely caring for and sharing with one another in love, operate together for our collective self-fulfillment.

In consideration of the spontaneous expression of concrete support and solidarity which we have received from our neighbours and all our foreign friends, I could not end this Address without publicly renewing particularly to President Ahmed Séku Touré and the People of Guinea, People of the Ivory Coast, our sentiments of deep gratitude and sincere appreciation on behalf of the Government and People of Liberia and in my own name.

My Dear Friends, with discipline restored to our body politic and the national spirit infused anew with an even greater sense of responsibility and commitment, let us go forth together and heal the nation's wounds. Let us reconstruct our country with faith in Almighty God and reliance on self. Above all, let us maintain at all times, one Nation, indivisible, with individual liberty and justice for all.

MAY ALMIGHTY GOD BLESS THE WORKS OF OUR HANDS AND SAVE THE REPUBLIC OF LIBERIA.

Appendix 5   Report of the Commission on National Reconstruction (Appointed by the President of Liberia – June 12, 1979)

Introduction

In a nation-wide broadcast delivered from the Centennial Memorial Pavilion on Saturday, May 5, 1979, exactly three Saturdays following the civil disturbances of April 14, 1979, the President of Liberia, Dr William R. Tolbert, Jr., announced a number of actions his Government had decided to pursue in an honest attempt to commence the process of healing the nation's wounds. (For the text of this broadcast, see Appendix 4.)

One of these actions was the constitution of a thirty-one man Commission on National Reconstruction. The President declared thus:

We remain continuingly open to new approaches. I have no monopoly over ideas; let us all join to build the new Liberia. This is why as we undertake to assess fully the implications of the events of April 14, we have decided to constitute a Commission charged with the responsibility of RECEIVING and ANALYZING suggestions from concerned citizens for the reconstruction of Liberia, and submitting recommendations for the attention of Government, and I assure you they will be given speedy attention by Government.

In faithful pursuit of the foregoing, and in order to facilitate its work, the Commission identified four principal problem areas and accordingly organized itself into four corresponding Committees. There was constituted a Suggestions Committee to receive and appropriately distribute to all subject area Committees suggestions from the people. The subject area Committees included: 1 The Socio-Political Committee (including problems relating to Education and Youth as well as Political matters); 2 The Economic/Finance/Business Committee; 3 The National Security and Preservation of the Rule of Law Committee; 4 The Long-Range Issues Committee.

There was also a Secretariat to co-ordinate the Commission's work, and a Drafting Committee.

The Commission fully recognizes not only the extreme seriousness of its undertaking, but also its inescapable responsibility before God, history and the People's Government. As such, and in consideration of our terms of reference, we have endeavored to convey the people's sentiments, for in the end, it is this quality of social control that inspires continuingly legal norms and public policy.

We approached the assignment fully cognizant of the time limitation (one month). As we progressed with our work insofar as problem identification was concerned, we reached a conclusion that, in consideration of the total situation now facing us as a people, some very serious concerns expressed by the people call forth immediate action, while others require further, more detailed and systematic study if the very roots of our problems are to be reached. We agreed that recommendations drawn from the two sets of concerns would be appropriately categorized.

The Commission emphasizes to the President the pressing need to consider the will of the people as expressed through the overwhelming flow of public sentiments ('more powerful than law'); and that prompt attention be given the people's preferences as conveyed in the recommendations. Any delay due to political considerations would not be serving well the interest of Liberia.

Fundamental Causes

The Commission sees in the Civil Disturbance of Saturday, April 14, 1979, a manifestation of serious social, economic and political problems with deep roots in our national society. These problems of justice, liberty and equity are neither exclusively the outcome of the national policies of the incumbent administration; nor yet can we convincingly characterize them as conspiratorial designs externally motivated. They are in a real sense a culmination of more than one hundred years of a national leadership that appears to have eroded its constituents' participation in a meaningful way. The surfacing of these problems which the events of April 14 occasioned could nevertheless be viewed as a consequence of the continuing decline of the quality of the social mores and principles provided for in our constitution.

Despite the fact that the Constitution guarantees to all the enjoyment of fundamental human rights, including the right to a decent standard of living, and in spite of these constitutional guarantees, there are serious ills which plague our society. A group of concerned citizens put it well when they wrote:

It is our view, based on all that we have heard and seen, that it is *economic* and *social* disparities that are at the root of present tensions. It is *not* 'Congo' versus Aboriginal, resident versus citizen, white versus black. It is simply that there are vast numbers of poor people in our society that are finding it increasingly difficult to cope.

What then has been responsible for these conditions of a widening gap between the few highly privileged and the many desperately poor, of continuing over-centralization of the decision-making process, of an unreliable national security establishment, all of this in spite of the pronouncements of our President? There are, from our analysis based on suggestions from the public, a number of contributory factors, foremost among which is a *lag in implementation* resulting from the lack of political will to execute policies and pronouncements of Government.

This problem of the lag in implementation, glaring defects in the structures of implementation, results, in the view of this Commission, from the prevailing social norms and practices which take precedence over law and public policy and which consequently render ineffectual any meaningful change. In such a situation, therefore, where progressive policies confront old structures and attitudes the result can only be progress circumvented.

Consider the following gleaned from 'suggestions' from the people.

We are committed to discipline, the rule of law and an open society, yet we seem to be afraid and apprehensive of the due process resulting from such commitments.

According to the Constitution and law, individuals are innocent of charges until proven guilty. But in practice they are presumed guilty until proven innocent.

We are committed to representative Government and a participatory system of checks and balances; why then is it so easy to get instant and unanimous votes without debate, regardless of the nature and circumstances of the issue?

Disagreement on views has been construed as destructive criticism or opposition. Freedom of speech which is encouraged by the Tolbert Administration is not an end, but an instrument to democratize the system. Yet the decision-making process of the system continues to be overly centralized.

Despite the call for 'total involvement', there remains a great gulf between the mass of the people and their political institutions.

Some social practices in Liberia create socially two worlds, of the rich and poor. And the gap continues to widen.

The Recommendations

A The Socio-Political

Within the Commission's terms of reference, we evaluated the afore-mentioned questions of equity and social justice as susceptible of adversely affecting the present and future of our country, if they are not speedily redressed.

Against this background, therefore, and based upon statements and letters ('suggestions') received from individuals from various sections of the Country, as well as its own evaluation of the situation, the Commission submits the following crucial *socio-political proposals* for immediate consideration of Government consistent with the promise made by the President in his speech of May 5, 1979:

1   On the crucial rice issue the Commission recommends the dissolution of the Rice Committee and that all interested parties be given the opportunity to import rice. This would lower the price of rice to less than the artificial official price a bag. Government's role should be to maintain standards, safety, supply, security and control of pricing in such a way that it would be compatible with the minimum wage. Government should also ensure by all forms of encouragement the domestic production of rice.

2   Over eight percent of the letters received and the people we talked to expressed concern not only for those imprisoned in connection with the April 14 incident but also about those directly responsible for the death by shooting of unarmed citizens. The Commission therefore recommends that general amnesty be granted those arrested. Such a step would help tremendously to bind the nation's wounds, promote the national image, diffuse tensions, and render more conducive the atmosphere for national reconstruction.

3   The people have suggested that the members of the Cabinet and

other officials who through their official conduct directly or indirectly contributed to the events of April 14, especially the Director of Police and the Ministers of Justice, Agriculture, Defense and Finance, stand indicted in the public eye. To restore full CREDIBILITY to the Executive Government, the Commission recommends that their official conduct in relation to the causes leading to April 14 be investigated.

4   With reference to serious conflict of interest involving Public Officials to the detriment of the struggling masses, the Commission recommends that the President appoint a Committee of Well-considered persons to prepare a *Code of Conduct*. Elements to be included in such a Code should be:
   a. That all principal Government Officials shall be required to declare their total property and cash assets before taking office and shall be fully audited before they are removed from office.
   b. With reference to the appointment of Commissioned officials of the executive and judiciary branches, Government will take the necessary measures to ensure a meaningful effectuation of the principle of advise and consent of the Senate.

5   The Commission recommends that the University of Liberia be reopened.

6   The Commission recommends that local scholarship recipients be selected by the local institutions on the basis of achievement results and the disciplines for which there is more national manpower need.

7   The Commission recommends that Government disclose any information it may have about the whereabouts of the Rev. Dr Nya K. Taryor in response to concerns expressed by some citizens, especially considering that his disappearance is related to the events of April 14.

B   *The Economic, Business and Financial*
Consequent on the Commission's assessment of the effects of the April 14 incident on the business atmosphere and the overall economy of the country, it wishes to make the following recommendations based on numerous statements and suggestions from the public, with the request that Government accord them prompt attention:

1   That Government allow businesses to make use of the lost carry-forward provision of the tax law by allowing businesses to write-off their losses over a period of five years.

2   That Government declare to local creditors debts owed by uninsured businessmen affected by the events of April 14 as 'Bad Debts' so that these creditors may write them off as such from their books.

3 That Government seek to grant where necessary assistance (for businesses that were hit) in securing long term credits to re-build their businesses. This is particularly applicable to uninsured businesses.

4 That Government seek to settle its outstanding obligation to all affected businesses.

5 That Government give very serious consideration to addressing the possible surge in unemployment that will result from the completion of certain OAU-related activities. In order to avoid the social problems that are imminent, a task force should be organized to design a program that would absorb the laid-off workers, at least during the period between August and the end of 1979.

6 The Commission recommends that the structure of wages be examined as a national priority and a policy instituted to ensure that minimum wages remain compatible with the cost of living.

7 The Commission recommends early implementation of the program of assistance for Liberian small businessmen. As a means of furthering this objective the Commission recommends the necessary measures be taken to organize immediate workshop training programs with assistance of the University of Liberia and the Institute of Public Administration.

8 The Commission sees a strong need for the enactment of a Credit Code for businesses. All persons defaulting on their business commitments should be prosecuted. To this end, it is recommended that the Ministry of Finance be made to accept personal checks, without certification and with order action to prosecute immediately anyone who presents a worthless check. This action would give confidence to the business sector, which is increasingly faced with accumulation of worthless checks.

9 The Commission recommends that Government locate a suitable area where the 'here-now' boys or petty peddlers could be taken to carry on their trade, and thus remove them from the streets where they now create social problems.

10 The Commission recommends that the Concession Investment Commission be made an independent agency of Government.

11 The Commission recommends that serious consideration be given the appointment of a Council of Economic Advisers to include individuals from the private sector.

12 Not unmindful of the many positive effects of Rally Time at an earlier stage, but moved by the people's indications that some officials of Government have exploited and abused the apparent good intent, the Commission recommends that features of Rally

Time *as an economic policy* be abandoned as there is the general feeling that this places undue burden on lower income people and is another form of the old system of *forced* contribution.

13   The Commission recommends that the requirements for establishing savings and checking accounts in Commercial banks be reviewed to bring them more into harmony with goals to encourage savings and financial intermediation and that charges for certain banking services such as certification of checks be considered for reduction.

14.   The Commission recommends that the Planning Process be rationalized with better adherence to planned programs and the Ministry of Planning and Economic Affairs made more effective in the monitoring of development projects.

15   The Commission recommends that there be a more equal balance of private sector and Government representatives on the Boards of Public Corporations and that no Minister should chair the Board of a Public Corporation.

16   The people have expressed serious concerns about monopolistic tendencies in our economy. Many have suggested that because of monopoly the rich are getting richer while the poor get poorer. Because the people desire an end to what they consider a public enemy, the Commission recommends that Government take all necessary measures to abolish monopoly.

More precisely, many letters and comments voiced serious concern about the high visibility of the President's relatives in certain business ventures, which they state impose unfair competition and create a monopoly in these areas. The Commission recommends that in the interest of our free enterprise system, the President gives serious attention to this situation.

C   *National Security and the Preservation of the Rule of Law*

1   As security concerns are central to the task of national reconstruction now at hand, and as the Commission has been informed that the national Government is also undertaking a careful analysis and review of the structure, role and efficiency of the existing Armed and Security Forces of the nation, the Commission recommends that arrangements be made for collaboration between the professional experts of the Commission and the appropriate Government Agencies.

Accordingly, we will have appended at the end of the full Report the studies (1) 'The Liberian Armed Forces And The National Crisis' and (2) 'The National Security Situation In The Light Of The

Recent Disturbance In Monrovia'. Both studies offer views that could be merged with other considerations in order to meet the requirements of more adequate national security.

2   Based on suggestions from the people, the Commission developed the definite feeling that public order must prevail within the framework of the Constitution and Laws of Liberia, as well as the Universal Declaration of Human Rights. Against this background, the Commission recommends that Government be vigilant in ensuring that all harassment, fear, intimidation and unfair imprisonment be fully guarded against so that peace and security may be enjoyed by all living withing the Republic of Liberia.

D   *General Recommendation*

Against the background of the request that the President be asked to enlarge, equip and extend the duration of the Commission to enable it accomplish Part II of its work (study of the Long-Range Issues), the Commission specifically recommends for Presidential consideration:

1   Enlargement of the Commission so that it may be nationally representative;
2   Employment of professionals to undertake basic research for the Commission:
    a) University of Liberia and Cuttington University College Personnel
    b) Others;
3   Revision of the Commission's terms of reference;
4   Duration of Commission not to exceed one calendar year.

Members of the Commission

1	Counsellor Nete Sie Brownell	Chairman
2	Counsellor Toye C. Bernard	Co-Chairman
3	Honourable Momolu Dukuly	Member
4	Honourable Henry Ford Cooper	–
5	Honourable J. Dudley Lawrence	–
6	Honourable Roland Cooper	–
7	Honourable Lawrence Morgan	–
8	Honourable Albert T. White	–
9	Dr Christian Baker	–
10	Mr Richmond Draper	–
11	Dr Flomo Stevens	–
12	Mrs Corina Van Ee	–
13	Dr Patrick L.N. Seyon	–

14	Bishop George D. Browne	Member
15	Mrs Sophie Dunbar	–
16	General Benyan Kesselly	–
17	Father Edward G.W. King	–
18	Honourable Nathaniel Baker	–
19	Professor Abraham James	–
20	Counsellor Robert Azango	–
21	Honourable Elizabeth Collins	–
22	Honourable Luvenia Ash-Thompson	–
23	Mr John Scotland	–
24	Honourable George Flama Sherman	–
25	Honourable Ellen Johnson-Sirleaf	–
26	Honourable David Farhat	–
27	Honourable Samuel Greene	–
28	Dr Stephen Yekeson	–
29	Mr Roland Dahn	–
30	Miss Massa Craytor	–
31	Dr D. Elwood Dunn	–

Addendum   *The Long-Range Issues Identified*

A   *Socio-Political*
  1   Reform of the True Whig Party
  2   Freedom of Association
  3   A National Youth Service Corps
  4   Required 'intern' Service for all College & University graduates
  5   A Liberian Research Association for Socio-Economic Development
  6   Review of Statute for Demonstration
  7   Review of Machinery and Operation of National Government
  8   Land Tenure
  9   Exercising the Right of Eminent Domain
 10   Review of Present Laws on Suits And Claims Against the State
 11   Implementation of The Due Process of Law Provision.

B   *Economic Business and Financial*
  1   Raising the Minimum Wage
  2   Making such Banks as the Development Bank and the Housing Bank more responsive to needs of the economy
  3   Transportation needs
  4   Housing needs
  5   Review of Taxes

Appendix 6   Report of the Committee to Devise a Code of Conduct for Public Officials

In early August, 1979, President William R. Tolbert, Jr. appointed a 'Committee to Devise a Code of Conduct for Public Officials'. This was in response to one of the recommendations made by the Commission on National Reconstruction. The President's reaction, made known in his broadcast to the Nation on June 26, 1979, was that 'Government accepts the *idea*, and will give timely attention thereto'.

The Committee appointed was composed of the following persons:

Hon. C. Cecil Dennis, Jr.
Bishop Roland J. Payne
Justice Angie Brooks-Randolph
Bishop Michael Kpakala Francis
Dr Doris Banks-Henries
Hon. Edward B. Kesselly
Dr J. Rudolph Grimes (Chairman)

Subsequently, Hon. Andrew H. Butler, Jr. was appointed Secretary of the Committee.

The Committee met and decided to request comments from citizens throughout the country as well as from professional and social organizations; and also agreed to undertake research to find out how other countries had handled the matter of conflict of interest in Government.

After several meetings of the Committee and the receipt of comments from the general public and a limited number of professional organizations as well as the receipt of documents from a few Governments, the Committee has decided to formulate and submit a report.

The Committee wishes first to emphasize that a Code of Conduct for Public Officials, if it is to be meaningful, cannot be a one-shot affair, nor can it be all-embracing. The world in which we live is constantly changing with the development of new circumstances and new problems. Therefore any Code of Conduct must be kept under continuous review and must also be made flexible by the issuance of rules and regulations as new circumstances and new problems warrant. In consequence of this the Committee's report may, to some extent, be general; but it will allow for the issuance of rules and regulations from time to time whenever the situations may arise.

The Committee recognizes that, in relation to a Code of Conduct, there are two basic concepts, coequal in importance, if the conduct and functions of Government are to meet the highest possible standards of efficiency, and simultaneously win the confidence and respect of the citizens in their Government. They are:

1 The ethical standards of the Government should be such as to make the actions of Government, as far as humanly possible, beyond reproach; and
2 The Government should be in a position to obtain and hold qualified personnel in order to cope with the complex problems with which Government has to deal.

The Committee is aware that, in order to attain these objectives, it is very important for Government to deal with what is generally termed 'Conflict of Interest'. Nevertheless, it is a term not easy to define. One definition which has been offered is interest incompatible with the interest of Government, and outside the official line of duties which tend to influence the judgement of Public Officials for personal gain. Some regard conflict of interest as anything which savors of corruption in Government.

The Committee believes that there are two basic interests of a Government employee/official that should not clash. If they do there is a serious conflict of interest. The first is the interest of the employee/official in the proper discharge of his duties. In this there is also a public interest. The second is the interest of the employee/official in his private economic matters.

Thus, whenever possible, the employee/official should not be placed in a situation or a position where the temptation exists for him to place his personal economic interest over and above the interest of Government; or in a situation where the public can develop reasonable suspicions that the private economic interests of the employee/official are being advanced at the expense of the public interest.

In short, Government employees/officials should be independent, objective and impartial. Government has an obligation to its citizenry not to permit public office to be used for personal gain, especially at the expense of the public interest. It is only on this basis that the citizens and residents of the country can develop and maintain confidence and respect in the integrity of the Government; and also develop credibility in the employees/officials of the Government.

A general theory has been advanced that a corrupt Government is an inefficient Government and the Committee expresses the opinion that this theory has much merit.

Hence, the Committee feels that there are three principal kinds of misconduct of employees/officials which should, as far as possible, be avoided or prevented. They are:

1 Government employees/officials should not be permitted to use Government to their special advantage or to the special advantage of

any entity on the outside in which they have a personal economic interest.

2 Government employees/officials should not be permitted to assist individuals or entities on the outside where the latter are seeking to move or influence Government action to their special advantage against the public interest.

3 Government employees/officials should not be allowed to use their position/office as a source of power or of confidential information for purposes of advancing their personal economic interests.

The Committee wishes to observe that, in the matter of conflict of interest, the President has to play an important or a key role since the conflict of interest problem seems to be a day-to-day problem. He can exercise this role, in our opinion, both by example and also by taking prompt and effective measures to curb, check or arrest potential or actual conflicts whenever they arise in Government as well as by taking measured punitive action in serious cases.

With this background and in this perspective, the Committee respectfully submits, for careful consideration of the President and of the Government, the following recommendations:

1 There should be enacted by the Legislature as early as possible a statute to deal with the problems of Government ethics, with appropriate and fair procedures for enforcement and proper penalties for violations since this would have the effect of probably heading off evils before they occur, especially if the statute is enforced.

2 The statute should provide for a special office, as a co-ordinating mechanism, that might lend guidance on, and give answers to, questions which arise affecting probity in Government, and that could also prepare and develop general and special regulations on conflict of interest problems for promulgation by the President.

In each Ministry and/or Agency of Government, including Public Corporations, there should be an office where administrative regulations can be drafted on the proper conduct of employees/officials for issuance by the Minister or the Head of Agency or the Managing Director in furtherance of the statute or the regulations promulgated by the President. It could be added that such regulations of Ministries or Agencies or Public Corporations be approved by the President before becoming effective.

3 The statute and the general regulations should prohibit *all* employees/officials of Government from receiving, accepting, soliciting or seeking gifts or gratuities or anything of economic value other than compensation from the Republic of Liberia for or in

consideration of personal services rendered or to be rendered to or for the Republic of Liberia, or to any person during the term of his employment by Government unless such services are not within the course of his Governmental duties.

The statute should also prohibit Government employees/officials from receiving, accepting, soliciting or seeking anything of economic value as a gift, gratuity or favor from any person if such employees/officials have reason to believe, or the circumstances or situations are such that would lead a reasonable person to believe, that the donor would not make the gift or gratuity or do the favor but for the position or office of such employees/officials within the Government.

The prohibition should be extended to include gifts, gratuities or favors to spouses, parents, children and close relatives of the employees/officials if there is the least possibility of implying, suspecting, or deducing that such gift, gratuity or favor is being made or done with the intent of influencing the actions of the employees/officials.

The statute should, in addition, include a prohibition against the making by individuals, firms, companies or any legal entity of gifts to, the offering of gratuities to, or the doing of favors for, any Government employee/official for acts done in the course of their employment or with intent to influence the action of such employee/official.

The statute should further make it unlawful for individuals, firms, companies or any legal entity to make gifts to, to offer gratuities to, or to do favors for, spouses, parents, children or close relatives of employees/ officials for acts done in the course of their employment or with intent to influence the action of such employees/officials.

Provision should be made as to how gifts when made or gratuities when given, should be handled especially when, for diplomatic or other tangible reasons, it might be impolite or discourteous to refuse them. In this connection consideration might be given to putting limits to the value of permissible gifts.

4   The statute should prohibit employees/officials from taking outside employment where it conflicts with their official duties or where it is incompatible with their positions; and should also prohibit them from receiving outside compensation in connection with their official services. The public, including firms, companies or any legal entities, should be also prohibited from making any contribution to, or supplement to, the salary of any employee/official for services performed by him for the Government.

It will be necessary to outline clearly some exceptions by general regulation if the Government adopts the policy of employing people for special duties without compensating them or if such employment is for a limited period of time.

5   The statute should prohibit the use of, or divulging of, information, confidential or otherwise, obtained in the course of employment, for personal economic benefit or for the economic benefit of employees/officials, their spouses, parents, children, close relatives or personal friends.

6   As personal property holdings sometimes create conflict of interest situations, the statute should forbid the acquisition of financial interests that may result in conflict between the private interests of the employee/official and his official duties.

   The Committee recognizes that this may be a very difficult and delicate matter, but the situation may be eased, to some extent, by providing for disqualification of the employee/official in the handling of matters in which he, his spouse, parents, children or close relatives may have personal financial interests, so that someone else in the Ministry or Agency can make the recommendation or the decision on the particular matter.

7   The statute should prohibit Government employees/officials from negotiating or awarding directly or indirectly any contracts for goods and services or special privileges such as tax exemptions or incentives to any business in which said employees/officials, their spouses, children or any close relatives may have a financial interest.

8   There should be a provision in the statute concerning post-employment relations of former employees/officials with a Ministry or Agency for a certain period of time. This will prevent the individual from handling the matter from both sides and also prevent undue influence over the actions and activities of employees/officials with whom the individuals may have collaborated during their term of employment.

9   The statute should prohibit all elected and appointed officials from engaging either directly or indirectly in the practice of law. This would prohibit all legislators and lawyers employed in Government from being retained by concessionaires, business houses or other clients while they have seats in the Legislature or positions in Government.

10   The statute should make it illegal for Government employees/officials, who have responsibilities or duties either for regulating or enforcing regulations in certain fields, from engaging in private business in the same field. This would mean that policemen or

police officers and their spouses would not be permitted to engage in public or commercial transport; Government employed lawyers would not be permitted to be members of law firms; Government employed doctors, dentists, pharmacists, nurses, technicians would not be permitted to engage in private practice or operate pharmacies; Government employed engineers would not be permitted to operate or participate in private engineering firms or companies; etc.

Whatever exceptions are permitted should be clearly outlined in regulations, but the regulations should ensure that there are no conflicts between the permitted actions and the Governmental duties of those involved. Moreover, the permitted actions should foreclose reasonable doubts and avoid legitimate suspicions about the potential and actual conflicts of interests in the given situations.

11 The statute should provide for full disclosure of all assets and liabilities at the time of election or appointment of *all* elected officials, cabinet ministers, their deputies and assistants and all judicial officials as well as at the time of retirement, removal or other form of withdrawal from office. It will be necessary for Government to determine whether such disclosures should be made public, wholly or partially.

The Committee suggests that these disclosures should be kept by an Agency to be designated by the statute to be made available for legitimate reasons.

12 The statute should make it illegal for any employee/official to keep ill-gotten gains and provide appropriate legal procedures for the Ministry of Justice to take action to recover such ill-gotten gains for the benefit of Government.

13 Payments received, fees obtained, or reductions in contract prices (discounts) granted on any Government transaction are properly the property of the Government. Therefore authorization should be given and procedure outlined to enable Government to recover such payments, fees or other things of economic value if they are not reported to Government by the employees/officials.

14 Appropriate sanctions should be provided in the statute to be imposed for all false information given under the statute and for all violations of provisions of the statute. Proper procedures for enforcement should be outlined taking into due consideration the rights provided by the Constitution of the Republic of Liberia to accused persons.

On the basis of letters and information received and made available to the Committee, there are a few suggestions we are submitting that need not necessarily be included in a statute.

There seems to be much concern about public servants being dismissed from public office for cause and within a brief period thereafter they are re-employed in responsible positions, sometimes with more responsibility and perquisites than they had before. The feeling of the public is that this encourages corruption. It might be helpful, in cases of dismissals for such cause, that the charges be clearly published and, if the individual is exonerated or vindicated, such exoneration or vindication should also be made public. A constructive balance should be sought in matters of this kind.

Proper rules and regulations should be established for the award of contracts and for Government purchases; and contracts, awards and purchases for Government should be monitored on a regular basis by an appropriate agency to ensure that the rules and regulations are being adhered to and are being complied with. In case of violations of the rules or regulations, the necessary corrective measures should be taken including sanctions when appropriate. Such rules and regulations should be extended to all Public Corporations where Government has the majority interest.

In addition, regular audits should be conducted of all Government Ministries, Agencies and Public Corporations with the reports being made public so that corrective measures can be instituted and penalties meted out to all who have violated laws or negligently or criminally handled public funds.

Such measures, in the opinion of the Committee, may reduce unsavory rumors and inspire more confidence in Government operations, activities and actions.

The tax laws of the country should be fairly and equitably enforced so that all persons who should pay taxes do in fact pay them. Further, elected and appointed officials should not be qualified to take office without a tax clearance from the Ministry of Finance indicating that all of their tax obligations have been met.

In order to effectuate these recommendations, the Committee wishes to observe that consideration be given to strengthening the Civil Service Agency so that appointments to the classified service will clearly be on the basis of merit, and promotions within the service can be handled also on the basis of merit. Remuneration of public employees/officials should be subject to continual review so that compensation is adequate; and well defined provisions for retirement with fair and adequate benefits be made.

In concluding, the members of the Committee wish to emphasize, once again, that ethics in Government must be kept continually and perpetually under review, the appropriate adjustments and revisions made from time to time in keeping with developments in our changing society.

The members of the Committee individually as well as collectively express appreciation to you, Mr President, for having selected us to undertake this important and delicate task; and we also express our strong belief that acceptance and implementation of these recommendations contained herein will be a continuing process in winning the confidence of the people in the integrity of their Government.

Respectfully submitted
C. Cecil Dennis, Jr. (*See Reservation attached as Annex I*)
Roland J. Payne
Angie Brooks-Randolph
Michael Kpakala Francis
Edward B. Kesselly
J. Rudolph Grimes, *Chairman*

Monrovia, January 3, 1980
NB Because of illness and absence from the country Dr Doris Banks-Henries did not participate in the deliberations of the Committee.

Annex I   Reservation to Paragraph 9 of the Report by Hon. C. Cecil Dennis, Jr., Member of the Committee

While I have no difficulty in agreeing with the proposal for a prohibition against *appointed* officials of Government engaging in the private practice of law, as a step toward minimizing the problems of conflict of interest and corruption among Government officials, nevertheless, I am of the conviction that such blanket prohibition should not apply to members of the *Legislature*. With respect to members of the Legislature, I feel that a distinction could be made between the category of clients they represent. While a prohibition against members of the Legislature who are lawyers representing concessionaires, business houses, firms, and companies is justified on the ground that there exists an apparent suspicion of probable conflict of interest, I feel that a Legislator should not be prohibited from rendering assistance to his constituents, (natural and not corporate, but excluding eleemosynary institutions) whether such assistance is of a legal nature or otherwise, especially those, for example, who might be in need of legal assistance but without means of affording it. I view this an obligation of a Legislator particularly to his constituents.

This reservation, nevertheless, is not intended to, nor should it be interpreted in any form or manner to the prejudice of the general intent and purpose of paragraph 9 of this Report.

Appendix 7 Report of the Special Task Force on Party Reform Submitted at the First Quadrennial Congress of the True Whig Party of Liberia, Lower Buchanan, Grand Bassa County, Republic of Liberia, October 24–26, 1979

Chapter One: Introduction

The Standard-Bearer of the True Whig Party of Liberia, Dr William R. Tolbert, Jr., convened a meeting of partisans in Bentol City, Montserrado County, on 13th October, 1979.

In uplifting and inspiring remarks, he indicated that he perceived a need for the Party to examine itself in order to determine whether it was capable of meeting the challenges and rising to the needs of a changing Liberian and world society. The Standard-Bearer averred that although the True Whig Party could be proud of its enviable record of 110 unbroken years of good and stable government, he sensed that there was now a necessity to make the Party more responsive to the needs and aspirations of the people of Liberia which it was instituted to serve. He then invited the assembled partisans to express their views and advance suggestions as to how this could be effectively achieved.

There followed much fruitful discussion during which many partisans expressed themselves frankly and forthrightly, putting forth many constructive and objective suggestions which in large measure called for fundamental changes in the structure and practices of the Party. A lively dialogue ensued, which evolved a consensus that the initiative of the Standard-Bearer was welcome and timely, and that these changes, if implemented, would result in a Party that was stronger, more vigorous, and better prepared to meet the challenges of the present and the vagaries and uncertainties of the future.

The Standard-Bearer then appointed a twenty-seven (27) man *Special Task Force*, and presented it with terms of reference as follows:

> Using the many suggestions for reforming the True Whig Party as advanced by Partisans during the meeting in Bentol on October 13, 1979, the Task Force will supplement those suggestions with its own ideas and solicit views from others as time will permit. From this exercise, recommendations will be drawn to be laid before the Party Congress in Grand Bassa County for timely consideration.

Outreach Effort

With only two weeks in which to accomplish its task, the Task Force nevertheless decided that it was vital to consult, as much as possible, a cross section of Liberians in each of the political sub-divisions of the Country. Subsequently, an Outreach Committee was established and an appropriate program was designed and successfully implemented which enabled members of the Task Force to directly contact hundreds of Liberians in each of the nine Counties and six Territories of Liberia, as set out more fully in the schedule below:

County or Territory	City or Town	Number of Persons Directly Contacted By Task Force
Bong	Gbarnga	100
Bassa	Buchanan	52
Cape Mount	Robertsport	250
Grand Gedeh	Zwedru	520
Lofa	Voinjama	291
Maryland	Harper	200
Montserrado	Monrovia	400
Nimba	Sanniquellie	200
Sinoe	Greenville	640
Bomi	Tubmanburg	200
Gibi	Kakata & Harbel Area	200
Kru Coast	Grandcess	100
Marshall	Marshall City	100
Rivercess	Rivercess City	86
Sasstown	Sasstown City	100
Total:		3,439

Contact in all the Counties and Territories listed above was by way of mass meetings, except for Monrovia, where partisans came individually over the course of three days to give their views and opinions. Additionally, several dozen written submissions were received from concerned partisans and citizens from many places in Liberia.

We consider it necessary to report here that all these meetings and contacts matched and indeed rivalled the Bentol meeting in eager enthusiasm, refreshing candor, and in earnest yearning for change, relevance, and responsiveness in the Party. Hundreds of Liberians spoke freely and frankly about the urgent need for revitalization, and a re-markable similarity was revealed in the views held by all – both urban and rural dwellers, educated and uneducated, men and women, and the young and old alike.

We sensed an air of relief as the people, as though for the first time, found an avenue through which they could be vocal about issues affecting their activities as partisans. It seemed as if a wave of disenchantment and an air of disillusionment had engulfed the people in their masses, due mainly to deficiencies and malpractices of the Party which they did not hesitate to articulate. The overwhelming feeling which we perceived all over the country is that we need a drastic overhauling of not only the Party, but the entire national fabric.

However, this was not mere hopeless despair. The vast majority felt that the situation could be reversed, and the damage repaired, if only the True Whig Party was prepared to change. There was a feeling that this task of revision and re-construction should begin *now*, and that as a people and a Party, we are quite capable of doing the job ourselves.

Nevertheless, there was deep-seated suspicion and strong skepticism as to the willingness and sincerity of the Party leaders to commit the Party to genuine and meaningful change in the light of existing reality.

In summary, it may be said that the overwhelming majority of opinion expressed the need for:

1   A restructuring of the Party Secretariat and organizations so as to make them more effective and responsive;
2   A change of personnel presently occupying certain Party positions in order to ensure a more vigorous implementation of Party policies and programs through full-time Party leaders;
3   A re-vamping of Party election procedures such that those elected will represent the true choice of the electorate, without the undue influence of the national or local Party leaders; and
4   A more highly visible and helpful Party, especially at the grass-roots level, which will encourage the active participation of the masses in Party affairs, and which will educate its partisans about its goals, aims, objectives and achievements.

In our work we have taken account of all of the views expressed by those who so kindly and willingly participated in this exercise. We have supplemented these with our own which, incidentally, were not substantially different, and have attempted to faithfully reflect those views in this Report.

At the beginning of each of the following Chapters, we have set out without comment a reasonable sample of views received on the subject of the particular Chapter. We then go on to place these in some perspective and logical order. Finally, in keeping with our terms of reference, we then submit for your timely consideration those recommendations which we, in our best judgement, consider as measures which, if implemented, will place our Party in a position to provide more effective, responsible, representative, and relevant leadership to our people and beloved country now and in the years to come.

In conclusion, we are grateful for the opportunity afforded us to perform this partisan task. We fully appreciate and accept the shortcomings of this Report. However, we hope that you will find it useful in some manner, no matter how limited. For us, it has been a labour of love, a privileged service, and a patriotic duty.

Chapter Two: Organizational and personnel changes

Summary of suggestions received

1 The National Chairman of the Party and all County and Territorial Chairmen should be employed on a full-time basis.
2 Abolish the elective positions of Assistant General Secretaries. Professionally qualified and competent staff should be hired instead.
3 Local Party headquarters should be established in each political subdivision of Liberia, where partisans can meet Party officials and obtain information on the Party.
4 The incumbent General Secretary should be retired.
5 Certain Party officials who seem to be impeding the progress of the Party especially at the local level should be dismissed.
6 A Comptroller should be added to the Secretariat.
7 The National Chairman and General Secretary should not attend Cabinet meetings.
8 True Whig Party officials should not have official license plates.
9 An ombudsman or grievance committee should be created in the Party where grievances of partisans can be dealt with.

Many partisans seem to share the view that there exists a large gap between the Party and its partisans. Some of them attributed this to the limited size and low level of professionalism of the Secretariat, which prevents it from effectively implementing the platform, policies and programs of the Party. Others held the view that this problem was exacerbated by the loose organization of the Party at the County and local levels, and the lack of an effective liason between the national and local party officers. Partisans told of complaints which went unattended, and letters which were often ignored.

We were startled by the fact that nearly every partisan with whom we spoke blamed the incumbent General Secretary for the general malaise and lethargy with which the Party seems to be chronically afflicted. The call for his retirement was virtually unanimous.

Of course, we are aware that the problems of the Party are much too numerous and complex to be solved or solvable by the simple expedient of changing a few individuals. Nevertheless, we are also aware of the potency of perceptions and symbols in politics, and we must not ignore the implications or ramifications of the strength and depth of conviction with which our sample almost universally expressed this view.

Moreover, many partisans bitterly called for the removal from office of several local party officials whom they felt were imposed upon them, who are by their activities, and in some instances by their prolonged absence from the locality, detrimentally affecting the image of the Party and alienating its members.

Additionally, it was felt that if the Party is to move vigorously and forcefully meet existing challenges, it must be led, as a matter of urgent priority, by officials who can devote their full time and energies to managing the Party's affairs. These leaders, managers, and political technicians should be competent, qualified and salaried professionals who will be able to control and direct the new thrust and dynamism of the Party into more fruitful channels of political and social achievement.

Suggestions and opinions were also received which tended to indicate that many partisans would prefer to see the separation of Government and Party emphasized by cessation of the practice whereby senior party officials are treated as officials of the Government, with privileges such as attendance at Cabinet meetings, official license plates and police protection.

Recommendations

In view of the foregoing, your Task Force recommends as follows:

Organizational changes

1 *The National Chairman* of the Party should be a full-time, salaried official who will be Chief Executive of the Party. He should be responsible for formulating policy guidelines in consultation with the National Standard Bearer, and monitoring the over-all direction and relevance of the Party to the needs of the people of Liberia. He shall represent the Party at home and abroad, and shall be Chairman of the Executive Committee.

2 *The General Secretary* should be the Chief Administrator of the General Secretariat, and should coordinate the Party's programs and projects on the national level and on the local level through the various Assistant General Secretaries. He should be a planner, organizer, and implementer who will travel regularly around the

country to supervise and give assistance to the programs and projects of the local parties, and thereby keep the national party fully abreast of local activities, and vice versa.

3   *Assistant General Secretaries.* The elective positions for Assistant General Secretaries should be abolished, and replaced by three salaried Assistant General Secretaries who shall be technically competent and professionally qualified. They should be designated in the following manner and have responsibility for the following functions.

a. *Assistant General Secretary for Public Affairs.* He shall be responsible for the proper projection of the Party's image through the publication of literature such as magazines, pamphlets, and newspapers, as well as through the use of radio, television, mass meetings and other communication media. All publicity, publications, and pronouncements of the party should be channeled to the public through the Assistant General Secretary for Public Affairs.

b. *Assistant General Secretary for Political Affairs.* He shall be responsible for the political socialization of the party members and the public. He shall work closely with the Public Affairs Bureau of the Party in the political mobilization of the masses, and shall address his efforts in this regard specificially to partisans, youth and student groups, women, labor unions, and rural and urban groups such as Marketing Associations, Farmers' Cooperatives, etc. Additionally, he shall co-ordinate political activities of the local parties, and shall be the functional link between the local parties and the General Secretariat.

c. *Assistant General Secretary for Research and Planning.* He shall devise and propose strategic political plans for the party. In conjunction with the Public Affairs and the Political Affairs Bureaux, the Research and Strategy Bureau shall engage in research and produce and maintain statistical data for the Party. He shall keep the Party abreast of current trends in public opinion, attitudes and reactions to the Party's plans and policies and recommend strategic responses in the best interest of the Party.

4   *The Comptroller.* If the First Quadrennial Congress gives new impetus and purposefulness to the Party and thereby widens its scope of activities, then there will be an increase in the number and complexity of financial transactions which the Party will undertake. It will therefore be necessary to employ a competent, professionally-qualified and experienced accountant as Comptroller within the Secretariat, in order to ensure efficient and accurate accounting and recording of the Party's financial affairs.

5   All County and Territorial Chairmen and Secretaries should be full-time, salaried employees of the Party, and should be per-

manently resident in their respective localities as a prerequisite for election.

6 Whilst recognizing and accepting that it is a matter of Presidential prerogative as to who may attend meetings of the Cabinet, we recommend that the practice of *regular* attendance by the National Chairman and General Secretary at such meetings be discontinued, as it only serves to further obscure the fine but definite line of demarcation which should properly and necessarily exist between the Party and the Government.

7 For the same reason indicated immediately above, officials of the Party should not be entitled to the use of official license plates on their cars, as they are *not* officials of the Government.

8 The policy already under way of establishing and constructing Party headquarters in each and every major political sub-division of Liberia should be vigorously continued.

Personnel Changes

9 We recommend that the First Quadrennial Congress should fix the term of office of all elected Party officials, except that of the Standard Bearer, at four (4) years each, in order to achieve a greater degree of accountability and responsiveness to the electorate on the part of incumbents.

10 We further recommend that election and appointment (as the case may be) of national officers of the Party be undertaken as part of the business of the First Quadrennial Congress.

11 We also recommend that, in the interest of the Party, the incumbent General Secretary should not be returned, and that a dynamic, active, and forceful partisan be elected at this Congress to fill the position.

12 A decision should be made at this Congress that County and Territorial conventions be organized and held in all counties and territories within three (3) months after the end of this Congress for the election of County and Territorial Chairman and Secretaries. Rules and procedures for the selection of delegates, the eligibility requirements and nomination of candidates, and convention voting procedures should be compiled, published and distributed well in advance of such elections.

Chapter Three: Internal democracy

Summary of suggestions received

1 End the domination of the Party by a hierarchy. This excludes partisans from fully participating in Party deliberations and election of officials.

2   The caucus as is presently conducted excludes full partisan participation.
3   Candidates pre-selected by only Party officials should not be imposed on the people in any given election.
4   Inputs from ordinary partisans should be encouraged for Party operations and deliberations.
5   Complete domination by a few elder statesmen should be abolished.
6   The Party must meet the needs of the masses, if it is to be identified with its policies and programs.
7   Party leadership should be broadened beyond Monrovia and Montserrado County.
8   Utilize the primary system for election of True Whig Party nominees for the Legislature and for local elective offices, as well as for convention delegates.
9   Make more effective use of the convention at both the national and county level for the election of Party officers and the determination of Party policies.
10 Party should not request popular candidates for party nomination to stand aside or 'ground arms' for any reason.

An important concern expressed to the Special Task Force almost universally by all those with whom its members came into contact is that the True Whig Party is not sufficiently democratic in the selection of its officers and nominees at both the local and the national levels.

It would appear that considerable frustration has been engendered by procedural abuses and high-handedness on the part of national and local caucuses which have made it virtually impossible for the rank-and-file of the True Whig Party to participate in the decision-making processes of the Party.... The consensus is that the nominating and selection process, and indeed the True Whig Party itself, is firmly entrenched in the hands of a few select, and internally appointed, and self perpetuating elder statemen, most of whom come from one main geographical subdivision, ie Montserrado County.

Many partisans indicated that once this group of Party leaders had made a decision as to nominee, candidate, or policy, they seemed to assume that all partisans would be in accord, and would accordingly confirm their actions and endorse the person or persons so selected. The professed end result of this process seems to be the achievement of a certain 'unity' in the Party which is supposed to strengthen it. However, it is a unity which is realized only in the minds of the decision-makers. At best, it is illusory, and at worst, it produces only disillusionment, frustration, and resentment in those partisans who see such heavy-handedness as a denial of their freedom to choose and an abnegation of their right to participate. As a result, many of them have become sympathetic to causes and groups expressedly committed to the destruction of the True Whig Party. In short, this striving for an artificial unity serves to weaken, rather than to strengthen the Party.

There is therefore a compelling need for the acceptance and efficient management of diversity within the framework of unity, to relate the parochial to the national, and to reconcile a vocal and vigorous individualism with a wider spirit of community and Party.

It is hoped that out of this exercise of the right of free speech on the part of citizens, and the willingness to change on the part of the existing Party machinery, there will emerge a revitalized Party that is both flexible and democratic; the credibility of which will endure that the unity and strength of those who comprise its rank and file will prevail.

The selection of nominees and candidates by inner caucuses must therefore be abandoned. The growing egalitarianism of today views the caucus as lending itself to bargains and deals of the few, leaving out the many who prefer the politics of choice.

It is a practice too aristocratic and undemocratic for this enlightened age. It negates the concept of the True Whig Party as a mass-based party, and isolates it from its constituencies.

As the only existing political party in Liberia, it is incumbent upon the True Whig Party to democratize its organizations and procedures for, so long as it continues to win at the polls, it is the only route by which the people can select their leaders and representatives. In such a situation, the formulating of the Party's program should not be regarded as the prerogative of the Party leaders alone, but as that of its representatives from throughout the Party's structure, from the grass roots up – from the smallest village to the largest and most sophisticated cities. This *must* be so. Changes in the Party system must come from the constituency level, as Party government cannot be fully effective without making nominations in the constituencies sufficiently reflective of the majority of the particular constituents. The greatest advantage that can be expected to accrue from this approach is that it will aid in making the political system free, open, and responsive to a greater variety of people and groups in the electorate.

There exists in Liberia today a larger number of articulate, vocal, and well-motivated persons who appear to be more interested in politics than ever before. They are interested in a party organization which will permit them to participate in an active and satisfying way. Such participation can be fostered through the revamping of Party institutions such as the Convention; through the adoption of new procedures such as primaries which are properly organized and conducted, with a view to providing members of the True Whig Party with more meaningful activity in every aspect of party life. These active partisans can thus help to shape and influence Party policy and also choose and work for the selection of fellow partisans who will carry out Party policies at the local and national levels, and in government, if victorious. This kind of party would truly make the people a sovereign people, and would give meaning and impact to a slogan that may well be adopted to characterize the Party's main thrust in the next decade: BRINGING THE PARTY TO THE PEOPLE AND THE PEOPLE TO THE PARTY. We must do our utmost to ensure that MASS PARTICIPATION is the PRIMARY criterion of the True Whig Party for the 80s and beyond.

Recommendations of the Task Force
To this end, we would make the following recommendations:
1) Nomination
Nomination of Party nominees for elective office and 60% of delegates for County and National Convention should be determined by direct closed primaries conducted by secret ballot.

We believe that the direct closed primary affords the constituent partisan the best opportunity for active participation in the affairs of the Party. The present practice is essentially an indirect closed primary, in which candidates for elective office either offer themselves or are petitioned at the ward level by way of resolution to run for office. The candidate then tries to get as many endorsements as possible for the other wards in his electoral district. All candidates then present these at the local caucus, where the candidate with the highest number of resolutions and endorsements is selected as the Party's nominee for the particular position.

In some places, especially in the rural areas, where partisans may not be able to differentiate their signatures on a resolution or endorsement, the primary is more direct, in that partisans are made to line up behind the respective candidates of their choice. In this case, the candidate with the highest number of votes is endorsed by the ward, district or Party.

Neither of these systems is satisfactory. In the case of the former, resolutions and endorsements are too susceptible to easy manipulation by ward and district chairmen. Also, no regard is given to the popular vote – it matters not that the successful candidate may not have as many signatures of partisans on his resolutions and endorsements as the loser – only that he must have more 'political actions', which is the generic reference which the Party ascribes to resolutions and endorsements.

Moreover, even where a candidate may have the highest number of political actions, there are numerous instances where that candidate, although successful by the Party's own practices, is asked by the Party bosses to 'ground arms' for one reason or the other. Often times, these reasons have to do with the rotation of the particular electoral district (e.g. left bank/right bank) or because of prior commitments which the Party has made to incumbents (the 2-term rule).

In the latter case of the more direct stand-in-line voting, the major drawback is that the partisans publicly indicate their choice of candidate, and run the risk either of intimidation prior to voting, or recriminations thereafter.

We are recommending direct closed primaries by secret ballot because we feel that there are several benefits to be derived under this system, besides the more obvious ones of increased democratization and the elimination of the present methods.

Firstly, all partisans participating in properly conducted primaries will gain experience and knowledge of the electoral process. They will become familiar with the marking of ballots, the location of polling booths, and in general become acclimatized to the entire atmosphere, meaning and procedures attendant upon the exercise of the right of franchise.

Secondly, the Party will have an opportunity to test and evaluate the strength of its organizational skills and abilities. Also, because it is a closed primary where voters will have to indicate their party membership before voting, either by prior registration or by show of membership cards at polling booths, the Party will be able to determine, and appreciate, its numerical support in each area locally, as well as nationally.

Thirdly, the proper conduct of primaries will lend validity to the eventual endorsement of the ultimate winner of single-party elections because this will provide the opportunity for those partisans who did not previously support that candidate to endorse him or her during the statutory elections.

We also feel that as many aspirants to office as so desire should be allowed to declare and stand in the first round of primaries, and that eventually the candidate in each primary with the highest number of votes should then participate in a run-off to determine the ultimate winner.

We have suggested *supra* that 60% of convention delegates allotted to each area should also be elected by primary – of course without benefit of run-off. We feel that 40% of the allotted number from each area should be reserved to accommodate ex-officio delegates such as Party officials and members of the National and Adminstrative and Executive Committees, which include members of the Cabinet, the Legislature, and County Territorial Chairman and Secretaries.

2) *Conventions*

Election of Party officials (including the Presidential and Vice Presidential candidates) at both the national and local levels as well as adoption of Party platforms, should be by open voting of delegates at conventions and national congresses. However, the convention as presently structured is inadequate and the rules are too loosely structured and ambiguous to assure that this major responsibility is executed in a manner that is both democratic and resistant to manipulation.

It is therefore recommended that a Special Commission on Convention Re-organization and Modernization be established to ensure that all subsequent county and national conventions will be able to achieve the following:

1 Oversee the long-term government and health of the TWP at both county and national levels;
2 Open the entire convention process to greater partisan understanding and delegate participation.
3 Establish and publish a set of guidelines as to its credentials, criteria and its management, voting, recording and reporting procedures.

Chapter Four: Improving Party's image

Summary of suggestions received
1 Designate specific officials to serve as spokesmen of the Party.
2 Improve the moral standard of the True Whig Party choices of candidates for elective offices through the elimination of candidates convicted of corruption.
3 The True Whig Party should establish information centers throughout the nation, publicize its election and nomination procedures and policies and train selected individuals from each area of the county through scholarship to return to their areas for service to the Party.
4 All bills including executive bills should be debated in the Legislature with a clear indication of the Party's stand on the issues involved.
5 The Party should undertake self-help projects in its own name.
6 The True Whig Party should provide benefits and rewards to its old and faithful members who may not be fortunate enough to hold positions in Government or Party.
7 The True Whig Party should conduct regular leadership training seminars and popularize its theme songs, motto and slogans.
8 Seek to clarify distinction between Party and Government.
9 Seek to establish and operate area co-operatives among its members in order to administer to their financial needs through loans, etc.

It is the general consensus of the more than three thousand persons contacted that the True Whig Party should maintain an image of constancy and credibility. Pronouncements, declarations and other expressions of the Party, both at the local and national level, must be consistent and in harmony with the Party's policies, platforms and programs.

The Task Force is convinced that the actualization of this consensus would indeed be the real and true interpretation of the Party's motto: 'Deeds Not Words'.

Increasing attention should be paid to the issue of the Party's image, especially by adherence to the Party's rules, regulations and platforms. Presently there is a gross distortion of the meaning and intent of the Party's motto. It is generally interpreted to mean the art of saying one thing and doing the opposite. This misconception has done much injustice to the intent and purpose of the motto; and hence the basis upon which the Party was organized and presently functions.

Secondly, the Party should become a functional organ in the lives of the people. Issues of concern to the community should be evaluated, and the Party should publicly declare its position on those issues. Many persons expressed the view that the Party is active during elections, but that after the elections and campaigning period, it loses touch with the people.

This has also given rise to the erroneous assertion that the Party is exclusive, does not cater to the mass of the Liberian people.

Recommendations of the Task Force

To the end of improving the image of the Party, we would make the following recommendations:

1　The Party should engage in self-help and other development projects in its own name.
2　There should be regular leadership seminars and workshops for Party leaders and members to popularize the Party through political rallies, involving songs, slogans and other activities of that nature.
3　The Party should set aside a day each year when there are scheduled simultaneous celebrations of the Party's day throughout the nation.
4　Handbooks should be published outlining the operations of the Party throughout the nation. This document should include the Party's history, policies and platforms over the years; the most recent platform and other highlights of Party activities.
5　Except for statements and pronouncements of the National Standard-Bearer or the National Chairman, all official declarations, statements or pronouncement representing the True Whig Party should be channeled through the General Secretariat.

Chapter Five: Strengthening the Party

Summary of suggestions received

1 Members of the Legislature elected on the True Whig Party ticket should be required to return home periodically and frequently to talk with their constituents on Party policies, inform them about activities in the Legislature, and discuss local issues and problems which should then be brought to the attention of the Party.

2 Local Party officials should periodically tour their areas, speak with their constituent-partisans, discuss issues, problems and Party programs, and make regular reports to the Party.

3 The National Chairman and General Secretary should make periodic tours of the country in order to inspect Party facilities and evaluate Party activities.

4 The National Standard Bearer should not commit himself to any candidate seeking election on the True Whig Party slate, nor in any way use his influence to elect a candidate.

5 All party members should be registered and should carry identity or membership cards.

6 Registration of Party members should begin at the First Quadrennial Congress.

7 Party organization and activities should be at all levels in the country.

8 Provide scholarships for Party members who are students.

9 TWP must undertake independent development projects.

10 The Party should assist the needy throughout the nation.

11 The Party should establish information centers throughout the nation.

12 Identification or affiliation with the TWP must carry with it certain benefits.

13 Party nomination procedures should be widely publicized.

14 A clear distinction between Party and Government must be made and maintained.

15 Leadership training should be mandatory for all Party leaders.

16 All non-TWP government officials should be dismissed.

17 Examine the staff of the 'Liberian Age', which is the Party's own newspaper, in order to ascertain loyalty of staffers to Party.

18 Establish annual youth camps for young partisans from throughout the nation where they can meet each other, learn about the Party, democracy and the virtues of the free enterprise system, TWP's platforms and policies, discuss and exchange ideas, and go out and seek the Party's interest when they return to their respective homes.

At the October 13th meeting in Bentol, the Standard-Bearer indicated that it was important for the Party to know who its members are. This was re-echoed by many partisans, who felt that partisans should be registered and carry membership cards, and that there should be direct benefits, both political and otherwise, which result from membership in the Party.

Others, especially those outside Monrovia and Montserrado County, conveyed a feeling of isolation from the mainstream of the Party and admitted to a sense of neglect on the part of their members in the National Legislature as well as the national and local officials of their Party.

Many suggestions were received as to possible ways and means of making the Party stronger. We feel that most of them point to a desire on the part of partisans for a more activist party, which would take bold initiatives and reach out into the various communities in which its partisans reside in order to assist in their efforts to better themselves. In keeping with this view, we would make the following specific recommendations:

Recommendations

1   Members of the Legislature elected on the TWP ticket should constitute a ready-made, permanent Task Force of the Party through a strong and effective liaison with their constituents. We therefore recommend that they be required by the Party to pay regular visits to their constituencies at least once a month and to report to the Party at the national level on the prevailing state of affairs. This should continue both during and between sessions of the Legislature. They should constitute the vanguard of the Party's efforts to reach out to the people.

2   Local party officials should undertake similar activity with respect to their respective areas, and should make every possible attempt to co-ordinate their efforts with the respective Members of the Legislature on the Party ticket from their area.

3   Plans should be adopted at this Congress for the launching of a massive membership campaign, and partisan registration should begin during the Congress.

4   Membership cards should be prepared and issued to *bona fide* members upon payment of a nominal fee of $1.00 to defray some of the costs of issuing same. Members should apply for and be issued their cards through ward chairmen, which will produce the benefit of mutual acquaintance. Partisans attending all meetings, congresses and conventions of the Party, or seeking admission to any Party

offices or headquarters, would be required to present their membership cards.

5   If candidates and nominees of the Party are truly to be the people's choice, we recommend that the Standard-Bearer should remain strictly neutral in respect of all candidates, and that he refrains from endorsing or committing himself to any particular person, or using his influence to ensure victory for anyone. Liberia is too small, and the Presidency is held in such high esteem, that when this is done the fairness of the electoral contest is compromised.

6   The practice of automatically returning a member of the Legislature to his seat for a second term must desist immediately. It was clearly the intention of the law that after one term, the incumbent legislator was meant to face his constituents and his challengers on the strength of his record of service and his popularity. The waning credibility of the TWP would be greatly restored if this recommendation is adopted.

7   Through the local Party offices and officials, partisans should be encouraged to invite the participation of the TWP in self-help development projects which they have already commenced in their various areas. These projects should be of general interest and benefit to the entire community.

8   During vacation periods, youths of the Party should be encouraged to engage in rural community development projects. These programs should be designed and planned in conjunction with local school authorities, Party officials, and development planners in the counties and territories. Youths participating in such projects should be provided with a stipend on par with that received by vacation students in urban areas in order to assist them with preparation for the ensuing school year.

9   Soft loans for low-income partisans and government employees should be made from the establishment of a loan fund by the Party, the proceeds of which would be used mainly for housing and educational expenses. A target group likely to derive maximum benefit from this scheme might be teachers and nurses.

Chapter Six: Revision of rules and recommendations

The Task Force strongly recommends the revision of the True Whig Party's Rules and Regulations adopted in Voinjama in 1975. These revisions should reflect those relevant aspects of the Task Force's recommendations endorsed by the October 25–26 Quadrennial Congress.

Because of time constraints the Task Force could not adequately prepare and present a completed version of the recommended revision of the Party's Rules and Regulations. Therefore, we present the below-listed items to be considered for incorporation into another revision of the Party's Rules and Regulations:

1 The Administrative Committee shall meet annually.

2 The three Assistant General Secretaries shall be technicians, professionally qualified, and shall be appointed by the National Standard Bearer, with the advice and consent of the Executive Committee, and be compensated.

3 All local Chairmen and Secretaries of the Counties and Territories shall be full time. No person holding a national office in the Party shall be allowed to simultaneously hold office in the local Party.

4 The Executive Committee shall have regular quarterly meetings.

5 The structure and functions of the Women and Youth wings of the True Whig Party should be recognized to reflect the need for their greater participation in the Party. This move will facilitate the utilization of the potentials of these groups for dynamic actions designed for Party promotions. Special program activities should be directed by the Party involving these two areas. Such programs include: retreats; workshops; seminars; social welfare programs; publications; panel discussions; and other activities directly sponsored by the Party.

6 The number of delegates of each political subdivision shall be proportional to the population of a particular area, based on the National Census at the ratio of one delegate to 1,250 persons. Each delegate shall have one vote. Delegates attending the Convention shall be elected by the various precincts and wards of the various political sub-divisions.

7 Every registered partisan of the True Whig Party shall pay one percent (1%) of his annual salary to the Treasurer of the Party.

8 Candidates endorsed by the Party to be carried forward to the electorate must be Liberians who meet the following conditions:
   a. Free of any tax obligation to the State;
   b. Must declare his assets prior to election by the Convention;
   c. Must submit evidence clearing him of conviction of any crime of a felonious nature.

9 We recommend that the Bolter rule of the Rules and Regulations be revised to reflect more equitable rules for discipline in the Party.

10 It is further recommended that no more than two national officials of the National True Whig Party should come from the same County.

Chapter Seven: Conclusion

In the performance of the special task assigned to us by our Standard-Bearer, we have looked at the Party in a novel manner which has proved to be surprisingly revealing: we have listened to the views, opinions, suggestions and recommendations of several thousand partisans and citizens throughout the length and breadth of this land. We feel confident that we accurately reflect the views of several thousand when we sadly conclude that they perceive the True Whig Party as neither popular, nor mass-based, nor united, nor democratic, neither is it known by the majority of the people.

If these views are representative of those held by most of our people (the probability of which is highly likely due to their startling similarity), in spite of its past glories and achievements, and its present advantageous position as the incumbent and only legitimate political party in Liberia, the True Whig Party is in danger of imminent collapse and disintegration.

Four years ago, in his Acceptance Speech made in Voinjama at the 33rd National Convention of the True Whig Party on the occasion of his election as Standard-Bearer, Dr Tolbert had this to say:

> There now exists a compelling need to make the True Whig Party more effective and more relevant to the needs of our society. This will warrant the formulation of dynamic and effective programs, extending from the Ward Precinct to the County and National Level, that will totally involve all the people, men and women, young and old, in pursuits that are beneficial to the Party and the Nation as a whole.

The record shows that the 33rd Convention did not share the Standard-Bearer's conviction – did not answer his call for change – did not take the opportunity to become more relevant and responsive.

During this First Quadrennial Congress, the Party now finds itself poised at a crossroads in its history, and on the brink of a new decade. There is much to be done if the Party is to survive; we must not only stamp out the evil, we must begin to build for 1983 and beyond.

The alternatives are clear, the options well defined, this First Congress, if it can find the wisdom and the courage, can catapult a revitalized True Whig Party confidently into the turbulence and uncertainties of the 80s as an enlightened, united, democratic Party of the People. Or, if narrow-mindedness and shortsightedness prevail, the First Congress might well go down in history as the Party's last. We hope and trust that this latter course will be avoided at all cost – for the good of the Party and the prosperity of the Republic.

Appendix 'A'   Suggestions for government from partisans

A view repeatedly expressed by several thousand partisans and individuals across the country was the apparent congruence of Party and Government. This perhaps may have led them to express to the Task Force many views which strictly had nothing to do directly with the Party. While the reform of the Party is properly the subject of this report, the Task Force felt an obligation to those who took the time to express these views, to append them to this report where they may be readily accessible to those persons and organizations who may find them useful. We are aware that they are *ultra vires*, and have refrained from comment thereon.

The following constitute suggestions received from partisans for Government:

1   All legislators and chiefs should serve one eight-year term.
2   Scholarship policies, both national and foreign, should be reviewed. Consideration should be given to providing scholarships to qualified and deserving students throughout the country.
3   Individuals seeking public office should declare their assets before and after their tenure of service.
4   Monopolies on locally produced commodities should be lifted as they serve to provide minimum benefits to the masses of the people.
5   The repatriation of money from Liberia should be carefully monitored and controlled.
6   Elected officials and those in positions of influence should not serve as chairpersons of companies and concessions.
7   The training of teachers and health workers should be intensified and more incentives provided to attract and maintain them in their respective professions.
8   The Liberian Broadcasting Corporation should be expanded to cover the entire nation.
9   Favorable consideration should be given to the recommendation for the removal of the property clause as a basis for voting.
10   Information services should be made more functional and relevant in projecting the image of Liberia.
11   There should be functional price controls for the following: housing/rent, food, health and educational services, consumer and other goods.
12   Workers in all sectors of the economy should not act as lawyers.
14   All senators and representatives, when not attending sessions of the Legislature, should be required to return to their people and report on their stewardship. They should also hold meetings with their

people to enable them to better advocate the people's expressed views, interests, problems and aspirations.

15 The Constitution, basic rights, and proper history of Liberia should be taught as a part of social studies in the schools throughout the country.

16 Paramount and Clan Chiefs' election should be by secret ballot, as all other elections for constitutional and statutory offices.

17 Text books and school uniforms should be ordered by and sold by the Government on a duty-free basis, to ensure mass education.

18 All elected officials of Government above the Paramount Chief level should be at least high school graduates.

19 There should be a uniform salary scale for all Government officials and employees of equal status and responsibilities. Salaries in the Judiciary should be on par with the Executive.

20 The salaries of the Paramount, Clan and General Chiefs should be increased. Consideration should be given to paying the Town and Quarter Chiefs.

21 Job opportunities and preceptorship/work-study services should be provided for students, particularly those in the rural areas. This would provide youths with constructive engagement in national development.

22 Social and public services (schools, health facilities, banks, etc.) should be provided on a balanced basis in each region of the Country.

23 Development budgetary allocations to the nine Counties, six Territories, statutory districts, cities, townships etc. of the country should be proportional to the population and development needs of the areas.

24 Incentives should be given to new industries to establish in regions where none exist. In addition, such incentives should also be given to existing industries to either re-locate or establish subsidiaries outside of major urban centers. This would provide employment opportunities, arrest the massive rural to urban migration and enhance development throughout the country.

25 Consideration should be given to revenue sharing between the national and regional levels on the basis of population in addition to their national development budgetary allocation.

26 Continued efforts should be made to expand and maintain the national road network: primary, secondary and farm-to-market roads.

27 Officials of Government or Party should desist from retainership by concessionaire in conflict with their official duties.

28 There should be local election offices in the Counties and Territories.

Respectfully submitted STANDARD BEARER'S SPECIAL TASK FORCE ON PARTY REFORM NATIONAL TRUE WHIG PARTY R. L.

Emmanuel L. Shaw II
CHAIRMAN

Hilary B. Wilson, Sr.
VICE CHAIRMAN

Mohamedu Fahnbulleh Jones
SECRETARY

Emily David Bruce
ASSISTANT SECRETARY

Jennie Johnson Bernard
George S. Boley
J. Emmanuel Zehkpehge Bowier
Benjamin Toe Collins
Edward A. David
William R. Davies, Jr.
Ernest E. Dennis
William E. Dennis, Jr.
Sadie L. DeShield
D. Elwood Dunn
Joseph W. Garber, III
Arabella Greaves
Christiana Harmond
Lawrence Kennedy
Alfred Kulah
Victoria Ricks-Marsh
R.P. Kpokpo Weah McClain
Peter Naigow
Thelma E. Nelson
Christine T. Norman
J. Montgomery Scott
R. Archibald Williams
T. Nelson Williams

24th October 1979

Notes

Chapter One
1 Winthrop D. Jordan, *White Over Black: American Attitudes Toward the Negro 1550–1812* (Baltimore, Maryland: Penguin Books, Inc., 1969) p.3
2 *Ibid.*
3 Jordan, *op. cit.*, p.6
4 *Ibid.*
5 Jordan, *op. cit.*, p.7
6 Jordan, *op. cit.*, p.4
7 *Ibid.*
8 Jordan, *op. cit.*, pp.4–5. See also Basil Davidson, *The African Slave Trade: Pre-colonial History 1450–1850* (Boston: Little, Brown and Company, 1961), originally published as *Black Mother*.
9 John Hope Franklin, *From Slavery to Freedom: A History of Negro Americans* (New York: Vintage Books, 1969), p.46. NOTE: Until the latter half of the eighteenth century a slave had no explicitly defined status and in fact the term was ambiguously used. See Oscar and Mary F. Handlin's article, 'Origins of the Southern Labor System' in Stanley M. Katz (ed.) *Colonial America: Essays in Politics and Social Developments* (Boston: Little, Brown and Company, 1971), pp.341–363. Note also the English playwright Shakespeare's use of the term in Act IV, Scene 5 of *Coriolanus*.
10 Franklin, *op. cit.*, p.46
11 Franklin, *op. cit.*, p.47
12 Katz (ed.), *op. cit.*, p.364
13 *Ibid.*
14 Felix N. Okoye, *The American Image of Africa: Myth and Reality* (Buffalo, New York: Black Academy Press, Inc., 1971), p.36
15 *Ibid.*

16 John W. Blassingame, *The Slave Community: Plantation Life in the Ante-Bellum South* (New York: Oxford University Press, 1972), p.7
17 *Ibid.*
18 Franklin, *op. cit.*, p.79
19 Jordan, *op. cit.*, p.375
20 Jordan, *op. cit.*, p.406
21 *Ibid.*
22 Jordan, *op. cit.*, p.407

Chapter Two
1 Charles Henry Huberich, *The Political and Legislative History of Liberia* (New York: Central Book Company, Inc., 1947), Vol. 1, p.29
2 *Ibid.*
3 Nat Turner was a Negro slave and preacher who led the famous slave revolt in American history. In 1831 Turner organized and led, with the aid of about seventy other slaves, a rebellion killing about sixty white persons in the state of Virginia. It took the militia of the State of Virginia to capture Turner and about twenty of his followers who were hanged in August, 1831. Because of fear and in revenge for the Turner incident, angry whites killed over one hundred innocent slaves while others freed their slaves to be shipped to Liberia.
4 Quoted in Huberich, *op. cit.*, p.25, footnote 14
5 Jordan, *White Over Black*, p.542
6 Jordan, *op. cit.*, p.543
7 *Ibid.*
8 Quoted in Jordan, *op. cit.*, pp.543–544
9 *Ibid.*
10 *Ibid.*
11 *Ibid.*
12 *Ibid.*
13 Jordan, *op. cit.*, pp.544–545
14 Jordan, *op. cit.*, p.546
15 *Ibid.*
16 *Ibid.*
17 Sir Harry Johnston, *Liberia* (New York: Dodd, Mead and Company, 1906), Vol. 1, p.125
18 Quoted in Jordan, *op. cit.*, p.552
19 Charles Morrow Wilson, *Liberia: Black Africa in Microcosm* (New York: Harper and Row, 1971), p.7
20 Wilson, *op. cit.*, p.5
21 Wilson, *op. cit.*, p.9
22 *Ibid.*
23 Wilson, *op. cit.*, p.10
24 Wilson, *op. cit.*, p.11
25 P.J. Staudenraus, *The African Colonization Movement, 1821–1865* (New York: Columbia University Press, 1961), p.62
26 Wilson, *op. cit.*, p.15

27 J.J. Ashmun, *History of the American Colony in Liberia from December 1821–1823* (Washington: Way and Gideon, 1826), p.8

28 *Ibid.*

29 Staudenraus, *op. cit.*, p.65. See also pp.64–67

30 Stanley A. Davis, *This is Liberia: A Brief History of this Land of Contradictions with Biographies of its Founders and Builders* (New York: William Frederick Press, 1953)

31 Davis, *op. cit.*, p.39

32 J. Gus Liebenow, *Liberia: The Evolution of Privilege* (Ithaca, New York: Cornell University Press, 1969), p.4

33 Charles Morrow Wilson, *Liberia* (New York: William Sloane, 1947), p.10

34 Wilson, *Liberia*, p.11

35 Andrew Hull Foote, *Africa and the American Flag* (New York and London: D. Appleton & Co., 1854), p.123

Chapter Three

1 Huberich, *The Political and Legislative History of Liberia* (New York: Central Book Company, Inc., 1947), Vol. 1, p.22

2 *Ibid.*

3 *Ibid.*

4 Huberich, *op. cit.*, p.23

5 Huberich, *op. cit.*, p.599

6 *Ibid.*

7 Huberich, *op. cit.*, p.600

8 *Ibid.*

9 Philip Sterling and Rayford Logan, *Four Who Took Freedom* (New York: Doubleday and Company, 1967), p.107

10 Huberich, *op. cit.*, p.577

11 Huberich, *op. cit.*, p.578

12 Huberich, *op. cit.*, p.569

13 Huberich, *op. cit.*, p.584

14 *Ibid.*

15 *Ibid.*

16 Wilson, *Liberia: Black Africa in Microcosm*, p.13

17 See Charles Morrow Wilson, *Liberia: Black Africa in Microcosm* (New York: Harper & Row Publishers, 1971), p. 13; Felix N. Okoye, *The American Image of Africa: Myth and Reality* (Buffalo, New York: Academy Press, Inc., 1977), pp.129–150; and P.J. Staudenraus, *The African Colonization Movement: 1816–1865* (New York: Columbia University Press, 1961), p.109, for other reasons why most free Negroes frowned upon colonization in Africa.

18 Jehudi Ashmun, *Journal*, August 21, 1821, in *American Colonization Society, Sixth Annual Report*, Appendix p.30. Still possessed by the American mentality (whites were masters and men, and black adults were boys), Ashmun referred to the recaptured African men as boys.

19 Margaret Rich, 'Objects of Benevolence: Recaptured Africans in Colonial Liberia.' Unpublished thesis, 1973. State University of New York College,

Brockport, New York, p.7, mimeographed. See also Sigmund Diamond's 'From Organization to Society; Virginia in the Seventeenth Century' in Katz (ed.) *Colonial America*, pp.3–31, and John P. Roche (ed.) *Origins of American Political Thought* (New York: Harper and Row Publishers, 1967).

20 *African Repository and Colonial Journal*, Vol. IX, 10 (December, 1833), p.308

21 J.J. Ashmun, *Journal*, August 31, 1822, p.32

22 Johnston, *Liberia*, p.195

23 The name New Georgia was adopted in memorial of Georgia, USA, from whence the first 'recaptured Africans' were sent to Liberia. Of these re-captured Africans, Ashmun remarked that they were 'rescued by the benevolence of our government'. *See American Colonization Society, Sixth Annual Report*, p.12. Marshall is now one of six territories in Liberia. Other territories are Sasstown, River Cess, Kru Coast and Bomi.

24 C.M. Waring, Letter, January 17, 1833 in *African Repository and Colonial Journal*, Vol. IX, 9 (November, 1833), pp.286–287

25 See Okoye, *American Image of Africa*, pp.20–21

26 J. Mechlin, Letter, April, 1832 in *African Repository and Colonial Journal*, Vol. VIII, No. 5 (July, 1832), p.135

27 From the letter of US Secretary of State Mr Upshur to a British Minister in Washington, D.C., September 25, 1843. See Supplement to *American Journal of International Law*, Vol. 4, 1910. (New York: Johnson Reprint Corporation, 1962), pp.212–213

28 J.P. Pinney, Letter, February 20, 1833 in *African Repository and Colonial Journal*, Vol. IX, 2 (April, 1833), p.60

29 Huberich, *op. cit.*, p.650

30 Supplement to *American Journal of International Law*, Vol. 4, 1910, pp.211–212

31 *American Journal of International Law*, Supplement, Vol. 4, p.214

32 Sidney De La Rue, *The Land of the Pepper Bird* (New York: G.P. Putnam and Sons, 1930), p.219

33 George W. Brown, *The Economic History of Liberia* (Washington, DC: The Associated Publishers, Inc., 1941), p.246

34 Brown, *op. cit.*, p.247

35 De La Rue, *op. cit.*, pp.213–214

36 Joseph Saye Guannu (ed.), *The Inaugural Addresses of the Presidents of Liberia: From Joseph Jenkins Roberts to William Richard Tolbert, Jr. 1848–1976* (New York: Exposition Press, 1980), p.241

37 *Ibid.*

Chapter Four

1 Raymond Leslie Buell, *The Native Problem in Africa*, Vol. II (Frank Case and Co., Ltd., 1965), p.795

2 *Ibid.*

3 *Report of the Special Committee of the House of Representatives on the Public Accounts*, adopted February 19, 1864, Vol. II, p.724

4 *Report of the Special Committee on the Public Accounts*, p.796

5   *Ibid.*
6   Johnston, *Liberia*, p.264
7   Guannu(ed.), *Inaugural Addresses of the Presidents of Liberia*, p.93
8   Guannu, *op. cit.*, p.94
9   Guannu, *op. cit.*, p.95
10 Buell, *op. cit.*, p.799
11 Buell, *op. cit.*, p.800
12 Buell, *op. cit.*, p.802
13 *Ibid.*
14 *Ibid.*
15 Buell, *op. cit.*, p.801
16 Buell, *op. cit.*, pp.802–803
17 *Ibid.*
18 Buell, *op. cit.*, p.804
19 *Ibid.*
20 Raymond Leslie Buell, *Liberia: A Century of Survival 1847–1947*, African Handbooks No. 7 (Philadelphia: University of Pennsylvania Press, 1947), pp.25–26
21 Buell, *Native Problem in Africa*, p.820
22 Buell, *op. cit.*, p.821
23 *Ibid.*
24 Buell, *op. cit.*, p.823
25 *Ibid.*
26 *New York Times*, August 31, 1928, p.5
27 Brown, *Economic History of Liberia*, p.188
28 *Hearings before the Committee on Interstate and Foreign Commerce*, House of Representatives, 69th Congress, First Session, p.254
29 Buell, *Native Problem in Africa*, p.829
30 Buell, *op. cit.*, pp.829–830
31 See Wilson, *Liberia: Black Africa in Microcosm* p.133
32 Wilson, *op. cit.*, p.134
33 Buell, *op. cit.*, p.834
34 Buell, *op. cit.*, pp.834–835
35 J.H. Mower, 'The Republic of Liberia' in *Journal of Negro History*, Vol. 32, No. 3 (July, 1947), p.290
36 Buell, *Native Problem in Africa*, p.847
37 Mower, *op. cit.*, p.280
38 Though President Tubman is credited as the architect of the 'Open Door' policy, he was, however, not its original proponent. The 'Open Door' policy is the first recommendation made in the 1930 *Report of the International Commission of Inquiry into the Existence of Slavery and Forced Labor in the Republic of Liberia.*

Chapter Five
1   Buell, *Native Problem in Africa*, p.833
2   Henry W. Nevison, *A Modern Slavery*, (New York: Schocken Books, 1968), Introduction by Basil Davidson, p.xiv
3   Nevison, *op. cit.*, Introduction, p.xv

4 Brown, *Economic History of Liberia*, p.117
5 Buell, *op. cit.*, p.777
6 *Ibid*. For an in-depth account of the Spanish and Portuguese cocoa plantations, the life-style and treatment of recruited laborers, see Henry W. Nevison, *A Modern Slavery*, (New York: Schocken Books, 1968), especially the Introduction by Basil Davidson. For an elaborate account of the so-called 'contract labor' system, see E.D. Morel's *The Black Man's Burden: The White Man in Africa from the Fifteenth Century to World War I* (New York: Modern Reader Paperbacks, 1969), first published in Britain in 1920. See especially pp. 149–160, but the entire script is very interesting.
7 Quoted in Buell, *op. cit.*, p.834
8 *Ibid*.
9 *Report of the International Commission of Inquiry into the Existence of Slavery and Forced Labor in the Republic of Liberia*, Monrovia, Liberia, September 8, 1930. (Washington: US Government Printing Office, 1931), p.25
10 Report of *International Commission of Inquiry, op. cit.*, p.22
11 Report of *International Commission of Inquiry, op. cit.*, p.163
12 The SS *Mesurado* took Postmaster-General Sherman to Greenville and was demonstrating the advantages of radio communication with points on the coast.
13 Report of *International Commission of Inquiry, op. cit.*, pp.176–177
14 *Ibid*.
15 Report of *International Commission of Inquiry, op. cit.*, p.29
16 Report of *International Commission of Inquiry, op. cit.*, p.30
17 *Ibid.*, footnote no. 29
18 Report of *International Commission of Inquiry, op. cit.*, p.31 footnote no. 51
19 James C. Young, *Liberia Rediscovered* (Doubleday, Doran & Company, Inc., 1934), p.73
20 Young, *op. cit.*, p.74
21 *Ibid*.
22 Report of *International Commission of Inquiry, op. cit.*, p.7
23 Report of *International Commission of Inquiry, op. cit.*, p.141
24 Report of *International Commission of Inquiry, op. cit.*, p.146
25 Robert A. Smith, *We Are Obligated: An Interpretive Analysis of Twenty-Five Years of Progressive Leadership* (Hamburg, West Germany: Hanseatische Druckstalt, 1969), pp.168–169
26 *Ibid*.
27 Smith, *op. cit.*, p.170
28 *Ibid*.
29 Young, *op. cit.*, pp.82–83
30 Young, *op. cit.*, pp.83–84
31 See the *Literary Digest*, November 7, 1936, pp.15–16

Chapter Six
1 Smith, *We are Obligated*, p.172
2 Smith, *op. cit.*, p.185

3 Smith, *op. cit.*, p.176

4 See details in Tuan Wreh, *The Love of Liberty: The Rule of William V.S. Tubman in Liberia 1944–1971* (London: C. Hurst & Company, 1976), pp.32–35

5 Buell, *Liberia: A Century of Survival*, p.9

6 Wreh, *op. cit.*, p.34

7 Guannu (ed.), *Inaugural Addresses of the Presidents of Liberia*, p.306

8 Guannu, *op. cit.*, p.311

9 Quoted in Stephen S. Hlope, *Class, Ethnicity and Politics in Liberia: A Class Analysis of Power Struggles in the Tubman and Tolbert Administrations from 1944–1975* (Washington, D.C: University Press of America, Inc., 1979), p.210

10 Wilson, *Liberia: Black Africa in Microcosm*, p.200. See Robert W. Clower *et al., Growth Without Development* (Evanston: Northwestern University Press, 1966) for insight into political and economic developments in the Tubman years.

11 E. Reginald Townsend (ed.), *The Official Papers of William V.S. Tubman, President of the Republic of Liberia: Covering Addresses, Messages, Speeches and Statements 1960–1967* (published for the Department of Information and Cultural Affairs, Monrovia, Liberia, by Longman, Green & Co. Ltd., 1968), pp.228–229

12 *Ibid.*

13 *The Daily Listener*, Monrovia, Liberia, 5-2-58, as quoted in Merran Fraenkel, *Tribe and Class in Monrovia* (London: Oxford University Press, 1964), p.59

14 *The Daily Listener*, July 19, 1958, Quoted in Fraenkel, *op. cit.*, p.227

15 Hlope, *op. cit.*, p.206

16 See Tuan Wreh, *The Love of Liberty*, especially pp.48–75

17 *The Liberian Age*, February 2, 1960, as quoted in Fraenkel, *op. cit.*, p.61

18 *Liberian Star*, May 2, 1968, quoted by Victor D. Du Bois in *American Universities Field Staff Reports Service*, West Africa Series, 'Liberia', Vol. XI No. 3, pp.10–12

19 Du Bois in *American Universities Field Staff Reports Service, op. cit.*, p.13

20 Wreh, *op. cit.*, p.54

21 Liebenow, *Liberia: The Evolution of Privilege*, p.115

22 Acceptance Speech of Edwin Barclay of nomination to Standard-Bearership of the True Whig Party and Reformation Party, delivered in Monrovia, August 27, 1954.

23 In 1951, Tubman bought a Presidential yacht, the *E.J. Roye*. When questioned by social critic Albert Porte about the merits of a Presidential yacht which would require a foreign crew and an annual maintenance budget of $125,000 when as an underdeveloped country there were many things of greater social value on which the funds could be expended, Tubman replied:

> How much taxes have you or any of the grumblers paid into the public treasury from 1944, when I took office...? Your spirit appears to me to be anarchical ... I think this an evil spirit or an evil eye which will not do you or the country any good ...

By 1961 there were two Presidential yachts the *Liberian* and *E.J. Roye*, maintained at a total cost of $264,147.38.

24 Wreh, *op. cit.*, pp.81–82
25 Wreh, *op. cit.*, pp.83–84
26 Wreh, *op. cit.*, p.105
27 Du Bois, *op. cit.*, p.3
28 Du Bois, *op. cit.*, p.5. For an account of the events associated with the trial, see *American Universities Field Staff Reports Service*, West Africa Series, 'Liberia', Vol. XI Nos. 3, 4, 5, 6, and 7
29 Du Bois, *op. cit.*, pp.5–6
30 Du Bois, *op. cit.*, p.15
31 William R. Tolbert succeeded Mr Tubman as President of Liberia in 1971 following the latter's death. He was deposed and assassinated in a revolutionary military takeover on April 12, 1980.
32 Richard A. Henries, following the Revolution of April 12, 1980, was arrested, tried and found guilty by the Supreme Military Tribunal of 'rampant corruption' and 'high treason'. Henries, along with twelve other high-ranking officials of the deposed Tolbert/True Whig Party régime, was executed by firing squad on April 22, 1980.
33 *American Universities Field Staff Reports Service*, West Africa Series, 'Liberia', Vol. XI No. 7, p.5
34 *Ibid.*
35 *American Universities Field Staff Reports Service, op. cit.*, p.14

Chapter Seven
1 Guannu (ed.), *Inaugural Addresses of the Presidents of Liberia*, pp.395–396
2 *Ibid.*
3 Guannu, *op. cit.*, pp.397–398
4 Wilton Sankawolo, *Tolbert of Liberia: A Biography of Dr. William R. Tolbert, Jr., 19th President of the Republic of Liberia* (London: The Ardon Press), p.26
5 Second Annual Message of William R. Tolbert, Jr., President of Liberia, to the Second Session of the Forty-Seventh Legislature at E.J. Roye Memorial Building, Monrovia, January 23, 1973, p.95
6 Address of the President of Liberia, Dr. William R. Tolbert, Jr., During the Program Climaxing the National Fund Raising Rally, May 13, 1973, Louisana, Liberia, p.4
7 Second Annual Message, p.94
8 Address Climaxing National Fund Raising Rally, p.5
9 Address Climaxing National Fund Raising Rally, p.9
10 Address Climaxing National Fund Raising Rally, p.7
11 *Ibid.*
12 Address Climaxing National Fund Raising Rally, p.8
13 Address Climaxing National Fund Raising Rally, p.5
14 Joe Wylie, Hiaimwoina Stewart and Wini Davies Debbah, *Poetry for the Struggle* (published by the All Peoples Freedom Alliance, Monrovia, Liberia, September, 1978), pp.9–10

15 See H. Tawile Cooper's *A Historical Light of Grand Gedeh's Yesterday and Today* (mimeographed, 15 pages, 1974).

16 At the outset of his administration, President Tolbert was fondly referred to as 'Speedy', a reputation he earned himself by moving swiftly against undiciplined public servants and corrupt officials. Several Cabinet Ministers were summarily dismissed by Tolbert in his seemingly genuine attempt to effect reforms in government.

17 The Grebo name for the *crioetomys gambienos liberiae* variety of opossum, commonly known in Liberia as possum.

18 The Krahn name for the species of the tree scientifically known as *tieghemella heckelii.*

19 Republic of Liberia, Presidential Papers, Documents, Diary and Record of Activities of the Chief Executive, August 1, 1974–December 31, 1975, p.234

20 Joe Wylie *et al., op. cit.,* pp.4–5

21 Report to the President of Liberia of the National Commission to Give Consideration to Possible Changes in the National Motto, Flag, Anthem and Constitution of the Republic of Liberia by McKinley A. DeShield, Sr., Chairman of the Commission, Monrovia, Liberia, January 24, 1978, p.4

22 Report of the National Commission, *op. cit.,* p.7

23 Report of the National Commission, *op. cit.,* p.47

24 Rufus Darpoh, 'Speaking Out: "Forerunners of the Revolution"' in *Outlook*, Vol. 3 No. 4, March 1981, p.35

25 *Ibid.*

26 Guannu, *op. cit.,* pp.409–410

27 *Bentol Times*, Vol. 1 No. 48, December 19, 1978, pp.1 and 6

28 *The Sunday People*, Vol. 1 No. 12, November 25, 1979, pp.1 and 8

29 See reference in *The New Liberian*, December 20, 1978, p.5

30 Joseph Saye Guannu, *An Introduction to Liberian Government: The First Republic and the People's Redemption Council* (New York: Exposition Press, Inc., 1982), p.99

Chapter Eight

1 An Official Account of the Civil Disturbance in Monrovia, Liberia, April 26, 1979 (Ministry of Information, Cultural Affairs and Tourism Press), p.8

2 An Official Account of the Civil Disturbance, *op. cit.,* pp.5–6

3 An Official Account of the Civil Disturbance, *op. cit.,* pp.7–8

4 Albert Porte, *The Day Monrovia Stood Still, April 14, 1979* (Pamphlet, May 1979), p.4

5 An Official Account of the Civil Disturbance, *op. cit.,* p.25

6 *Matthews Recants – Tolbert Replies* (MICAT Press, April 25, 1979), p.4

7 *Matthews Recants – Tolbert Replies*, p.5

8 Address to the Nation by Dr William R. Tolbert, Jr, President of the Republic of Liberia, Centennial Memorial Pavilion, Saturday, May 5, 1979, p.11

9 Report of the National Commission on National Reconstruction to Dr

William R. Tolbert, Jr, President of the Republic of Liberia, Monrovia, Liberia, June 12, 1979, p.3

10 Report of the National Commission on National Reconstruction, pp.5–6
11 Report of the Committee to Devise A Code of Conduct for Public Officials, January 3, 1980, pp.4–5
12 Executive Ordinance No. 2 (1980). Measures for the Regulation of the Importation of Rice into the Republic of Liberia, February 27, 1980, pp.2–5
13 Special Message by Dr William R. Tolbert. Jr, President of the Republic of Liberia, to the First Session of the 49th Legislature on Attempts made by the Progressive People's Party to Overthrow the Government of Liberia, Monday, March 10, 1980, pp.1–2
14 Special Message to the First Session of the 49th Legislature, *op. cit.*, pp.3–5
15 Special Message, *op. cit.*, p.7

Chapter Nine

1   The first four presidents were from the Republican Party, and of fairer complexion. J.J. Roberts, first president of the Republic, was called upon to serve following the deposition of President Roye in 1871.
2   Buell, *Native Problem in Africa*, p.712
3   *Ibid.*
4   *Buell, op. cit.*, p.713
5   Buell, *op. cit.*, p.714
6   *Ibid.*
7   *Ibid.*
8   Buell, *op. cit.*, p.715
9   Quoted *ibid.* (footnote 27).
10 *Ibid.*
11 Acceptance Speech of Edwin J. Barclay as Presidential Candidate for the Independent True Whig Party, delivered August 27, 1954.
12 Liebenow, *Liberia: The Evolution of Privilege*, p.115
13 Dew Duan-Wleh Mayson, *Susuku in Grand Gedeh County: A Response to Poverty in Liberia* (Monrovia: March 1978), pp.2–3
14 PAL Special Release, September 27, 1979.
15 An Interview with Amos Sawyer by Neville Best, p.2
16 *Ibid.*
17 *True Whig Party in Step with the New Liberia* (Public Affairs Bureau of the TWP, Monrovia), p.2
18 *Ibid.*

Select Bibliography

Adams, John, *Remarks on the Country Extending from Cape Palmas to River Congo, Including Observations on the Manners and Customs of the Inhabitants* (London: Frank Cass, 1966).

African Repository and Colonial Journal, IX, 10 (December, 1833).

American Journal of International Law, Supplement, Vol. 4, 1910 (New York: Johnson Reprint Corporation, 1962).

American Universities Field Staff Reports Service, West Africa Series Vols. VIII–XII, 'Liberia', XI, Nos. 3, 4, 5, 6 and 7.

Anderson, Benjamin K., *Narrative of a Journey to Musardu, the Capital of the Western Mandingoes, together with Narrative of the Expedition despatched to MUSAHDU by the Liberian Government under Benjamin J.K. Anderson Esq. in 1874* (London: Frank Cass & Co., Ltd., 1971).

Anderson, Robert Earle, *Liberia, America's African Friend* (Chapel Hill: University of North Carolina Press, 1952).

Annual Report of the American Colonization Society for Colonizing the Free People of Color of the United States, Vols. 44–53, 1861–1870 (New York: Negro Universities Press, 1969).

Area Handbook for Liberia (Washington: Government Printing Office, 1972).

Ashmun, Jehudi J., *Journal*, August 21, 1821, in *American Colonization Society, Sixth Annual Report*.

———, *History of the American Colony in Liberia from 1821 to 1823* (Washington: Way & Gideon, 1826).

Azikiwe, Benjamin Nnamdi, 'In Defense of Liberia', *Journal of Negro History*, 17 (January, 1932) pp. 30–49.

———, *Liberia in World Politics* (London: Arthur H. Stockwell, 1934).

Beard, Charles A., *An Economic Interpretation of the Constitution of the United States* (New York: The Free Press, 1965).

Bixler, Raymond W., *The Foreign Policy of the United States In Liberia* (New York: Pageant Press, Inc., 1957).

Blassingame, John W., *The Slave Community: Plantation Life in the Ante-Bellum South* (New York: Oxford University Press, 1972).

Blyden, Edward Wilmot, *Hope for Africa*, A Discourse Delivered in the Presbytherian Church, Seventh Avenue, New York, July 21, 1861. '*Liberia*', pp. 95–167 (New York: John A. Gray & Green, Printers, 1865).

———, '*Our Origin, Dangers, and Duties*', The Annual Address before the Major and Common Council of the City of Monrovia, July 26, 1865, the Day of National Independence, and Repeated on Tuesday, August 1, 1865, at Caldwell, St Paul's River (New York: John A. Gray & Green, Printers, 1865).

———, *The African Problem and Other Discourses*, Delivered in America in 1890, *The Liberian Government Concessions and Exploration Company, Limited* (London: W.B. Wittingham & Co., 1890).

———, '*The Needs of Liberia*', A lecture delivered at Lower Buchanan, Grand Bassa County, Liberia, January 26,1908 (London: C.M. Phillips, Printer, 1908).

Boone, Clinton Caldwell, *Liberia as I Know It* (New York: Negro Universities Press, 1970).

Brawley, Benjamin Griffith, *Social and Political History of the American Negro* (New York: Collier Books, 1970).

Brown, George W., *The Economic History of Liberia* (Washington: The Associated Publishers, Inc., 1941).

Buell, Raymond Leslie, *The Native Problem in Africa*, Vol. II (Frank Cass & Co. Ltd., 1965).

———, *Liberia: A Century of Survival 1847–1947* (Philadelphia: University of Pennsylvania Press, 1947).

Cassell, Christian Abayomi, *Liberia: History of the First African Republic* (New York: International Publishers Inc., 1970).

Clower, Robert W., George Dalton, Michell Hartwitz and A.A. Walter, *Growth without Development* (Evanston: North-western University Press, 1966).

Cole, Henry Benoni(ed.), *The Liberian Yearbook 1956* (London: Diplomatic Press & Publishing Co., 1957).

———, *The Liberian Yearbook for 1962 (Monrovia: A Liberian Review Publication, 1962)*.

Dalton, George, 'History, Politics and Economic Development in Liberia', *Journal of History*, **25**, 4 (December 1965) pp. 561–569.

Davidson, Basil, *African Slave Trade: Pre-Colonial History 1450–1850* (Boston: Little, Brown and Company, 1961).

Davis, Stanley A., *This is Liberia: A Brief History of this Land of Contradictions with Biographies of Its Founders and Builders* (New York: William Frederick Press, 1953).

De La Rue, Sidney, *The Land of the Pepper Bird: Liberia* (New York: G.P. Putnam & Sons, 1930).

Douglass, Frederick, *Narrative of the Life of Frederick Douglass, An American Slave: Written by Himself* (Boston: Published at the Anti-Slavery Office, No. 25 Cornhill, 1845).

Dow, George F., *Slave Ships and Sailing Port Washington* (New York: Kewikat Press, 1969).

Dow, Luther Henry, *Liberia, the Inside Story: A Travel Report of an American Union Man* (New York: Exposition Press, 1963).

Foote, Andrew Hull, *Africa and the American Flag* (New York: D. Appleton & Co., 1854).

Fraenkel, Merran, *Tribe and Class in Monrovia* (London: Oxford University Press, 1964).

Franklin, John Hope, *From Slavery to Freedom: A History of Negro Americans* (New York: Vintage Books, 1969).

Guannu, Joseph Saye (ed.), *The Inaugural Addresses of the Presidents of Liberia: From Joseph Jenkins Roberts to William Richard Tolbert, Jr., 1848 to 1976* (New York, Exposition Press, 1980).

———, *An Introduction to Liberian Government: The First Republic and The People's Redemption Council* (New York: Exposition Press, 1982).

Hale, Sarah Josepha, *Liberia, or Mr Peyton's Experiments, Upper Saddle River* (New York: Greeg Press, 1968).

Heard, William Henry, *The Bright Side of African Life* (New York: Negro Universities Press, 1969).

Huberich, Charles Henry, *The Political and Legislative History of Liberia*, Vols. I & II (New York: Central Books, 1947).

Hlope, Stephen S., *Class, Ethnicity and Politics in Liberia: A Class Analysis of Power Struggles in the Tubman and Tolbert Administrations from 1944–1975.* (Washington: University Press of America, 1979).

Johnston, Harry, *Liberia*, Vol. I (New York: Dodd, Mead and Company, 1906).

Jordan, Winthrop D., *White Over Black: American Attitudes Toward the Negro 1550–1812* (Baltimore, Maryland: Penguin Books, Inc., 1969).

July, Robert W., *A History of the African People* (New York: Charles Scribner and Sons, 1970) pp. 101–121.

Katz, Stanley M. (ed.), *Colonial America: Essays in Politics and Social Development* (Boston: Little, Brown and Company, 1971).

Kpor, Woanta Johnny, *A Nation of Two Worlds: Liberia* (Unpublished M.A. thesis, Atlanta University, Atlanta, Georgia, May 1977).

Liebenow, J. Gus, *Liberia: The Evolution of Privilege* (Ithaca, New York: Cornell University Press, 1969).

Literary Digest, 'War in Liberia', November 7, 1936, pp. 15–16.

Marinelli, Lawrance A., *The New Liberia: A Historical and Political Survey* (New York: Fredrick A. Praeger, 1964).

McCall, D.F., 'Liberia: An Appraisal' in *Annals of the American Academy of Political and Social Science*, 306, July 1956, pp. 88–97.

McLaughlin, Russell U., *Foreign Investment and Development in Liberia* (New York: Praeger, 1966).

Morel, E.D., *The Black Man's Burden: The White Man in Africa from the Fifteenth Century to World War I* (New York: Modern Reader, 1969) pp. 149–160.

Mower, J.H., 'The Republic of Liberia' in *Journal of Negro History* 32, (1947) pp. 265–306.

Myrdar, Gunnar, *An American Dilemma* (New York: Harper Bros., 1944), pp. 879–907.

Nevinson, Henry W., *A Modern Slavery* (New York: Schocken Books, 1968).

Nimley, Anthony J., *The Liberian Bureaucracy: An Analysis and Evaluation of the Environment, Structure and Functions* (Washington: University Press of America, 1977).

Okoye, Felix N., *The American Image of Africa: Myth and Reality* (Buffalo, New York: Academy Press, Inc., 1971).

Padmore, George, *Pan-Africanism or Communism* (Garden City, New York: Doubleday & Company, 1972), pp. 22–82.

Pinney, J.P., Letter, February 20, 1833 in *African Repository and Colonial Journal*, IX, **2**, 1833.

Reeve, Henry Fenwick, *The Black Republic: Liberia, Its Political and Social Conditions Today* (London: H.F. & G. Witherly, 1923).

Report of the International Commission of Inquiry into the Existence of Slavery and Forced Labor in the Republic of Liberia, Monrovia, Liberia, September 30, 1930.

Rich, Margaret A., *Black Colonialism: Territorial Acquisition in Liberia 1821–1847*, N.P., November 1972, mimeographed, 25 pages.

————, *Objects of Benevolence: Recaptured Africans in Colonial Liberia*, N.P., Summer 1973, mimeographed, 15 pages.

Roche, John P. (ed.), *Origins of American Political Thought* (New York: Harper & Row Publishers, 1967), pp. 193–247.

Sibley, J.L., *Liberia: Old and New* (London: 1928).

Slaughter, Philip, *The Virginian History of African Colonization* (Richmond: Macfarlane & Fergusson, 1855).

Smith, Robert A., *The Emancipation of the Hinterland* (The *Star* Magazine and Advertising Services, Monrovia, Liberia, 1964).

————, *We Are Obligated: An Interpretive Analysis of Twenty-Five Years of Progressive Leadership* (Hamburg, West Germany: Hanseatische Druckanstalt, 1969).

Starr, Frederick, *Liberia* (Chicago Book Co., 1913).

Staudenraus, P.J., *The African Colonization Movement, 1816–1865* (New York: Columbia University Press, 1961).

Taylor, Wayne Chatfield, *The Firestone Operations in Liberia* (Washington: National Planning Association, 1956).

U.S. 28th Congress 1st Session, *Colony of Liberia in Africa: Message from the President of the United States accompanied by a Report of the Secretary of State relative to the Colony in Liberia*, House Executive Document No. 162 (Washington: Government Printing Office, 1844).

U.S. 33rd Congress 1st Session, *Message from the President of the United States*, House Executive Document No. 1, Vol. 3, Part 3 (Washington: Government Printing Office, 1853).

U.S. 33rd Congress 1st Session, *Message from the President*, House Executive Document No. 1, Vol 1, Part 3 (Washington: Government Printing Office, 1854).

U.S. 41st Congress 2nd Session, *Colonization of Persons of African Descent,*

Letter From the Secretary of the Treasury, House Executive Document No. 222 (Washington: Government Printing Office, 1870).

West, Richard, *Back to Africa: a History of Sierra Leone and Liberia* (New York: Holt, Rinehart and Winston, Inc., 1970).

Williams, George Washington, *History of the Negro Race in America, 1619–1880* (New York: Arno Press, 1968).

Wilson, Charles Morrow. *Liberia* (New York: William Sloane, 1947).

———, *Liberia: Black Africa in Microcosm* (New York: Harper & Row, 1971).

Wood, Donald S., 'Patterns of Settlement and Development in Liberia'. *Journal of Geography*, 62 (December, 1963), pp. 406–413.

Wreh, Tuan, *The Love of Liberty. . . . The Rule of President William V.S. Tubman in Liberia, 1944–1971* (London: C. Hurst & Company, 1976).

Young, James Capers, *Liberia Rediscovered* (New York: Doubleday, Doran & Company, Inc., 1934).